Heartache and HOPE in Haiti

THE BRITNEY GENGEL STORY

Making Our Daughter's Last Wish Come True

LEN AND CHERYLANN GENGEL

WITH GARY BROZEK

A PUBLICATION OF TRIMARK PRESS, INC.
368 SOUTH MILITARY TRAIL
DEERFIELD BEACH, FL 33442
800.889.0693
WWW.TRIMARKPRESS.COM

LIBRARY OF CONGRESS CATALOGING-IN-PUBLICATION DATA

Heartache and Hope in haiti: The Britney Gengel Story: Making Our Daughter's Last Wish Come True

Len and Cherylann Gengel with Gary Brozek

P. CM.
ISBN: 978-0-9849568-4-5
Library of Congress Control Number: 2012947982

A13
10 9 8 7 6 5 4 3 2 1
First Edition
Printed and Bound in the United States of America

A publication of TriMark Press, Inc.
368 South Military Trail
Deerfield Beach, FL 33442
800.889.0693
www.TriMarkPress.com

Authors' Note: There are many opportunities to help us bring hope to Haiti, from donating, to fundraising, to volunteering as a Britsionary in Grand Goâve. For information on how to share Britney Gengel's dream and keep her spirit alive, please visit us at www.BeLikeBrit.org or call (508) 886-4500.

DEDICATION

We dedicate this book to . . .

Our three children, Britney, Bernie, and Richie!!!

To our family and friends who have supported us
over the past three years.

To everyone who has helped us to make
Brit's last wish come true.

To those who lost their lives on a Journey of Hope,
and their families, who are always in our prayers!

Stephanie Crispinelli
Christine Gianacaci
Courtney Hayes
Dr. Richard Bruno
Dr. Patrick Hartwick

To those who survived

Lindsay Doran
P.J. Tyska
Tom Schloemer
Daniela Montealegre
Mike DeMatteo
Julie Prudhomme
Melissa Elliot
Nikki Fantauzzi
Leann Chong

To the children of Haiti

CONTENTS

CONTENTS

FOREWORD

*"Lenny and Cherylann are regular, down-to-earth people . . .
I am in awe of their compassion and their perseverance."*

—U.S. REP. JAMES MCGOVERN

On January 12, 2010, a terrible earthquake devastated Haiti. The news coverage showed countless men, women, and children stunned as their homes and livelihoods were destroyed. They had no food or water. No shelter. And with each passing moment, the death toll continued to rise.

I learned that one of my constituents, Britney Gengel—a college student at Lynn University in Florida—was in Haiti as part of a student team working with Food for the Poor. I immediately reached out to her dad, Lenny, to see if I could be of any help. He asked me to call the State Department, or whatever appropriate government agency, for help in locating his daughter. Shortly after, Lenny called me to say that he was assured she was safe and would be on a plane back to the United States. I was relieved.

But Britney wasn't on that plane and no one could account for her whereabouts. I couldn't imagine the anguish and horror that both Lenny and his wife, Cherylann, were going through. I have a daughter myself—and the thought of losing her is unbearable.

I called Lenny again. He asked me to call the President or the Secretary of State to find Britney. He wondered whether she had been injured or if perhaps she was still trapped. But time was of the essence and, like any father, he wanted action immediately.

I called everyone I could think of, frustrated that I couldn't do more. I remember attending a candlelight vigil at St. Patrick's Church in Rutland, Massachusetts, the Gengels' hometown. The church was so crowded that I joined hundreds of others and sat on the floor. One of the organizers asked if I wanted to speak. I declined because I couldn't find the words that would give anyone comfort. I just sat there and prayed that this story might have a happy ending.

Over the next several days, I watched Lenny give one news conference after another. He was grief-stricken. Understandably impatient, he publicly asked President Obama to do more. "What if it were one of your daughters, Mr. President?" he asked.

Then, about a week after the earthquake, Lenny called me again and asked me to take him to Haiti. He wanted to see for himself whether everything possible was being done to rescue his daughter. I didn't know whether it was even feasible, and I certainly did not want to take personnel from the search-and-rescue operation to accompany a congressional visit.

I talked to Cheryl Mills, Secretary of State Hillary Clinton's incredible chief-of-staff, telling her I wanted to visit Haiti with Lenny. Senator John Kerry also called, urging that such a visit take place. Cheryl, at first, pointed out all the logistical challenges with arranging such a trip—and then, understanding that we were going no matter what, helped pave the way for Lenny and a few other families to go to Haiti. I will forever be grateful to her and Secretary Hillary Clinton.

On January 23, eleven days after the earthquake, we went to Haiti. I flew from Boston to Santo Domingo, Dominican Republic, and then drove to the María Montez International Airport in Barahona, where I met up with Lenny and the other families.

We hitched a ride on a U.S. aid convoy and drove into Haiti. We witnessed tragedy everywhere we looked. We went to the Hotel Montana, where Britney had been staying, and saw how that hotel was completely crushed by the earthquake. We also saw the unbelievable search-and-rescue operation taking place. I was relieved and proud to see that everything that could be done was being done—and I think Lenny felt the same.

Len and Cherylann Gengel are two of the bravest people I know. After it became clear that Britney did not survive, they turned their grief into something remarkable and inspiring. They decided to honor their daughter by building an orphanage and school in Haiti.

They have given hundreds of talks highlighting Britney's commitment to the poor and, especially, the children of Haiti. They have invested their own funds and raised tens of thousands of dollars from others to pay for the construction of the orphanage.

Lenny and Cherylann are regular, down-to-earth people. They love their family and friends. They love a good meal and they love a good laugh. They are the kind of people you want to be around. That's why it seems so unfair that they have suffered the tragic loss of their daughter. No parent should have to go through what they have.

I am in awe of their compassion and their perseverance. They have made sure Britney made a real difference—that she accomplished more in her short life than most others do in decades. They are the type of people who change the world. And I am privileged to call them my friends.

—U.S. Rep. James McGovern
November 2012

INTRODUCTION

"They love us so much and everyone is so happy.
They love what they have and they work so hard to get
nowhere, yet they are all so appreciative. I want to
move here and start an orphanage myself."

—BRITNEY GENGEL
January 12, 2010
Three hours before the Haiti earthquake

CHERYLANN

I was just about through sorting the invoices from the lumberyard when my cell phone rang. I looked over at Doreen, the office manager at C&S Builders, and smiled, knowing we'd just talked about people's ring tones and how funny some were, though mine was just the standard one that came with the phone. My husband, Len, was the president of the company, and I was in the office lending an extra hand around the holidays while a bunch of people were out on vacation, so the place was pretty quiet. We'd known Doreen long enough that I didn't feel the need for privacy.

My smile got bigger when I saw the call was coming from Britney, our soon-to-be twenty-year-old daughter.

"Hey, how's things in Haiti? You doing okay?"

"Things are okay. They're good."

I picked up on something in Brit's voice. She sounded different from how she had the day before when she'd first arrived. Some of the excitement was gone.

Len and I had told Brit to expect some ups and downs. As we sat at the dinner table before she left, we tried to prepare her for what she would see: the extreme poverty and all that went with that. Still, we knew this discussion was in the abstract—she'd have to see and experience this herself.

Only a few hours earlier I'd gotten an ecstatic text message from her saying, "They love us so much and everyone is so happy. They love what they have and they work so hard to get nowhere, yet they are all so appreciative. I want to move here and start an orphanage myself. I already know this is what I want to do with the rest of my life."

I was thrilled to see Len's and my prediction—that this was going to be a life-changing experience for our college sophomore daughter—was coming true. When I read those words, I was gushing with pride and pleasure. I thought to myself, maybe there really is something to this J-Term experience. Maybe Brit is learning more about herself and how to get along in the world outside the classroom of Lynn University than she is in any sociology or other class.

"Remind me again of what you've been doing today," I said, imagining what she was looking at as we talked.

"We were with the little kids this morning. This afternoon we were at a kind of nursing home, helping old people with meals and feeding them."

"Sounds like you loved the kids." I was a bit surprised by that. Brit was never one of those girls who couldn't wait to babysit and was eager to start having babies of her own. She liked kids well enough, but didn't go out of her way to spend time with them. Now there she was in Haiti saying she'd found her calling. I was waiting for the other shoe to drop.

"This woman made me cry," Brit said, an edge of hurt sharpening her words.

"What do you mean she made you cry?" I knew that Brit wasn't a crier, so something bad had to have happened. Or maybe this crying was just another part of the emerging new Britney I was seeing.

"We were just sitting there, all of us, and this woman started going off on me. On Americans. What were we doing in her country? We don't need your pity. You can't just come here one day and then leave and feel good about yourself."

"Oh my God, Brit, that's horrible. What did you do?"

"I just sat there and took it and kept helping the other people."

I bit my lip, knowing this must have really upset her, but I made sure to sound upbeat. "Did any of your teachers step in and do anything?"

"No. What could they do? I mean, we weren't there to defend ourselves, we were there to do something good for these people. By the end, though, I think because we didn't get all up in their faces or say how great the U.S. is or anything like that, we won them over. They knew we weren't there pitying them. We just wanted to help them. No judging."

"I'm glad it turned out okay," I said.

"It did, but it's still hard to have people question your motives. I just can't believe it."

I heard a tone on the line. I had another call coming in. Earlier I'd spoken with our travel agent about our spring-break trip to Disney World. She needed some information and was going to call me at the end of the workday to get it. I asked Brit to hang on for a second and then asked the travel agent to do the same.

Back on with Brit, she filled me in a bit more on the day's activities. I was feeling bad leaving the travel agent hanging, and as hard as I tried to, I couldn't really keep straight in my head everything that Brit was saying.

Finally, after about ten minutes, I said to Britney, "Can I give you a call back?"

"We're all going to dinner together later. I have to go upstairs and shower. I'll call you around seven."

"Okay, I love you. Have a good dinner."

"Love ya'," she said.

"Love ya'," I replied, both of us laughing at having adopted the current slang term of endearment.

I looked at the clock. It was a little after 4:00 p.m. I clicked over to my other call, hoping it wouldn't take too long. I had to get home and get dinner going for Len and the boys.

LEN

"Hey, John, I think a few from this angle and we'll call it good. I don't like shots with any of the backfill in them. Makes it look too much like a destruction site and not a construction site."

I pulled my jacket collar a bit tighter around my neck and looked at John in a thin windbreaker and no hat. John was a family friend—his mother and I grew up together—and he was like a cousin to Brit. He was a good, smart kid, and I had hired him as a graphic designer to help with my C&S Builders website and brochures. I remembered when I was young and just starting out busting my hump on construction sites. Of course, I had a nailing apron and a hammer with me and not a digital SLR. But I was like John back then; cold didn't bother me. Nothing could bother me. "Strong like bull," my family used to tease me.

While John snapped a few more shots for our website, I looked across what was going to be, in a few months, the

Highlands of Holden development. It had been a tougher than usual start to the winter, but I was grateful we'd been able to dig the foundation for the model home. A step forward is a step forward no matter how you look at it.

I walked up a nearby hill to take in the surrounding acres. A backhoe, a pay loader, and a dump truck still sat parked at the entrance of a cul-de-sac. From this distance, they looked like Tonka toys. And I was still a kid who took pleasure in seeing those things do their work. Though we were in the first days of 2010 and the housing industry had taken a real hit across the country, we were blessed to be doing well. The Lord had been very good to us.

I heard footsteps crunching across a crust of frozen snow.

"I'm not sure how these are going to work for us, Mr. Gengel," John said, "With the sun setting like this, the light's a little tough to work with."

I followed his gaze to the west. The horizon was a brilliant orange with a little bit of smoky gray frosting it and then a beautiful blue layer above it.

"Oh my God, John. That's beautiful. I don't care if it doesn't work for the brochures. You have to take a picture of that."

"Wow. Cheesy sunset pictures. Things sure have changed. I bet Brit would be all over you if you tried to use that in one of the commercials." John smiled, taking away any hint of unkindness from his words. He knew how much fun Brit and I had doing our television commercials together. She was a natural. The camera loved her, and she loved being in front of it. Nothing was sacred with Brit, and we spent as much time laughing and cutting up in the studio as we did actually filming the spots. That didn't make the director and crew too happy, but it did us.

"I don't know, John. We'll figure out some way to make those cheesy photos of yours look good." I clapped my hand on his shoulder. "I'm not sure I like the idea of having to do your job and mine, but if I have to . . . "

John and I laughed, knowing that my limited technology skills would have made it a challenge for me to even turn on his camera, let alone do anything with the images.

We stood and admired the sunset for a few more minutes. My thoughts drifted thousands of miles to the tropics and Brit. I imagined her lounging by the pool at the Hotel Montana, taking in the same view as I was. What a world: digital cameras, cell phones, a kid in college in a third-world country I could reach out to in a second. All that stuff, but still you miss your kid when you get home at night and her place at the dinner table is empty.

What I didn't miss was some of the screaming fights, the times she'd tell me she hated me when I took away her cell phone as punishment, the times her mother and I lay awake at night hoping she'd party safely.

"Let's get back to the office. I've got things to do."

CHERYLANN

"Hey, Ruthie, what's up?" I said as I preheated the oven and got dinner prepared.

Ruth is Len's sister and was most likely calling for an update. "Just checking to see if you'd talked to Brit and how she's doing," she said.

"I just spoke to her a few minutes ago and she sounded terrific!" I said. I filled her in on the details about Brit's arrival and told her the story that she had just shared with me. We continued chatting when another call started beeping in. I didn't switch over because I wanted to finish my conversation with Ruth.

A little while later after Ruth and I hung up, I dialed my voicemail to see who had called. It was my friend, Ines. I didn't listen to her message but instead called her back to see what she wanted.

"Cherylann, I don't want to alarm you, but I heard there was an earthquake in Haiti. Have you heard anything from Brit? Is it anywhere near where her group is staying?" Ines said.

"What?" I couldn't believe it. Brit hadn't said a thing about it, "No, I didn't know, but I just spoke to her and she was fine."

While we were finishing up our conversation, the call waiting beeped again. It was Lynn Doran, Lindsay's mother. Lindsay was Brit's roommate and she hadn't taken her cell phone on the trip, so I called Lynn the day before to let her know that the girls had arrived safely and all that. I figured she was calling for an update.

After we exchanged hellos, Lynn said, "Did you hear that Haiti had an earthquake?"

"I just heard about the earthquake from my friend, Ines," I answered.

"Have you heard from the girls?" Lynn asked.

"Oh, God yeah, I just talked to Brit. She's fine."

"But there are all these reports coming over the news," Lynn continued. I didn't know Lynn at all, but I could tell she was a bit panicky. I couldn't blame her really, with her daughter not having her cell phone.

"Listen, I'll call Brit right now and check on her. I'm sure it's no big deal. I'll call you right back."

"Thanks."

I dialed Brit's number and got her voicemail. "Hey, it's Mom. Just give me a call. I guess there's an earthquake or something like that in Haiti. Just wanted to make sure you're okay."

I didn't think much of her not answering. She'd told me that she was going to shower before dinner. I called Lindsay's mom back and told her the same thing. I told her as soon as I heard from Brit, I'd let her know.

I went back to the kitchen to finish dinner, and then another call came in telling me the same thing about Haiti and the earthquake. Then another call came in. And another. All telling me the same thing.

I felt a little buzz in my stomach, but I wasn't going to jump to the worst possible conclusion. I remember thinking, there must be something to this incident because everybody knew about it. I yelled down to my son, Bernie, who was in the cellar, and said, "Hey, Bern, I heard there was an earthquake in Haiti. Can you see if you can find anything on the computer?"

I went into the living room and switched on the TV. The local news was on, but they had nothing about Haiti, so I flipped through the stations trying find something—anything—about the earthquake. CNN was the first station, but they didn't have much information, just a report that there's been an earthquake.

I felt a cold shiver run through my body. Still, I told myself, there's no reason to get hysterical. Haiti is a big place, I'd just talked to Brit, and we planned to talk again at 7:00. All I had to do was pick up the phone and get her on the line again, so I dialed the number. No answer. I dialed again. No answer. Then I thought it's kind of stupid of me to think that if there was an earthquake all the phones would be working. Haiti was the poorest country in the western hemisphere, and we'd been told infrastructure wasn't very good. I set the phone down and finished peeling potatoes while watching the news. All anyone would say is that there'd been an earthquake. That was like telling me there was going to be a meeting the next day at some time and at some place and that maybe I should go. I needed specifics, anything to make this seem more real.

I didn't like hearing that the quake had struck at 4:53 P.M. That was not long after Brit and I had spoken. Still, the whole thing was surreal enough that I wasn't going to let my imagination run with this. All I needed to do was keep busy, and the phone would ring and it would be Brit telling me that she was fine.

At 5:30, I called Len.

"Are you coming home?"

"I have a few things to finish up here."

"Len, there's been an earthquake in Haiti."

"Yeah, Doreen said something about that."

"I haven't heard from Brit."

"I'll be there in a bit. Give me a few to get this thing done. I'm sure it's no big deal. She's in a five-star hotel, remember? We made Brit show us the website. I'm sure she's fine. There are earthquakes in California every day."

I went to the basement stairs and called down to Bernie to see if he'd found anything on the Internet. Suddenly, this whole thing was starting to feel more real.

LEN

After Doreen mentioned the earthquake to me, I went to AOL News to see if they had anything about it. Nothing. I wasn't as certain that it was no big deal as I'd made it seem to Cherylann, but I wasn't thinking doom-and-gloom thoughts. On the drive home, I listened to WBZ on the radio, the biggest station in New England for news, but the lousy AM reception made it hard to hear a whole lot. We're a family of Catholics, and I have my faith, but I'm also a bit of a Doubting Thomas. I need to see something with my own eyes before forming an opinion.

As I pulled into the driveway, I still believed that just like that solid foundation we'd been taking pictures of earlier, our lives were anchored very firmly to the ground.

Little did I know.

After kissing Cherylann, we went into the great room and turned on the big-screen TV. We flipped to CNN and across the bottom of the screen, the crawl stated a major earthquake had struck Haiti. Its magnitude was 7.0 and its epicenter was 15 miles WSW of Port-Au-Prince, at 18.443°N, 72.571°W. At that point, the numbers meant nothing to me; they might as well have been giving me the formula for cold fusion or something.

Five minutes later when the first images coming out of Haiti hit the screen, I needed no explanation. I don't know how, I don't know why, but as my heart fell and the bile in my stomach rose into my throat, I knew I had to get my ass in gear and start to do something.

"Oh my God. Oh my God." Cherylann's words echoed the ones in my head.

I held my wife to my chest and then at arm's length. "Get the number for Food for the Poor. You've still got the file and the contract, right?"

Cherylann nodded and walked to her office area.

Five minutes later, P.J. McDonald, a dear friend of ours who is the headmaster at Eagle Hill School, the high school where my sons attended, walked into the room. A few minutes later, our youngest, Richie, came home accompanied by his advisor at school, Jenna. We all sat staring at the screen as some minister or the other in Haiti's government spoke, saying there was great devastation and Port-au-Prince was in chaos.

I sat there, my jaw tightening into a clench, rocking back and forth, back and forth in an armchair, barely feeling how precariously balanced I was on those legs, not yet understanding but somehow sensing that the shock waves that had torn into an island sixteen-hundred miles away were bearing down on us, as powerful and as bent on destroying us as it had Haiti. As upset as I was, I had already begun marshalling allies and supplies for the long struggle ahead of us.

SIGNS AND WONDERS

*"God's blueprints are so massive and so all encompassing that
we can't possibly see every detail and every perspective and
every elevation and every floor plan at one time.
He can."*

—LEN

CHERYLANN

As parents, we're constantly on the lookout for signs: are
our kids fitting in, are they doing drugs, is their health
okay, are they developing mentally, socially, spiritually?
Life provides us with some markers to help us better measure
our kids' progress. As Catholics, we saw Britney move through
the sacraments—Baptism, Reconciliation, First Communion,
and Confirmation. School also helps us out with graduation.
Then there were the family trips and birthday remembrances.

I didn't think of it until now, but we mark most of those
events with some kind of party. Even as a little girl, our Brit

1

loved parties. She loved the attention even more than she did the food, the cake, the balloons, or whatever went along with the gathering of family and friends. Still, just because the calendar, the school, the church, or whoever or whatever says that our kids have reached some sort of rite of passage, that doesn't mean that our kids have really grown in the ways that we want them to or feel that they should. If you have kids of your own, I'm sure you know what I mean. Just because your kid has reached the age that the state you live in says they can drive, that doesn't mean they are as responsible and mature as they should be.

Before my eyes Brit was maturing into an independent young woman—free spirited and headstrong, opinionated as all get out. She also could be difficult sometimes. Just ask her brother, Bernie, who once said, "Yes, Britney was mean as nails, would kick you when you were down, ruin your day just because she was having a bad day, and everything always had to be about her. But she was also the 'caring princess,' as most of Brit's roommates from Lynn U. described her."

Bernie saw that side of her more than other people did, but that is typical of siblings. Brit was strong willed, that's for sure, but she evened that off with a sunny disposition that often swayed people in unexpected ways. I remember how, when she was fifteen, we wanted to teach her the value of working for things. The restaurant I owned also had an ice-cream window. Brit didn't want to waitress ("I don't want to take people's orders!") but she didn't mind working the window. I tried to explain that waiting on tables was a better way to make money. In addition to the minimal salary she'd get tips. Lots of tips. She didn't care. She was going to do what she was going to do, even after I explained to her that at best she might come home with five dollars for a three- to four-hour shift.

The inside tables were for full-service customers—those who ordered appetizers, main-course meals, and dessert. The window was where ice cream was served. It was occasionally busy, but the restaurant was usually busy, so waiting tables was the place to be if you wanted to make any money.

I should have known better. The restaurant was across from a Little League diamond, and lots of families stopped by after the baseball games. That often meant fathers, who were usually the coaches, and their sons. I think many of the boys may have had a crush on Brit. Some of them would look at her wide-eyed and say, "I think you're pretty!"

After Brit came home from her first shift, I asked her, "How'd it go?"

"Fine." Brit couldn't keep from smirking.

"Oh, yeah, what's fine mean?"

"Fifty-eight dollars!"

Eventually I'd see how she managed to make more money in tips at that window than anyone before or after that. Brit wasn't manipulative; she genuinely liked people, and her smile and her compassion charmed the dollar bills into that jar. She had a knack for remembering people and the things they'd told her. "Oh, hi, Mr. Jones, what can I get you? Your usual vanilla swirl with jimmies? How's your brother doing with that new job? Does he like it?" That kind of thing. She was great with people. She and Bernie had their normal sibling rivalry stuff. What wasn't typical, based on what I've read and seen about other mother-daughter relationships, was the lack of tension between us. She was never ashamed of Len or me, never hesitated to introduce us to her friends. A lot of times she'd invite me to go along with her and her girlfriends, "C'mon Mom, please go to the movies with us. It'll be fun." I didn't go very often, but it was nice to be asked to the movies, shopping, or to get some ice cream with her.

Brit and her cousin, Shelly, spent a summer living in a trailer home in Maine. At one point, just before Brit went away to school her freshman year, Shelly talked a lot about their time together: Brit letting the lawn go to the point that a neighbor took over cutting it, and Brit convincing her cousin that he actually was the hired help; her bringing Brit breakfast in bed, asking for "butter, please" in her fake wealthy heiress voice—what we all knew as her "fabulous tone."

Shelly also talked about how the two of them made friends so quickly at work, teasing one of the cooks to the point that the other one had to join in. The first time they went out with co-workers, they were at a place where a reggae band was playing. It wasn't long before my daughter jumped on stage, singing "One Love." In addition, Brit proved herself to be the best housewife, cleaning, cooking chicken parmesan for her cousin, greeting her with, "Honey, I'm home!" after work, and jumping next to Shelly on the couch so they could plan the rest of the evening's entertainment. We trusted Brit, letting her live independent of us for that summer. We knew she'd make good choices. They'd mostly be motivated by having a good time, but not always.

So, in October 2009 when Britney came to Len and I and said that as part of her schoolwork at Lynn University she wanted to go to Haiti to do some work with an organization called Food for the Poor, I was really happy.

"How are things going to be different this time?"

"You mean Haiti?"

"Yeah, Lindsay went last year, and you wound up staying on campus and eating at a restaurant and tanning at the beach."

"Trust me. You know that Lindsay said that her experience changed her life. She's going to Haiti again. Food for the Poor is a great organization. I want to go. I have to go."

I knew that my bringing up the previous year's J-Term, the first time Lynn had offered the program, was a sore point for Brit. She'd backed out of going and instead took a movie/dinner course. They would watch a French movie, then go to a French restaurant. She and Meghan, Brit's freshman roommate and one of her BFFs, went to the first class and decided they couldn't be bothered, so they went to the beach instead. She was so honest about it, I had a hard time getting upset with her. Luckily, it was a pass/fail class—though with that kind of attendance, I doubt she passed!

As far as this trip to Haiti was concerned, Lindsay's word was as good as gold. She was very focused and wanted to change the world—which I don't doubt she will do someday. I knew this experience had the potential to be a life-changing experience for Brit.

I also wondered how this fit into a larger pattern I'd seen emerging in Brit's life. She had started out as a communications major; she saw herself as a trendsetter, becoming the next Nancy Grace, and I had no doubt if that was what she set her mind on, she'd achieve it. Lately she was talking about switching over to social work as a major. A little bit of Nancy, a little bit of a Good Samaritan. I didn't really care what she chose, just so long as she was going to be happy doing it.

Rutland is a small town of about six thousand people and is very family oriented. I had grown up here and love the town. Still I sometimes thought that Britney suffered more because of our family's accomplishments than she let on. Len's business success as a builder wasn't something we could hide, and we didn't feel like we had to. Along with the TV commercials he and Brit did, you couldn't really drive anywhere in the area without going past a development that C&S had done. We provided well for our kids, but they had no sense they were privileged or better than anybody else. Still, kids can be cruel, and there were more than a few times when Brit came home upset about some kid insinuating that she was a "rich bitch."

We tried to instill in our kids the idea that you had to give back to the community. Even that can backfire on you. Len was a trustee at Becker College in Worcester. One day Brit wore a sweatshirt to school that said "Becker" on the front. Along with the sweatshirt, she had on a pair of dungarees and flip-flops. I mean, we're not talking a million-dollar outfit here. As she walked down the hall, some kid said, "What, your father owns that college too?"

I asked her how she dealt with that, and she said in typical Brit fashion, "What are you going to do? The kid was an idiot. I just walked by him." In some ways, I thought that those things might have made her stronger, but I couldn't help but wonder if her change in major had something to do with how other people perceived her. We helped build a couple of homes through the Habitat for Humanity program when Len was president of our local chapter and coordinated Blitz Builds long before *Extreme Makeover: Home Edition* did their things in a week. Brit helped out a little bit, but wasn't a Mother Teresa type going out into the streets to minister to the sick and the homeless.

Brit was complicated. She could be demanding, but she also would be the first one to lend you a hand. She was a genuine person with a heart of gold.

LEN

As a father, I'm always going to feel concern for my kids' safety. That's job one. When Brit brought up the idea of going to Haiti, I wanted to know as many facts as I could. I looked over some of the information Food for the Poor provided and learned it was the second-largest charitable organization in the United States in terms of dollars collected and distributed. They were also going to provide security personnel for the group of students and faculty who were going to be down there. In my head, I imagined them like Secret Service agents, kind of blending into the background but still visible enough to make anybody with any bad intentions think twice and then move on.

The J-Term session program with Food for the Poor was called "Journey of Hope," and Cherylann and I had our own hopes for our daughter. College is a time for exploration and trying to find your way in the world. We hoped this journey would help Brit find her purpose in life. She was going to be joining thirteen other people from Lynn University that included the dean of education and another professor. Knowing that school officials also were going to be down there in Haiti, I was pretty certain the right steps were being taken to ensure my daughter's safety.

I also wanted to know about the type of accommodations they were going to be living in during their time in Haiti. I knew that they wouldn't be out doing relief work twenty-four seven, and I knew my daughter—who was fiercely independent—would probably want to go out socializing with the other kids in the evening. I was concerned about her being in a big city like Port-au-Prince during their off hours. Thus, I was relieved to find out that she'd be staying well outside the city in a very nice hotel on a hillside overlooking the capital. The Hotel Montana seemed as modern and as luxurious as anything we'd ever stayed in. We're discount hotel people—Super 8, Motel 6, with the occasional Holiday Inn throw in when we're splurging. So to see the leafy grounds, the pool, the gardens and all that on the Hotel Montana's website made me comfortable. There was a gated entrance, and that would help keep out anyone who didn't belong there.

When she told me that Father Marty, the man who ran the campus ministry at Lynn, was going to accompany them, I felt even better about the opportunity. Father Marty had gone to Jamaica the previous year, so he had some experience in doing this kind of work.

Given all that, I didn't really fear for Brit's safety. I knew she had a good head on her shoulders, but as anyone knows, what you can't control is what other people are going to do. I was satisfied that Lynn University and Food for the Poor were putting in place the things they needed to do to keep my daughter safe. I also knew that Brit could take pretty good care of herself. Some people might think it strange that I took pride in my daughter's toughness, but I did. Brit had the looks and the charm of what most people envision of a high-school cheerleader, but pardon my French, the girl had balls. No pun intended, but some of her toughness was the result of her playing baseball and softball most of her life, including through high school.

She was always a tough little kid, and one story from her junior year in high school should be enough to get my point across. Brit didn't cheer in high school, but her best friend Tara did. That winter, the Mountaineers had to travel to Worcester to play an away game. Now, you have to understand this. I'm from Worcester. I love my hometown, but it's fallen on some hard times and some of those neighborhoods are pretty rough. If it were up to me and it was just me, I'd still live in Worcester. But I've got a wife and family to think about and their safety, so we moved out into the suburbs.

Tara was a little scared about going into that part of town. She didn't know much about the city, except what she'd heard and read. Brit had experienced Worcester first hand. We still go to church at St. Johns in one of the most impoverished areas. So, Brit and about twenty other kids volunteered to go with Tara to the game as her kind of escort.

"Don't worry about it, Tara. I'll go. I'll be up in the stands." All one-hundred-ten pounds of her up in those stands looking out for her best friend. She flexed her arms and laughed.

Later that night, Brit came home all wound up, and I noticed that her right cheekbone looked a little bruised.

"So, what's going on?" I asked.

"Things were going okay at first," Brit settled into her storyteller's voice and her eyes sparkled as she flopped onto our bed and rested her chin on her hand. "Then kids from the other school started yelling things, not nice things. The cops were there, but what could they do?"

"We were winning in the fourth quarter and the yelling got worse. Some of our teachers were there. They told us we should leave before the game ended because they thought things might get out of hand, so we did."

Brit paused and checked her phone.

"And that was it?"

"Hold on!" I watched Brit's thumbs flashing across the phone's keyboard. "So, we were walking in the parking lot, and I heard someone yell, 'Run for it!' I looked back and there were all these kids from East coming after us. I got in the car, and these kids started pounding on it, calling me rich bitch and a bunch of other stupid names. So, I got out of the car and started swinging."

"You did what?" Cherylann and I were both out of our minds at that point.

"Don't you know someone could have had a gun?" I said.

"I wasn't going to take any more shit that night from any-one." Brit shrugged her shoulders and then popped up and walked out of the room saying, "Goodnight. I love you both."

Cherylann and I lay there looking at one another, stunned. I don't think either of us slept that night thinking about what might have happened.

Even so, I was proud of her that night. I have a friend who says that when push comes to shove, there's going to be pushing and shoving. Violence isn't the answer, but sometimes you have to do what you have to do. Brit understood that. We always told her that nobody can take your dignity from you. Those kids had crossed a line with her.

CHERYLANN

You tell your kids the old line about sticks and stones. Brit understood that pretty clearly. So she got teased about being a rich kid a little bit. No big deal. But I did wonder what kind of effect that was having on her once she got to Lynn. It's a private school in Boca Raton, Florida, and that area has a certain wealthy element. Brit would tell me a few times about how uncomfortable she felt when some of the people in Boca would treat service people—cafeteria workers, sales clerks, and other people—very poorly. More than a few times she'd call home yelling to me about how someone had given a waitress a hard time. Her not wanting to take orders aside, she did work as a waitress a few shifts. Her first job in Maine was waiting tables, and she knew that I had done some of the same work. Maybe she shouldn't have taken how those people were acting personally, but I'm glad she did. She stuck up for the little guy all the time, mostly because that's how she viewed herself.

I think Brit learned that while she was a big fish in small pond here in Rutland, she was a small fish in a very large ocean populated with huge fish at Lynn. Though we had done well for ourselves with our businesses back here, she met some kids whose lives made hers look like she was one of those inner-city girls. Not all her friends were like that, and she never told me exactly who were the worst offenders, but Brit's sense of defending the underdog was not something new to us. In fact, when Brit was in the fourth grade, her teacher, Mrs. Dumas, called the parents in for a conference. There wasn't a lot of physical bullying going on, but some of the girls were getting way too catty. Afterward I asked Brit about it, and she said it didn't matter if you were fat, skinny, had glasses, had crooked teeth, straight teeth, or whatever, someone was going to pick on you. This was about the time when the movie *Mean Girls* had come out.

I was proud that Mrs. Dumas singled our daughter out and said to us, "Brit's not one of them. She doesn't say a bad thing about anyone. Doesn't tease anyone."

"That's good. That's how she was taught," I said.

I think Brit carried around that sense of right and wrong, and who had advantages and who didn't for a long time. Brit was a B-average student, but as she got older and especially into high school, her grades began to drop. We thought she wasn't studying hard enough and had more than one discussion about her putting more time into her studies. During her sophomore year, her German teacher told us she thought Brit had a learning disability, and we said, "No way!" Our two boys have severe learning disabilities and were diagnosed at a very early age—like two or three years old. We thought for sure a learning disability would have showed up with Brit much sooner than this.

After much discussion we decided to have her tested and

were shocked by the diagnosis: attention deficit disorder (ADD). Dr. Connors, who performed the tests, said because she was a girl, a lot of the symptoms don't present themselves. Brit's personality and ability to function in every other area is probably why we never picked up on it. The day we received the results was terrific and sad all at once. I'll never forget her looking at me and saying, "I just thought I was dumb this whole time." I was crushed that she had thought of herself this way. I'm sure she saw all the other kids breezing through their work and wondered what was wrong with her and why she couldn't do the same.

After she was diagnosed, we decided not to put her on medication, but instead made a few changes with how she took tests and did her homework. While academics were never easy for her even after this, at least we could pinpoint the problem and work within the parameters of the disorder.

Brit was so gifted socially, so much a free spirit and a leader, that her grades and her academic status probably didn't matter a whole lot to the rest of the kids anyway. Still, there was something about her decision to change majors and do the Haiti trip that signaled some kind of change in her.

When I think about it, I see that Brit didn't have this magical breakthrough moment when she was one person one minute and a different one the next. She was evolving. I can see now that even as far back as the Christmas of '08, there were some signs.

Every year at St. John's, Len, the kids, and I help coordinate a Christmas-gift program. We have done this for more than twenty-two years. St. John's is right downtown in my hometown, and people have really fallen on hard times there. So, to help out at Christmas, we collect, purchase, wrap, and distribute gifts for people in the neighborhood. We've been doing it for years, and the kids are kind of involved but kind of not. Brit was a high-school senior that year, and I thought it was time for her to step up a bit in her efforts. You have to understand that Brit LOVED Christmas.

The October that Brit came to us and told us about her desire to go to Haiti, she started cranking the holiday music immediately after our conversation. I couldn't say anything to her about it; after all, she was obeying the "not before October 1st rule" I'd had to institute. Otherwise, Brit would have played holiday music all year round. For her, Christmas was the best time of year, and it was about the gifts, of course, both getting and giving them. We wanted her to understand she was blessed with a family that could afford some nice things, but that not everybody is. I mean, that sounds kind of hokey, and of course, she knew that in theory. But did she really understand that in reality?

So, in '08 I decided that Brit was going to be my assistant. It was going to be just her and me doing all the coordinating and the handing out. One Saturday before Christmas, it was just Brit and I in a room in the church's hall. One of the parishioners had donated a huge box of gifts—hundreds of whistles, pencils, and other little things that you might find at a dollar store.

A woman and her kids came into the room, and of course, we weren't ready at that point to give things out. Few of the things were wrapped, we hadn't inventoried everything, marked what age and gender they were appropriate for, and all that. Still, how could you not want to help them out?

I can still picture Brit. She was pretty much a by-the-book kind of girl. Rules were rules, and unless she was the one breaking them, they had to be adhered to.

She was marking things down on a sheet of paper with a clipboard in her hand. I saw her brow furrow when this family walked in. Brit was never one of those girls who adored babies and had to scoop them up and hold them. So, when the family's little girl, a toddler of maybe three, her hair all done up in corn-rows and ribbons, spotted Brit and walked unsteadily toward her, I didn't know what was going to happen.

Brit saw the little girl coming toward her, and she set down her clipboard and got this huge grin on her face. She knelt down so she was eye level with the little one, and I heard Brit say, "Hey, do you want to pick something out of this box?"

Brit hauled the big box down onto the floor, and the little girl's eyes lit up like a Christmas tree.

With Brit's help she selected a tiny necklace. The thing couldn't have cost more than a few cents, but you would have thought this was a grab bag at Tiffany's.

Brit helped her put on the necklace, and I expected that was going to be it. Instead, though, Brit sat down on the floor with the little girl and spent time talking with her. I couldn't catch much of what they were saying because I was helping the mother with some canned goods and a few other things. But they stayed there together on the floor, chatting away like old friends reunited, and when it was time for the woman to go, Brit leaned into the child and gave her a hug. Brit had a huge smile on her face that was reflected in pure pleasure in the little girl's eyes.

I could tell that not only was Brit reaching out to this little girl, but she also was discovering how very fortunate our family was.

LEN

By Thanksgiving, everything with Lynn University and Food for the Poor was signed, sealed, and delivered. Brit was Haiti's for J-Term!

This is hard for me, talking about those weeks before she left, knowing what happened on January 12, 2010. As I said, I'm a Catholic, a believer in God. Some people say the Lord moves in mysterious ways. That's true, but I've come to think of God as a mystery writer—true-life mysteries, though. (Maybe that's also partly because Brit loved true-crime books and TV shows.)

But like Cherylann said, she was looking for signs and wondering how these decisions fit into a larger picture of who our daughter was becoming. Me, I'm also interested in looking back, leafing through the pages of the script that God had written, seeing how he had planted clues for us to figure out the mystery. And maybe it's like those books and TV shows; when the outcome is revealed, those clues suddenly stand out better, the pieces of the jigsaw puzzle fit together in ways more obvious than they did before.

I guess that one way to look at it is that in our grief, we're trying to make sense of things, put together a picture that doesn't just appear rational but offers comfort. Personally, I think the ways of God are knowable. I don't think he wants to trick us, make us feel any less intelligent or aware. I think he plants those clues so we can look back later, see his guiding hand in all things, let us know he was present at all times, that he hadn't abandoned us at all.

Jesus was a carpenter, and the Father is the great architect. As a builder it brings me comfort to put it like that. God's blueprints are so massive and so all encompassing that we can't possibly see every detail and every perspective and every elevation and every floor plan at one time.

He can.

We just have to take it in a page at a time, remember what we saw in the past, and try to keep it all fresh in our minds.

All that to say, when Brit came home in December 2009 prior to going to Haiti, I sensed some things were different about her. I really couldn't have articulated exactly what. My impressions were mostly based on observations, and I was pleased, really pleased with what I saw.

As you know, Christmas is a big deal in our house, and Brit was the ringleader of many of the things that went on during the holidays. After getting home from school in mid-December, she had a few weeks to do her gift-buying, helping at St. John's, and all that. In the past, when she was in high school and during her freshman year at Lynn, that also meant going out nearly every night with friends. But that year was different. Not much, but enough for me to notice that she was sticking closer to home a little bit more. One afternoon, the kids and I were all in the family room. We videotape everything in our family. If aliens come down to Earth and want to know what family life was like at the latter end of the twentieth century and the beginning of the twenty-first, we'll invite them over, pop some corn, and show them.

So, that afternoon the three kids, Cherylann and I were all sitting around watching some of the old home videos. We were laughing at the bad haircuts, bad outfits, and just enjoying being with one another. At one point, there was a scene of Brit and Kelly, a girl who at one time was my daughter's best friend. We were at some function in Rutland, and there were Kelly and Brit lip-synching to some Britney Spears song up on stage. They were so good; they won the competition against girls much older than them. Instead of jumping up and down and pumping her fists in the air reliving the victory, Brit sat there smiling but quiet.

She excused herself, and the rest of us sat there looking at one another. A moment later, a light came on the phone next to me, indicating that someone had picked up in another part of the house. I didn't want to eavesdrop, but I was curious. After dinner that night, I asked Brit whom she had called.

"Kelly."

"How come? The two of you haven't been in touch in years."

"I know. I felt bad about that. We were such good friends and then—"

To me, her silence said a lot. The Christmas before I had come home from work, and Brit was in her car in the driveway, her cell phone in her hand. She was just staring at it and sobbing. I tapped on the glass, and she stepped out of the car and into my arms.

I asked her what was wrong, and she said, "Why can't they just be happy for me?"

I didn't know the specifics of who "they" were and what "they" were doing, but I was able to guess. Most of Brit's high-school friends had stuck close to home instead of going away to college. I wasn't worried about Brit adapting to life in Florida a thousand and something miles from home. She was independent and strong. What I didn't anticipate and can't really figure out about girls is why her friends would give her grief for having chosen a different way from them.

15

The point is, that in a way, Brit had done the same thing with Kelly. Her friend was incredibly smart, one of those really gifted kids who excels at the books. I'm not speaking from experience here, but from what I've heard, it isn't always easy being a smart kid in school. I can't say for sure, but I suspect that's why Kelly and Brit drifted apart. They moved in different social circles.

I don't know exactly, but Brit said seeing that video of her and Kelly and how much fun they had then made her want to get back in touch to let her know she was sorry for whatever, and that she missed having her in her life.

"Christmas can be a time of getting in touch with old friends, right?" Brit asked. "Letting them know they're still part of your life?"

"That's true. It's important that people know you haven't forgotten them, that they're a big part of who you are today."

Almost thirty years ago, a woman came into my life and gave a struggling carpenter who did framing jobs a real opportunity to move up in the world and make a name for himself and a better life for his family. Her name is Carla. I knew her from a summer community where my seven siblings and I grew up. I can never repay her for the kindness and faith she showed in me, but she's the reason why as a family we give back to the community as much as we can.

Also, to let Carla know how much we appreciate what she did for us, we visit her every Christmas Eve. She's a part of our lives and our Christmas Eve routine. We leave the house around 2:30, get to Carla's place in Worcester about 3:00, and leave forty-five minutes later in time to get to Christmas Eve services at 4:15. Like clockwork for the past thirty years, we've been doing that as a family. Carla's been widowed for more than thirty-five years, she has family, but we still want to thank her by bringing her a little Christmas gift and visiting with her.

In 2009 Carla was ninety-four years old, in a wheelchair, wracked by spinal pain, and frailer than ever. It was really hard for the kids to see her like this—they felt so bad for her. As they got older they understood what Carla had meant to me and appreciated her for it.

They'd sit there politely through the visits. As younger kids I imagine they were thinking of what was going to be under the tree for them; as older kids they likely were wondering what text messages they were missing. One thing they could count on, was that for the past ten or so years, just as we were saying Merry Christmas to Carla and making our way to the door, she would say, "This is going to be our last Christmas."

Not exactly festive, but given her age and health, realistically speaking, she was in the ballpark with her estimation. We noticed and expected her to say that, but that year, we were standing there shrugging our way back into our winter coats, not saying anything but waiting for it. It was like we were actors and it was in the script, and this line had to be delivered or the rest of us couldn't go on with ours.

That year, Carla didn't deliver the line. I could hear wool ruffling and zippers zipping, but not the line.

So then, totally out of character for Brit because she's not one to openly express affection physically, she stepped up and bent over to Carla and hugged her. Not one of those A-frame, just-brush-your-shoulders-together-and-get-your-head-out-of-the-way kinds of hugs, but a big hug.

In the car, I said to Brit, "That was nice of you to hug Carla like that."

Her voice sounded kind of funny to me, a little bit pinched. "Dad, that's the first time she didn't say, 'This is our last Christmas,' so I thought this really was going to be the last time I saw her."

Months later and in a seemingly different lifetime, I called Carla to wish her a happy birthday on April 1. Who would have thought that what Brit said was going to be true, but that the ninety-five-year-old was going to be the one who would remark, "Do you know what I didn't say to you this year? 'This will be my last Christmas,' and Brit came in and hugged me?"

She knew why Brit hugged her. I couldn't see the sign then, but I see it now.

And just so you don't think this is a father imagining things through his grief, a while ago Bernie was talking about that same holiday, that same incident I referred to earlier when we were all sitting around watching home videos. Sure, the kids were laughing and all, but at several points Brit said to her brothers, "I love you guys." Okay, so there was a bit of mockery in her tone a time or two when she said it, but at others there was a poignant sincerity that I'm not imagining, a tenderness in her voice that ears beaten up on by the sounds of hammers and circular saws can't attribute to some lessening of my auditory ability.

"It was almost like she knew. Almost like she knew she had to say some things," Bernie said.

Of course, in the immediacy of the moment, none of that really registered with any of us on a conscious level. After all, Brit grew tired of the videos, cranked up the stereo, and Bruce Springsteen's "Santa Claus Is Coming to Town" ran into Mariah Carey's "All I Want for Christmas Is You." Instead of visions of sugar-plum fairies, I had visions of Brit and her cousin, Jillian, on a video of them dancing away to those songs.

In our house we sure knew it was Christmas. The halls were decked, the crown pork roast was in the oven, and our daughter was everywhere, literally sometimes with bells on, ushering in the most wonderful time of the year.

I'm no Wise Man, and even if the stars in the east had spelled it out for me in great big letters, I don't think I could have anticipated what was going to happen next, wouldn't have been able to believe that those signs and wonders had such an awful and beautiful message to deliver.

STANDING TOGETHER

"We deal with what we're given and sometimes can grow to appreciate it more than we ever thought possible."

—CHERYLANN

LEN

When I said that I had to start marshalling resources like I was about to fight a battle, I had no idea at the time that it would sometimes prove difficult to know who was on our side.

One thing was never in doubt: Cherylann's and my family's devotion and support. Sure, there was bound to be some tension during the hours, days, and eventually months that followed, but everyone pitched in as best they could. No Gengel is very good at keeping an opinion unvoiced, and we wear our hearts and our guts on our sleeves. But when

19

the chips are down, you always know where you stand with everybody—shoulder to shoulder ready to fight.

I came from a family of eight kids, and we had fourteen children of our own. As my oldest sister, Christine, said, "We were taught that children in our family are a gift to be cherished—and we did that." When Brit was born, thirty-two family members came to the birthing suite to greet her entry into the world. We helped raise each other's children and the cousins had strong bonds. Our house was usually the family meeting place for parties and celebrations. Today we needed family more than ever.

Along with our worries about Brit, we wanted to be sure the boys were okay. Richie's a sensitive kid, a big kid whose physical appearance doesn't clue you in to how kindhearted he is. When he walked in the door, his face ashen, eyes darting, I walked up to him and gave him a big hug and a kiss on the cheek.

"It's going to be okay," I told him. "We all have to stay strong and believe and pray."

Richie nodded and went upstairs to his room.

Cherylann's mom, Kathy, and her sister, Jodi, came right over. We gathered in the great room, watching the television coverage, none of us really saying anything. We knew Port-au-Prince was a big city, sprawling, and we knew Brit's precise location—the Hotel Montana. The Lynn University group was being housed on the outskirts of the city, and we were grateful for that. I'd seen the photos of the structure and believed that it was far more sound than anything I'd seen of the other buildings that were either damaged or still intact.

Since he'd gotten home, Bernie had been sitting right there with us, working at his laptop.

"Hey Dad, the epicenter of the quake was in Port-au-Prince. According to Google Maps, the Hotel Montana is ten miles away from there."

That gave me some hope, but still, we wanted someone to mention the hotel itself. Brit had told us a lot of foreigners stayed there, as well as some higher-ups in Haitian society. Bill and Hillary Clinton had stayed there during their first year of marriage. This was one of only two five-star hotels that we knew of. I figured that might be newsworthy, but as the clock ticked past 6:30, still nothing on the news.

Cherylann had been dialing Brit's number over and over again, knowing it was unlikely that any kind of cell phone towers would still be up, but still you had to try. I had called my sisters, Christine and Ruth, and they'd joined our vigil. I was grateful for them being there, but not even their presence in the room could keep my heart from collapsing minutes after they'd arrived.

We watched CNN, and they were interviewing a Haitian ambassador. He was home over the holidays from whatever country he served in. He must have been a pretty important official because he had access to a helicopter. He said that he had flown over the site of the Hotel Montana. At the very first mention of those words, I felt every hair on my arms rise. When he continued by saying the building was completely leveled, I felt a chill creep up my spine.

After that, I lost it. I can't remember exactly what I said and what I kept contained, but I do know a cascade of thoughts came rushing to my mind. How could this happen? This is a nightmare. This is just not true. Our Brit has to be okay.

I told myself I had to keep it together for the sake of Cherylann and the kids. At that point the house was in a bit of an uproar, to put it mildly, but I knew I couldn't feed into that. Panicking wasn't going to do anyone any good. Besides, we had a logical explanation for everything. Brit couldn't reach us because there were no cell phones operational at that point. Several news accounts had mentioned that fact. Bernie had demonstrated that Brit's location was far away from the center of the city, the place where we'd seen the only images of the destruction.

That report from the ambassador? That was hard to dismiss, but it's easy to go with what you know firsthand versus what someone else says. When you're desperate to believe something good, it's easy to reject the bad. Besides, that first report at the Hotel Montana was quickly contradicted by others stating that it was only partially damaged, that it was still

21

standing but some areas of it crushed. Which do you choose to believe? Besides, we had other things to do, other means we'd hoped would provide us with a message of certainty.

We'd been trying to reach someone at Lynn University since I'd gotten home but hadn't been able to reach anyone there. Cherylann and I alternated making phone calls to Food for the Poor and had, to that point, no success there either.

Finally, hours into our vigil, I spoke with a man from Food for the Poor. Now, I have a lot of respect for the organization and for other charitable organizations like it, but this individual I had no respect for prior to and following this tragedy. At first I was in contact with a woman at Food for the Poor who'd served as the guide who had taken the group from Miami to Haiti. She was now back in the U.S. She assured us that all of the Lynn University people were at the hotel and they were all fine. She wouldn't say anything beyond that. That wasn't very comforting or helpful, but I understood she was stating the party line. When I asked to speak to this other person, she put him on.

"Tell me who you have at the Hotel Montana who can verify for a fact that they're all there and okay," I said.

There was a pause and then in a kind of an undertaker's hushed and falsely soothing tone, he replied, "We have no one from the organization with whom we have direct communication." I felt my jaw go tight as he continued. "However, we do have communication from another person outside the organization in Haiti who has seen the Hotel Montana, and it is okay."

"You're certain?" I pressed him.

"Go to bed, Mr. Gengel. They are all at the Hotel Montana and doing fine. We spoke to them just before the earthquake. They're going to be okay. We'll talk in the morning."

We said good-bye, and I put the phone down, feeling more than just a bit of relief coursing through my body. I worked it out in my head.

Food for the Poor had someone inside Haiti who'd confirmed that the Hotel Montana was okay.

Brit had been at the hotel at the time the earthquake struck.

Therefore Brit was okay.

CHERYLANN

As the evening turned into night, I held my cell phone in my hand, pressing redial, hoping that I'd hear that familiar voice on the other end of the line. I didn't, of course, and I'm not sure if I was acting like a kid with a loose tooth poking and probing at it to give my thoughts some place to go, or if I was somehow on autopilot, doing the only thing I could to offset the feelings of helplessness.

At one point, the clamor of the thirty or so people in the house got to be too much for me, so I went outside with the dog. Bruno was still a pup, an English bulldog, appropriately enough. It seems like everybody in our house had the kind of tenacious attitude that makes that dog so legendary. Thinking of how we got Bruno gave me a bit of relief.

One of Brit's friends had an English bulldog, and my daughter loved that thing. I use the word *thing* now even though my attitude toward Bruno has changed since those first days when we got him. You see, Bruno was a "present" for me, a surprise gift. A real surprise since I'd been against us having a dog for quite some time. With the kids and their busy schedules, Len's and my even more jam-packed lives, I knew that whatever time and attention a dog got would likely fall to me. Not fair to the dog. Not fair to me.

So, when we flew down to Boca for Parents Weekend during Brit's first semester away at Lynn and wanted to go out for ice cream, the last thing on my mind were four-legged friends and the possibility that I might have one.

I'm smart enough to recognize an ambush when I see one, but I was pretty powerless to defend myself when, ice cream in hand, Brit suggested we walk next door to "look at" the puppies.

"Don't you just love him?" Brit's infectious tone and smile were difficult to resist. She placed a warm, squirming bull-dog puppy in my arms, then stepped back, pressed her hands

23

between her legs, and then brought them up to her face. Brit took a picture with her phone and sent it to her co-conspirators: Len and the boys.

That was so Brit. As I later found out, she and some of her girlfriends had discovered this ice-cream shop and the next-door pet store far earlier than Parents Weekend. On one visit to the ice-cream place, Brit had gone in to look at the puppies. She instantly fell in love with one of them, the English bulldog who would become Bruno, and had called Len. He recruited Richie and Bernie, and together they hatched this scheme. So, instead of just one scoop of watermelon sherbet, Brit came home at Thanksgiving with a bag of bulldog—all six pounds of him, most of it in his head. Len still has the video of Brit sashaying down the staircase to the baggage claim area at Logan, a shopping bag held daintily in front of her, her mischievous grin and eyes giving her away. She looked like *Reese Witherspoon* in Legally Blonde. I'll always cherish that memory of her.

As I stood there that cold and clear January night, I was grateful to have Bruno, another bit of Brit with me, but this one I could see, hear, and touch. I knew Brit wanted a dog, and this was one way for her to get one, but I also knew she wanted me to want to have a dog and to be happy in his company. There's a distinction there, but it's more about Brit's generosity, her belief that people should do the things they want to and not get caught up in the possible negative consequences of things. In her heart, she knew things would work out between Bruno and me, and that, in the long run, she would be right about the place that Bruno would take in our lives, the comfort and companionship he would bring us.

I couldn't have known what form her belief in the power of that gift would take. Obviously, I'd prefer to not have grown to need Bruno, both in those immediate moments after hearing the news and even today. But we deal with what we're given and sometimes can grow to appreciate it more than we ever thought possible.

Brit was strong-minded, and her little scheme to get a dog

for us fits into a larger picture of a test of wills that she and I waged for years. I remember standing out in the driveway with Bruno, feeling him tugging at the leash, straining to go the way he wanted to go, to spend as much time as he wanted sniffing what appealed to him regardless of whatever agenda I had in mind.

"You remind me of someone," I said to him. He turned and looked at me, his so-serious expression softened for a few seconds as if to tell me he understood. An instant later he was back going about his business, only vaguely aware, if at all, of what I needed from him.

* * *

Brit could stick up for herself, and as Len's story about the fight after the basketball game should tell you, she was also there for her friends. And not just her friends; she stuck up for the underdog. Of course, she could be pretty brutal in teasing her brothers, but she didn't like it when anyone else said anything too harsh about them. She'd laugh and say she didn't like anybody else cutting in on her territory, but I knew she felt protective of them. Those weeks before Christmas when we all were sitting around and the kids were sharing some of the exploits had frightened and comforted me.

Frightened me because knowing that your underage daughter had been out joyriding with friends, going to a Dunkin' Donuts in a not-too-safe part of Worcester, and breaking the law, let's not forget, was not the kind of thing you want to hear about, even after the fact.

"Oh, Mom. Don't worry. It was me and Shauna." Shauna was one of Brit's best friends.

"As if that makes a difference. You took our car and went out to Dunkin' Donuts in Worcester? I can see going around the neighborhood, but my God, Brit."

She smiled and shrugged her shoulders in that no-big-deal kind of way that she could have taught a master class in.

"We wanted ice cream."

I said to her, "You know, I can still ground you for that."

She opened her beautiful blue eyes wide as though she was frightened. She shook her head. "No, you can't."

We both laughed.

I came to the end of the driveway and looked down the sidewalk toward the other houses. Ice cream. Does it always have to come down to food in this family? I let out a little laugh and that felt good.

I stood there for a few minutes, my hands thrust in my pockets and tried to imagine what was going on in those houses. I was sure that the TV was on, that some of those people were watching the coverage of the earthquake, feeling a bit of sympathy for those poor people in Haiti. Others were upset that their usual program was being pre-empted or that they had to use the remote to get to some distant part of the TV universe to escape. I knew that for me there was no getting away from it. Haiti had happened. It had happened to our daughter. It had happened to us.

I remembered 9/11 and how bad I felt not just for the people in New York and D.C., but the people who had dropped their loved ones off at Logan or kissed them good-bye before they drove themselves so that they could make that fateful flight that was hijacked and detoured.

I had to push those thoughts away, just as I kept pushing that redial button. I didn't like the idea that it was a cell phone that I had to carry with me as another reminder. Len struggled with Brit's independent spirit sometimes. She loved to party, and to her a curfew was more of a suggestion than a requirement. For periods of her life, Brit didn't just test boundaries, she pulled up the stakes we'd pounded into the ground, sometimes moved them to a location more convenient for her to do what she wanted and sometimes tossed them away. It wasn't like she was in a bunch of legal trouble or anything, maybe just typical teenage stuff, but still it hurt Len.

Cell phones can connect us and brings us pleasure. They can also cause us pain. Len knew that, and he also knew that the most effective punishment he could give Brit wasn't just to ground her but to take away her cell phone. As he used to say, "If you want to make a punishment that hurts a teenage girl, taking that cell phone is the only thing that works."

As I made my way back up to the house, I thought of those times when Brit stood in front of Len, her expression grown hard, her eyes narrowed and defiant.

"Hand it over."

She'd reach into her pocket, cocking her hip to her side, her eyes never leaving my husband's equally stern face.

The phone slapped down into his open palm, and she spun on her heel, her hair like a curtain drawing close at the end of a scene. Except there'd be that last line of dialogue: "I hate you."

I knew she was not just acting out, but also really acting out a part like a stage performer when she said those words.

Still, they had to hurt. As I pressed the phone to my ear and heard the ring repeating endlessly, I knew that no words hurt as well.

I needed to get back inside and find Len, hoping that he'd learned something more definite. I wasn't sure for how long I could go on standing on such unsteady emotional ground.

3

WE ARE FAMILY

"I know Brit's my older sister and I'm her younger brother, and we're supposed to hate each other a lot of the time. Then there's other times I think she's the best."

—BERNIE

LEN

I f it had been anyone else doing some of these things, I might have been really angry, but it was my family, so I understood.

In those earliest hours, the family's reactions ran the gamut from optimistic to shattered. As the first images came onto the screen, the gasps and oh-my-God's were whispered and wailed. That was okay with me. We had only one ground rule: You could react and respond in whatever way you felt you needed to, and the rest of us had to respect that everybody was going to behave differently. If you didn't like it, then either walk away or ignore that person's response. We weren't going to tell anybody how they should be acting.

I was struck by how different the tone in that house was since we had gathered there just a little bit more than a week ago. Brit's birthday is January 21, and we knew she was going to be in Haiti on that date, so we "decided" to give her an early party. That means Brit came to us asking us to do something for her birthday with the whole family. We had some back and forth about that because it was so close to the holidays, and we didn't want to burden anybody with more gift-buying. Brit chimed in that she didn't want presents; she just wanted everybody to get together. Cherylann didn't need the extra duty of hosting and cooking for another Gengel gathering, but she did and it was great.

We gorged ourselves and as the night went on, the music got cranked up, the furniture got pushed aside, and we were all out there dancing. Everybody was having a great time, and I stepped aside for a couple of numbers and just watched everybody.

The holidays had been a lot of fun, of course, a little stressful as they always are, but they were different somehow this time around. Brit seemed more at ease with herself, more grown up. And there she was dancing and singing, her head thrown back, her hair whipping around, acting like a goofball.

The kid never lacked for self-confidence, really, and a smile still comes to my face when I remember opening day of our Little League season when Brit was nine. She loved baseball and was one of the few girls in our league, but she was as tough and hardnosed as they come and didn't give an inch to any of the boys—or to anybody else for that matter.

So, Brit heard through the grapevine that one of her fourth-grade classmates, a girl whose name I forget, had been selected to sing the national anthem at some local event. Well, if someone else could do it, so could Britney. Although she had no vocal training and had never performed in front of a large crowd before, she decided she was going to belt out "The Star-Spangled Banner" at her Little League game, and not just any game. Opening day of the Little League season was still a big deal back then in our town, with many more kids playing than today. All the teams paraded in and gathered on the field. So, a week after letting us know she wanted to sing just like her classmate, in front hundreds of parents, her teammates, and opponents, Britney stood at home plate. I watched as she squared her shoulders, spread her legs a bit to get firm footing (I couldn't help but think she was digging in just like she did as a batter), and took the microphone off the stand. She paused for just a second and looked around, then jumped in with both vocal chords. Once she was through, she set down the microphone, pulled on her hat, tucked her glove in the crook of her arm, and trotted out to her position to begin the game.

No big deal. Our kid was fearless.

I'd overheard a few of my family members asking her why she was going to Haiti; what in the world was she thinking? My wife and I had a similar conversation with her, but it was good to hear her telling other people the same thing and with the same conviction she had when she spoke with us. She wasn't sure, but she most likely was going to switch her major from television communications to social work. She wasn't so interested in being well known as she was in doing good things. Those are my words and not hers, but she'd said just as much herself.

The day after the party, the day before Brit left for Florida to begin her training for the Haiti trip, Cherylann and I took her out to dinner. Normally it's all of us together, but that night we told Richie and Bernie that we wanted to spend some time with their sister alone. They were fine with that, and we had a nice dinner with our daughter. We told her how proud we were of her, and we tried to prepare her as best we could for what to expect. Neither of us had been to Haiti, but we knew this was going to be a life-changing experience for her.

Brit laughed and said in her self-mocking way, "I know that. It's going to be fabulous."

We laughed along with her, sensing she was using her catch-phrase ironically. A family friend of—how do I put this—some advanced years, used the expression "fabulous, darling"

31

in a way that Thurston Howell III or his wife, Lovey, might have used it on the old TV show *Gilligan's Island*. I'm not sure why, but it struck Brit as absolutely hilarious, and over time, she used it in the same way as you might expect a toting-a-little-dog-in-a-purse-Paris-Hilton celebutante type to be using it. Sort of sarcastically but not entirely. Only in Brit's case it was almost all irony, unlike what we'd come to think of as some of the "Boca bitches" she'd encountered while in Florida. Too much money. Too many privileges. Too little moral grounding.

I guess that's what I saw and heard in my conversations with my daughter over the holidays. I knew she had a strong moral compass. She sometimes sailed away from her own true north as most kids do, but she was making the necessary course corrections by deciding to follow through on her J-Term project. Even more, her decision to switch majors was her deciding that maybe life was less about becoming Oprah the media mogul and more about being the Oprah who helps people and builds schools and all the rest. And I'm sure she would do it with her own sass and style—like a cross between Oprah and Nancy Grace.

If Haiti was going to be transformational for Brit, that was because she was already moving in another direction. We were eager to see where she was going to wind up. For all the changing Brit seemed to be doing, one thing remained the same. The light in her eyes and her smile was still high-voltage electricity, only it was made up of few bits of mischief and more mission than before.

CHERYLANN

Brit always cared about other people and their feelings. Unlike most kids, though, she didn't seem to care too much about what other people thought of her. Sure, she wanted to dress nicely at times, but she wasn't one of those overly-obsessed-with-appearances girls with their nose in a fashion magazine and their head in their closets trying to figure out what combinations would wow everybody. Pajama bottoms, sweatshirts, and flip-flops seemed to do a lot of school days.

In high school Brit was one of those rare kids who seemed to able to cross the traditional boundaries. She would tell me about the cliques but just laugh and say they were stupid. As a result, she had friends from all the different high-school social groups: jocks, partiers, preps, nerds, or whatever other terms exist for the suburban teen social strata. Len likes the story about Brit sticking up for her girlfriend, but I think Brit and her attitude toward prom say something just as important about her.

Don't get me wrong. Brit loved the idea of a high school formal, and she went her senior and junior years. She spent just as much time picking out a dress, getting her hair and nails done, and all of that. More than a few guys asked her to go with them her junior year, but she turned them down with a simple and truthful explanation.

"I just want to go and have fun. I want to be with my friends. I don't want to make it into anything more than that."

Among Brit's really good friends were Shauna and her cousin, Shelly. Brit struggled a bit academically until she was diagnosed with a learning disability. We didn't talk about it much, but I knew that it wasn't easy for her to see how some of her classmates breezed through high school. Eventually having a label applied to her and being marked as different was probably tough. (She was given extra time on some tests and was given some reading assistance but remained in regular classes.) Even before any of this, Brit was always on the side of the underdog, and she hated seeing anyone else getting picked on or being left out. She had a huge heart, and that's the reason why Shauna, a girl Brit knew since second grade who eventually grew to be her best friend, came to live with us for a couple of years for personal reasons. Brit was thrilled—finally a sister! We moved in an extra twin bed, gave Shauna some drawer space and half the closet. Of course, they already shared *all* their clothes, so what was Brit's was Shauna's and what was Shauna's was Brit's.

Maybe that's why Brit and I were so close. Being outnumbered by the boys in the house, we had to stick together. The thing is, though, we genuinely liked each other's company.

Brit also reached out to her cousin, Shelly, who was quiet and didn't get invited to her prom. Brit knew how much Shelly wanted to go to prom, so instead of going with her boyfriend her senior year, Brit took Shelly, knowing this was Shelly's opportunity to enjoy that special night.

At her birthday party, I sat and listened as Bernie told us about his "special" relationship with his sister.

"Brit could beat the shit out of me until I turned fifteen." Brit took great delight in invading Bernie and his buddies when they were down in their "cave"—an area underneath the house that was an addition and never backfilled. He had even set up a bench, a recliner and a table out there. "She came up to me, gave me a cheap shot to the side. I picked her up and threw her! Not until this past Thanksgiving did she try beating me up again.

"One minute my buddies were texting me about how hot my sister looked, and the next they'd be grossed out by something foul she'd say. I knew she was doing it to just get a reaction out of them, but still you don't think of girls saying the same kind of rude stuff about taking a smelly dump like Brit would."

Not one of my prouder recollections of Brit.

Of course, that was followed up the night after I took Brit to Logan so she could get to Lynn U. for her training. After Brit had gotten home from dinner with Len and me, she needed ice cream. And I mean *needed*. So, she asked Richie and Bernie if they wanted to go to the grocery store with her. They all bundled up and piled into the car.

I didn't hear about this until after Brit was gone and Bernie and I were alone after dinner doing the dishes. He was drying. He leaned against the counter with his hip, as he was turning a plate and wiping it down.

"I know Brit's my older sister and I'm her younger brother, and we're supposed to hate each other a lot of the time."

"Yeah? Hate's kind of a strong word for it," I said, but knew Brit could get to Bernie in ways that made me think she could have had a future as an interrogation expert.

"Then there's other times I think she's the best."

"Such as?"

"Well, last night we went to the grocery store, right? Brit had to get some watermelon sherbet." He stood shaking his head. "That stuff is so sweet, I don't know how she can eat it. Anyway, we're at the Big Y in Holden in the ice-cream aisle, and I had gone to get some chips and there was Brit standing in front of the cases. Next to her was this old guy. I swear he had a hump on his back. He turned toward me, and he had crossed eyes and his tongue was hanging out, and he was walking like a penguin with a broken leg."

"That poor man."

"I guess, but I burst out laughing when I saw him. I couldn't help it." Bernie paused and twirled the dish towel into a rattail and snapped it a few times. "The thing was, though, Brit didn't laugh. She stood there chatting with the guy, talking about ice milk versus low fat, flavors, that kind of thing. Then she opened one of the cases for him and helped him get what he needed. She had the watermelon sherbet cradled in her arm like a baby or something, and she just stood there talking to the guy for a couple more minutes. Talking with him like he was just a regular person. She's like that, I've noticed. She doesn't give a shit if you're black, white, purple, fat, old, skinny. She's nice to people. Other people. I don't think I've ever been prouder of her. "

"Did you tell her that?"

Bernie smiled. "Of course not. You kidding?"

Hearing that story made me feel good and made me worry a bit. I knew Brit's big heart was a blessing. You know how it is as a parent. You trust your kid, but you don't always trust other people. In the days leading up to Brit's departure for Haiti, I was hoping the students and staff were going to get good instruction from the advisors at Food for the Poor. I wanted Brit to experience the reality of what life was like in Haiti, but I didn't want it to be too real, too up close and personal. I wanted her heart and mind to be opened, but I didn't want it to be broken. I knew too many people who didn't want to look at the harsher realities of life and turned their back at any mention of them. They didn't want to be knocked out of their comfort zone and did as much as they could to protect their ignorance-is-bliss world view.

Bernie's story about the man in the grocery gave me hope and reconfirmed what I'd already been seeing in my daughter. She wasn't going to turn her back. She was going to reach her hands out to help whoever needed her. I just hoped that no one would take advantage of her generous spirit. My daily prayers went unchanged. I always asked God to look out for my family.

LEN

That first night when we heard the news about what happened in Haiti was, to put it mildly, a tough one. I'm a big sports fan, so this analogy makes sense to me. That first night and the next day or so were like the early minutes of a game or the first rounds of a boxing match. You always hear broadcasters saying the two teams are feeling each other out, probing for weaknesses, assessing the opponent's strategy. At the same time, it felt like I'd already been battered by blows to the head. That made it difficult to really be able to know for certain if my brain was functioning properly.

I thought I had a pretty good idea what I was going to be dealing with, but I also had some doubts. After all, I'd never had to face anything that was as much of an unknown as Haiti. The country was the wild card in all of this. Add in the fact that I'm somebody who is used to and likes to be in control, and the news that the situation on the ground was growing worse as more information became available, you can understand my anxiety. The only thing close to what I was experiencing was my reaction to the attacks on the World Trade Center. In those first few hours I was feeling a lot of the same helplessness I felt back in 2001—though this was intensified and personal since it was my daughter. I wanted to do something, and besides making a few phone calls, trying to connect with other families who had their kids down there with the Lynn University group, there wasn't a lot I could physically do.

My mind was screaming for me to get on a plane and get to Haiti. I knew that wasn't going to be possible, but still that's what I wanted. Call me a Doubting Thomas, but until I could hear Brit's voice, until I could hold her in my arms, I was going to be on edge. I had to balance those doubts and anxieties with not raising too many alarms with Cherylann and the boys. I'm somebody who likes to tackle problems head on, so in most ways, just having to sit around and wait for word from other people was my worst-case scenario.

That first night, Cherylann and I went to bed with both of us feeling drained but wired—our bodies were dragging but our minds were racing. Like most married couples, we'd developed a kind of shorthand language, so when I asked her as she lay with her head on my chest, "Do you trust me?" she knew I was suggesting something more complicated than those simple words. Same thing when she answered by saying, "Yes."

Cherylann knows me better than anyone, and she knows how I approach situations. Still, I wanted to hear from her that she would support whatever I was going to do. It was beyond important that the two of us stay united in all of this. I was prepared for our friends and family to have different kinds of reactions and ways to deal with the uncertainty, but I needed from Cherylann what I've always been able to count on—her constant support and level-headedness.

Of course, that didn't mean we were going to hide our emotions from one another. That night we clung to one another and cried and cried, the two of us bawling with great chest-heaving sobs. We'd have moments of calm, but then we'd start up again, the worry tearing at us, exposing every raw nerve in our bodies.

Everything that first night had been spastic like that. One minute this. The next minute that. I can't think of a better word for it than spastic. The media was giving all kinds of conflicting reports. We were hearing from CNN that the Hotel Montana where the kids were staying was 100 percent leveled. Then we'd hear it was only partially damaged. We knew that Port-au-Prince was heavily damaged, but we didn't know exactly where the Hotel Montana was in relation to the capital. Thank God for Bernie. He's a self-proclaimed computer geek. He started an Internet consulting business when he was fifteen, and he put his skills to use that night for us.

He used Google Maps to show us Haiti and Port-au-Prince and how the Hotel Montana was outside the city by about ten miles. That was a relief. He also went on CNN's site, and I don't know all the details of how he did this, but he put a message out on Facebook as well. He asked people to repost his message. Somehow, one of the lead reporters from CNN got in touch with him. They seemed to be as much in the dark information wise as the rest of us, and knowing that Bernie had some insider knowledge through his connection with the Journey of Hope, I guess they were hoping he'd be able to help them out. I didn't have a whole lot of time to consider this, but I do remember feeling a bit unsettled by the idea that a major worldwide news organization was essentially in the same situation as our family, desperate for insight and information.

Our "newsroom" was the great room of our house. It seats thirteen people, but more than thirty of us crammed into the space, people sitting on the floor, draped over the arms of chairs and the couch, lined up along the walls. Those whose eyes weren't glued to the TV screen were often on their cell and smart phones, taking turns at the family computer, every one of them hoping our journey would end well. For the next two days, it was standing-room only in our house, the big-screen TV on constantly, and it was as if the on-air people at CNN were becoming a part of the family. Cherylann's mom and her sister,

Jodi, joined with my sisters Ruth, Joan, and Chrissy in holding down the fort. Nearly everybody who came over stayed the night. I don't know how they all got fed, but they did.

Cherylann and I had been scrambling to make phone calls that night, trying to cover as many bases as we could. When I attended Central Connecticut State University, the campus priest was Robert Lord. He's become a very dear friend, so to my family and me, he's Father Bob. As that first evening wore on, I called Father Bob in Florida where he lives in semi-retirement. Brit had always been like a granddaughter to him, so I had a hard time holding it together when I let him know Brit was missing in Haiti. At one point, I really lost it and was just begging him to pray for us and to help us get through this. Father Bob was great and tried to reassure me it was still early in the process, but I could hear the concern in his voice. We promised to stay in touch, and I hung up feeling awful about having to share such bad news with him. The man was seventy-five years old and had dealt with a lot of things as a priest, but I suspected this was a first for him.

We'd also contacted Lynn University right away. I think like everyone else, they weren't aware initially of how bad things were. We were put in touch with Dr. Phil Riordan, the vice president of Student Affairs. At that point, he knew nothing but assured us they were doing everything in their power to assess the situation and contact the Lynn University group. He would contact us as soon as he learned anything. A bit later, I would get frustrated because we learned that any of the news reports coming out of Haiti were being transmitted by satellite phone. Haiti is known for not having the greatest infrastructure in the world, so why hadn't Brit's group gone down there with a backup satellite phone in case cell-phone service was somehow interrupted? While Lynn University and Food for the Poor couldn't have known an earthquake of that magnitude was coming, the lack of a contingency plan in case of any kind of communications outage was an early frustration for me.

Again, things were so chaotic and spastic. While we were hearing that the cell-phone towers were down and no communication was possible, Lindsay Doran, Brit's best friend at school and one of the other students down there, had contacted her parents letting them know she was okay. We were thrilled to hear that, for the Dorans' sake and because it gave us some additional hope. Brit was Lindsay's roommate and if she was okay, then chances were that Brit was too. We knew Brit and Lindsay were essentially inseparable, so that if the Dorans had gotten the official word that Lindsay was okay, it was only a matter of time before we got the same.

Phil Riordan later contacted us and let us know that another student, Daniella, had sent a text saying, "We're all safe and we're all together." When I heard that, I wanted to get down on my hands and knees and throw my hands up in the air and thank the good Lord. Still, even with that, we weren't going to do any celebrating yet. So far no one had mentioned Brit specifically, and we hadn't heard from her directly. I live in a business world where I have to deal with enough the-check-is-in-the-mail type of people that my threshold for accepting something as true is maybe a little bit higher than most people's.

I'd hear that kind of news and feel great for a few minutes, but then I'd start thinking about it some more and listening to what my body was telling me, and doubt would start creeping in. I was on a rollercoaster ride emotionally and intellectually—a rollercoaster that had some elements of a fun house. What was true? What I was seeing and hearing on the TV? What I was being told by other people?

Don't get me wrong, I don't think anyone was flat out lying to me, but I also wondered if, as is so often the case, I was hearing what I wanted to hear, believing what I wanted to believe, and hoping that I wasn't falling victim to the desire that pumped through my veins with every beat of my battered heart: that my daughter was safe.

When I shared these positive reports with everyone, I could see the relief on their faces, and that was good. I knew that like Cherylann and I, they wanted to believe that Brit was safe. Human nature is a funny thing, and I don't know if my family has had more or less of its share of difficulties—the hospitalization of my mother for long periods of time throughout my childhood, the early loss of our parents, the death of a nephew when he was only a day old, various bouts with serious illness, death of spouses and what not—but I do believe for the most part we are an optimistic bunch. That doesn't mean we don't have our moments of doubt, don't have at the tail end of a long procession of faith a few worst-case scenarios straggling behind. We've always been hope-for-the-best-but-plan-for-the-worst types. I wasn't close to thinking about the very worst and wouldn't even allow those words to creep into my mind, but still they were out there and lurking in the shadows, waiting for a moment of weakness to pounce.

I know from experience it is possible to have hope and heart-ache simultaneously—the two of them battling it out, just like the sports teams early in the game that I talked about earlier.

Those first few days were all a jumble of shifting facts and emotions. Things felt slippery and elusive, like I had made the catch but then the ball squirted out of my glove, that I had made solid contact, driven the ball hard and deep only to have the wind push it into foul territory. I had no idea how cruelly the battle between hope and heartache could take shape. Like I said, it was the early days and I had a lot to learn. Some of the lessons were good, some were painful, but I can't forget any of them.

CHERYLANN

At one point during that first day or so, Len's sister, Ruth, talked to me about Brit. She was saying she knew that Len was really hurting. She told me about a time when Brit must have been four or so. She couldn't remember the exact circumstances, but she was over at the house and as sometimes happens even in the best of families and the most loving of brother and sister relationships—surprise, surprise—she and Len exchanged some harsh words with one another. She didn't think much of it at the time. Those kinds of dustups were pretty common.

As the day progressed, she tried a couple of times to get Brit to come sit in her lap. She got the stare that could freeze you to the bone. She tried again later. Same result. Finally, she was able to get Brit to sit down next to her, and she asked, "Why are you giving me the silent treatment? What did I do?"

"You were mean to my daddy!" Brit said and wagged her finger at her aunt with a shame-on-you look spreading across her face.

Ruth tried to explain what had happened, but Brit would have none of it.

"You mean you don't forgive me?" Ruth asked.

Brit took in a deep breath, folded her arms across her chest, and shook her head fiercely from side to side.

Brit eventually did forgive her aunt. Ruth also told me about how touched she was many years later when she was undergoing cancer treatment. She was home alone and heard some sounds coming from the backyard. She got up and peered out the kitchen window, and there was Brit raking out the beds of her beloved flower garden.

"No one had asked her to do it, but she was out there."

Ruth thought about going outside to thank Brit, but she decided against it. She figured Brit had wanted to do her that favor anonymously.

"She wasn't looking for any kind of attention or thanks, and it wasn't until just before she left for Haiti that I told her I knew it was her. And you know what she said when I finally thanked her? 'That's quite all right, darling. Anything to keep the place looking fabulous.'"

Hearing that story and others was good for me. They kept my mind from wandering too much. I wondered if Brit was scared, if everything that had gone on during the earthquake had frightened her. Brit wasn't easily scared, and given everything that was going on, I thought of one time that I'd seen her on edge. Ironically, it had to do with one thing I'd never thought we'd end up agreeing to: getting her navel pierced. We knew all the girls were doing it, and Brit begged and pleaded, but we told her she couldn't. Then I came up with a plan. Brit's grades needed improving, so I told her if she made the honor roll, she could get her belly button pierced. Of course, I never expected her to make those grades. Never underestimate the power of a teen's desire. One day she came home from school her sophomore year. I was in the kitchen getting dinner ready.

Brit sat down at the kitchen table. She wagged her finger at me, summoning me to join her, her mischievous grin lighting up her face.

I wiped my hands on a tea towel and joined her.

"You're probably going to want to be seated."

A dozen thoughts passed through my mind in an instant. She paused for dramatic effect and then pulled an envelope from her purse.

She handed it to me. It had the school's insignia on it. Before I could even pull the letter out, Brit said, "Bet you weren't counting on this, were you?"

I shook my head, "Congratulations, you made the honor roll!"

A week later, we were at a tattoo parlor on Park Avenue. I wanted to be sure the place was not some dive, and this one was absolutely spotless. Brit lay on her back, and I could see her eyes starting to dart around the room. She gulped hard a couple of times, and I could see her blood pulsing at her temple as the technician went about his business.

"You want me to hold your hand?"

I expected Brit to refuse the offer, but she said in a tiny voice, "Yes."

I held her hand and thought some football lineman had taken over my daughter's body. I sat in a chair beside her and watched as the first tear pearled at the corner of her eye. She flinched and squeezed harder, something I didn't think was possible, while the procedure was carried out.

The technician went on and on about some details of

follow-up, and I could see Brit was not doing well. Finally she whispered to me, "I need to get out of here."

I helped her get to the car, and she sat in the passenger seat, then the flood of tears came. I didn't know what to say to her, really. Be careful what you wish for? I'd never say that to her. Finally, I said, "Congratulations on making the honor roll."

"I can't believe I just did that," Brit said, shaking her head slowly. In a minute the tears subsided and she started to laugh.

I sat there that January night, hoping that at some point soon, I'd hear that laughter on the other end of the line.

THEY GOT HER ... NOT

"I was so upset because I was thinking what kind of a mother doesn't know her own daughter? I never thought it was Brit on the stretcher, but I wanted it to be her in the worst way."

—CHERYLANN

LEN

For the most part, sleep eluded me that first night. I may have nodded off for a minute or two, but I would wake up again with a start, like someone had hooked me to a car battery and shocked me. Then my mind would take off, trying to process and put into some kind of order all the pieces of the puzzling night. Once I'd made my way downstairs, I saw the overnight crew really hadn't moved. Cherylann's sister, Jodi, my sisters, Joan and Ruth, were still watching TV, all bleary eyed, nearly all with mugs of coffee held in front of their faces, their bodies wrapped in blankets. They were stalwarts, each of them, as were so many other family members and friends. Though it was a workday, none of them were going to their jobs. Nothing was discussed, none of that, "Are you sure you want to do that? We'll be okay," kind of false politeness crap. They knew we needed them, they knew what needed to be done, and they went ahead and did it.

At first, I didn't realize how important a role being the keeper of the gate was going to be. I'd made a couple of calls first thing to Lynn University and Food for the Poor. Both of those were more check-in, wait-and-see kinds of conversations. While the TV networks were getting some of their first real images out of the country and the scope of the devastation was becoming clearer, our focus became more single-minded. We wanted to know about Brit, about the Hotel Montana, and about the others from Lynn University who were down there. I know that sounds callous, and believe me, in our hearts and in our prayers were the people of Haiti and anyone affected by the earthquake, but that was like what happens to objects on the periphery when you are staring intently at a TV screen. They are there. They are mostly out of focus. They aren't fully on your mind. So, I guess I had my own internal gatekeeper. I gave not a single thought to my business or anything else going on in the world outside of those few hundred square yards comprising the walled, fortress-like area my daughter had shown me in the brochures for the Hotel Montana. That was my ground zero.

At about nine o'clock, the doorbell rang. That was a bit strange, because if it was anyone who knew us well, family or friend, they would have come right in. At the door stood Ron Sanders, a veteran reporter for Boston's NBC affiliate. He was familiar fixture, and after he introduced himself, he expressed his hope that Brit and the others would be fine and that he hoped we wouldn't mind answering a few questions.

This was our first face-to-face experience with the media, and Ron was very polite and respectful.

"We're in no shape to talk to anyone on camera right now," I told him. "But when we get the good news we expect to get, we'll let everybody know."

Ron nodded and smiled at me. "I understand. I have a son in college. I don't blame you."

Next, he leaned his head over his right shoulder. I could see three or four vans with the logos of their various networks emblazoned on them, their antennae masts rising into the morning light. "Just so you're aware, we're going to be out here. We're waiting for you to get the good news that we know is coming your way today."

I shut the door and tried to shut out all the questions that the media's presence in our lives raised. I knew I was going to have to figure out a way to use them to our advantage, but I was hoping I wouldn't end up needing them. We live in the Information Age, and I'm as aware of that as anybody, but now that a new day had begun in this tragedy, I was becoming even more keenly aware of how getting, managing, and spreading information was.

On my first call that morning to Food for the Poor, I was told that Lee Ann, the guide the organization provided for the kids on the Journey of Hope, was missing. They'd had no word from her. They had no other information they could share whatsoever. That was troubling but not unexpected. What I didn't expect was that when I spoke to someone there later that afternoon, I was told Food for the Poor was no longer going to communicate directly with the families whose children were involved in the program. They would issue no statements, and they said we should direct our inquiries to Lynn University, which had made this request.

A part of me was pissed off by their refusal to answer any more questions. This wasn't just a financial issue. Yes, we'd paid them $1,800 to take of our daughter down there and house her and all the rest. But this was their program. They were the experts in Haiti. Lynn University had contracted with them, but the school wasn't the organization with vast experience in a number of third-world countries. If we wanted advice on what to do, insight into what was being done to contact them, or just have someone offer some kind of reassurance that they had gone through anything remotely like this before, I didn't want that filtered through the university and some spokesperson. I know companies and organizations seem to think that it's important to go into cover-your-ass mode whenever something goes wrong. That's not how I do business. If something is not being handled properly, even if it's by one of my subcontractors, you better believe I take control and accept full responsibility for making things right.

The people at Food for the Poor were overwhelmed as much as everyone else, but to cut off one link to possible information about our daughter or any of the fourteen Lynn University volunteers seemed unconscionable. We were at the stage where you are so eager for information, yet so little of that precious resource was available; not having it there for us probably hurt more than it might have otherwise.

Everyone at the house, including Cherylann and I, despite the constant presence of the TV, the Internet, and telephone, felt starved for information, and we eagerly devoured what few scraps there were.

From the outset, I was concerned that knowledge and information were of vital importance, especially as the scale of the disaster grew larger and larger. We weren't alone in thinking that initially this earthquake was a minor event, likely to not really have affected Brit or any other Americans for that matter. I was well aware as those devastating images came in, but my focus narrowed. That's reality. Yes, I cared about the thousands and thousands of Haitians who were undoubtedly killed or injured. In my head and in my heart, that mattered to me, I felt compassion for them. But that paled in comparison to the worry and concern I felt for the Lynn University group, and nothing compared at all to how I felt about my daughter.

I wanted other people, particularly those in power in the government who might be able to do something tangible and immediate, to be on the ball from the get-go. For that reason, my sister-in-law, JoAnne, called my congressman, Jim McGovern, early on Tuesday. She and Chrissy were good friends with him and I knew Jim from having served on a board of directors with him, and through a couple of other connections. We weren't buddies, but I was one of his constituents, and Jim was the kind of guy who cared deeply about more than just getting elected. He got it immediately: We needed to let people in the government know there was a group of American college kids on the ground in Haiti who were missing.

I didn't know just how many Americans there were in Haiti, working at the embassy, serving various functions with aid groups, non-governmental organizations, and all the rest. That knowledge would come later and hit hard. Jim got on the case immediately and contacted Senator John Kerry. This was key because not only was he one of the senators representing our home state, he also was the chairman of the Senate Foreign Relations Committee. As I saw it, that was key. If we wanted and needed information, if we wanted someone with some pull, he was our man.

I get tired of saying this, and I'm sure you'll get tired of hearing it, but I never would have expected to have Senator John Kerry sitting in my living room thirty-six hours after receiving word about an earthquake and my daughter being unaccounted for in its destruction. But there he was, looking grave and serious, but being as gracious and comforting as could be. He was clearly used to dealing with people in crisis, and just having him in the room offered us a small dose of comfort.

His words, however, didn't. We appreciated his honesty and told him that was what we wanted from him. He said that his sources told him there were literally thousands and thousands of dead bodies in the streets of Haiti. The destruction was widespread and on a scale that was difficult to comprehend. There were countless people trapped, buried, and otherwise unaccounted for. Travel within the country and particularly within the capital was haphazard at best and dangerous to impossible at worst. His thoughts echoed what Cherylann and I had talked about. We had to hope for the best but prepare ourselves for the worst. He told us that President Obama, Secretary of State Hillary Clinton, and other key people were monitoring the situation, coordinating with the military, and doing everything they could at those early stages to do whatever possible to help.

Cherylann and I thanked him and reminded him again,

that our daughter and thirteen other members of the Lynn University group were down there at the Hotel Montana. I kept with the message that we felt needed to be made. Our ground zero was that spot outside the confines of the city, those fortified acres of hotel property where it seemed few people had been able to reach.

Later that day, we were encouraged to hear from our other senator, the newly elected Scott Brown, who called to offer us words of encouragement and hope. It was good to know we had important people on our side. We also knew this was out of our hands, their hands, and firmly in the hands of God.

CHERYLANN

Fortunately for me, I didn't have to worry about feeding those gathered at our house—either food or information. My sister, mother, and Len's sisters, took care of that. Normally, I would have preferred to be in charge of meals, and I was somewhat surprised at myself for not wanting to have those kitchen duties as a distraction, but I had other traditional roles to play in the house.

By nature, I'm not really a demonstrative worrier. I think one of the reasons why Len and I have worked so well together over the years and I've meshed with his family is that I tend to be more low-key emotionally. It's not that I don't feel things as deeply and as passionately as the Gengel clan; I just don't show it as much. That can be a good thing or a bad thing depending on the situation.

Fortunately, I know enough about myself and how our temperaments have been passed down to the kids to have pretty good insight into how to deal with them. Bernie has some of Len's take-charge energy and intensity. His way of dealing with the fact that his sister was involved in the crisis was to work on his computer to gather information. I'd check in with him every now and then, more under the guise of asking him if he'd seen anything posted about Brit or the others on Facebook or some other site. He was so busy typing or reading that all I would get from him was a quick shake of the head or a brief nod and an even briefer summary of what he was learning. It was from him that we found out the Hotel Montana was its own special kind of deal. In a way it was like the United Nations. Lots of diplomats and agency workers and other non-Haitians lived there. Being on the outskirts of Port-au-Prince, it was protected from some of the protests and turmoil that went on in the capital.

From what we could see coming from the news agencies that now had live video feeds, if Brit and the others needed to get anywhere, it was going to be a long and difficult trip. It seemed as if most of the buildings that were leveled had collapsed into the narrow roads. Debris was piled high all around. Walking would have been extremely difficult, and any kind of vehicle would have had to wind its way around to find a clear passage anywhere, if such a route even existed.

I kept telling myself to be patient, but I was anything but. We were still making the quarter-hour calls to Brit's cell phone, and even though those moments when I heard the static ring were agonizing, I at least felt like I was doing something, making some kind of contact.

I also had to keep an eye out on Richie, our youngest. In some ways, he's more like me. With Brit and Bernie, you always knew what was going on in their heads because they were likely to just tell you or reveal it through their actions. I felt bad that Richie had to come home from school to such a wild scene of us gathered around the TV. I was so preoccupied at first, that even the few minutes I spent with him letting him know the basic facts and telling him that it was far too soon to know much about the specifics of Brit's situation felt inadequate. When you don't have a whole lot of facts to draw from and all you're left with is the kind of false reassurances that you hope prove true, you'd almost rather not speak at all.

I knew I couldn't insulate Richie from everyone's reactions, and as much I wanted to keep him away from the center of the action where emotions were thrown together into some kind of stew, I couldn't do that. This wasn't a time for me to tell him to go to his room; this was something for the adults to deal with. We don't usually handle things that way, anyway. But this was his sister, and he had his own kind of relationship with her, and he deserved to be there in the mix along with everybody else. As a mother, that was a hard call to make; you want to protect your kids, but we had to let him make the choice for himself how he wanted to approach things.

It nearly broke my heart when I saw Richie coming down the stairs from his bedroom to join the vigil in the great room. So, while seeing our youngest wearing his NCIS hat and his tatty robe joining the collective in front of the TV was painful, it was also perfect. Richie and Brit shared a love of true crime and detective shows like NCIS. Brit teased him about that robe, but he wore it like a badge of honor. At least his older sister paid him enough attention to tease him about it. Seeing him dressed that way was a kind of show of solidarity between the two of them. Maybe that seems kind of silly or like I'm reading too much into it, but that's how it is with family. You have these little inside habits, routines, or what have you that to anyone outside the circle would make little sense. You might think he was just wearing whatever made him comfortable. In reality, he was wearing that as a sign of respect. It was his way of saying, I'm here waiting for you, Brit, knowing that you're going to be home soon and firing away at me with your best verbal ammo. I'm ready for that and I welcome it. Bring it on.

Probably the hardest part for me, besides the not knowing about Brit, was my wondering about Len and his health and how all this stress was affecting him. At the age of forty-one back in 2001, Len had undergone major cardiac surgery for a heart defect. He had two stents sutured into him then, while later in

2005 after nearly dying from other complications and additional arterial blockages and things, they added an additional three. Len's a vibrant, energetic man, but I sometimes kid him about the eight medications he's on for various things. We'd watch the nightly news and see the ads for things like Plavix and Crestor and a bunch of other prescription drugs, and I'd ask him why he wasn't on them all.

I knew that all of this was emotionally distressing, but when you're dealing with someone who's got a physically damaged heart, that brings another level of anxiety. Len's mom and dad had died relatively young as well. So, that first night when Len asked me if I trusted him, part of my "yes" response was that I trusted that he wouldn't do too much to harm himself. Like I said, Len's a very intense man most of the time, and there's not a lot I could do to change that about him. All I could do was make sure he was still taking his medications, taking a little bit of time away from the phones, the Internet, and the TV to decompress—at least a little bit.

I also knew if I showed signs of cracking, it would be hard for him to deal with my stress complicating matters. As protective as he was of the kids, the same was true of his feelings about me. The two of us were in this thing together, and we'd have to lean on each other a lot. I knew the spirit was willing, but I also knew that part of his flesh was weak. Len would do whatever it would take to get Brit back home and safe, that was for sure, but what toll it would take on him, I had no way of really knowing.

To make sure Len didn't drive himself too hard all day, every day, as we waited for word from Britney, the two of us agreed that we would take walks with Bruno. The fresh air did us some good, gave us a few minutes alone to check in with one another on how we were doing, and allowed us to feel for a few minutes like we weren't under a microscope. Everyone was really well intentioned, and I know that if the situation was reversed, I would have been asking whoever I was there with to support how they were doing, but in time that question gets old and it's difficult to say anything meaningful. So, while we were out walking together, Len and I kind of let loose, crying and holding onto one another, letting the shock and disbelief and the absurdity of it all kind of climb over the walls we'd built up.

That Wednesday night as we were heading back toward the house, we saw someone in the road. Turned out it was an old friend of ours who had driven up to the house. He said he thought he recognized us by our silhouettes, and he asked us what he could to help us out. Len and I looked at each other. We were so grateful for the outpouring of support, but we didn't know what else to say except to ask for his prayers. I could see the sadness and the helplessness in his eyes, and I knew they mirrored what we were experiencing. I looked away and up and down the road, and I could see the houses with their lights glowing in the window. People were sitting down to supper or had just finished and were settling in front of the TV. How I wanted to be one of them. Sure, I would have been sad, and I would have been watching the news and shaking my head and hurting for those poor people. But this was different—a different kind of hurt, a different kind of anguished interest in what was being fed into our homes, our heads, and our hearts.

We all stood there in the dark, the silence lingering. Our friends had asked the million-dollar question. What could we do? What could any of us do but sit and wait? I looked beyond him to the western sky where a bright light shone. A planet, I remember Richie telling us, correcting Len's belief it was a satellite. Whichever. I don't know if the stars or satellites had much to tell us.

A moment later Len's cell phone rang, and I was certain a minute after that something in the heavens had spoken loud and clear.

LEN

As upset as I was about Food for the Poor's no-talk policy, I was glad for one thing that policy produced. I got to speak with and to begin to establish a relationship with one person at Lynn University. Phil Riordan was assigned to be the point person for six of the immediate families of the Lynn people affected by the earthquake. Phil served as the university's vice president for Student Affairs. Another member of the administration was assigned to work with the other eight families.

My heart skipped a beat when I saw it was Dr. Riordan calling me. As far as I was concerned in those moments, our friend who was speaking with us had ceased to exist. My whole universe shrank down to me, that cell phone, and the person on the other end of the line. I liked Phil and the fact that he cut immediately to the chase. He's a very genuine man, a very caring man, and I sensed from the beginning that he was torn up about those kids and the faculty members down there.

"Len, we've got some good news. We've started to hear from some of them. They've been rescued, and they've been taken to a location from where they've been able to email their families. I don't have many more details than that."

I barely heard the rest of what Phil had to say.

I focused on: "Emails. Some of the kids are starting to send emails."

I'm a big man with a torn-up heart, but I can still get a move on when I need to. Cherylann and I muttered something to our friend, and the three of us, Bruno included, started sprinting for the house.

By that time, our house looked like a Best Buy or Apple store or something. Everyone there had a laptop or some other electronic device to monitor the situation. We came busting into the house, and I said, "I need the computer! I need the computer!"

People started scrambling, and I don't know who was on my computer, but I sat down with Cherylann at her computer, waiting for an email, wondering if maybe it came to my AOL address instead. She sat right alongside me with her smart phone, both of us staring at our screens trying to will that stupid tone that indicates a new mail has come in to sound.

People were asking us what was going on, and together Cherylann and I managed to piece together a brief explanation. I heard a few people sniffling and crying, more than few saying their prayers, and my eyes were boring into that screen and the inbox icon as if I could somehow turn my prayers into pixels.

Ten minutes went by.

Nothing.

Phil Riordan called me to let me know that a family had gotten the good word.

Another ten minutes.

Nothing.

Another phone call. Family number two was overjoyed.

Another twenty minutes.

Nothing.

Phil again. A third family got confirmation that their loved one was rescued.

I looked at Cherylann. "We're next. I know it. I can feel it. Please, dear God, let it be Britney."

Cherylann wrapped her hand around my biceps and pulled me closer.

"I know you're right, Len. I know you're right."

Phil Riordan got on the line again, "I'm sorry to say this, Len, but so far none of my group has gotten a message. I just need one win tonight. Just one. I just want to be able to share the good news one time tonight."

It's funny how in that moment I started to feel so bad for Phil. That feeling never stopped. Phil was a father; in fact, his daughter attended Lynn and was the same age as Britney. I think we connected for that reason, plus a whole lot more. I knew Phil wanted to get more than just the one win, and that it wasn't really about keeping score. He didn't care really that the other contact at Lynn and that group were the ones who had been rescued and were making contact. He was feeling what I was feeling, what I imagined Cherylann and the other dozen or so families were feeling. Just one bit of good news to offset the shit ton of bad news we'd been seeing, hearing, and feeling for the past forty-eight or so hours. We were all dying of thirst, and just one drop was all we needed to tell ourselves the rains were going to come.

That night, they didn't.

Instead, a storm of disappointment and devastation blew through me. Cherylann and I were grateful that some of the families had found relief. We took comfort in knowing the Hotel Montana was a place where some could survive. We'd been frustrated that during all the hours of coverage to that point, all the accounts we read online, no one had shown images of or had heard from anyone at that location. It was all about Port-au-Prince. Intellectually, I could understand why. Emotionally, that gutted me.

We spent a fitful night clicking between channels, scanning our computers for incoming messages, and praying to God to deliver us all and our daughter from what seemed to be a hell on Earth.

* * *

I'm generally a pretty optimistic person, but I have to admit that at 9:30 the next morning, Thursday, January 14, 2010, when I saw Phil Riordan's name and number pop up on my cell phone's screen, I was expecting more of the same from the night before. I couldn't let myself get that high again only to be let down. Still, I rallied a bit, and told Phil I hoped he at least got his first win. "Hey, Phil, what's the good word."

"Len, they've rescued Britney and two other girls. I'll be very clear about this. They rescued Brit and two other girls. They're on a helicopter as we speak, and they're being transported to Port-au-Prince airport. We're lining them up to be on a plane out of Haiti with the other eight we've had rescued so far."

At that point, I sank to my knees and started crying like I have never cried in my life. All I could manage to say was, "God is good. God is good."

To take the call, I had gone into a hallway connecting the

kitchen and the great room. I was half-sitting, half-kneeling, leaning up against the wall.

"They got her! They got her!" I shouted past my tears. My sister, Chris, came running up along with Cherylann, and they started crying. I got to my feet and hugged and kissed them, and jumped up and down.

I know all the clichés about feeling like a load has been lifted from you and all of that, but that's exactly what it felt like. I had been feeling for days like someone had knocked me over with the bucket of a backhoe and then put that bucket on me and was trying to mash me into the ground.

I could hear Phil saying something else to me, but I couldn't make it out. I don't know how long it took for me to get some place where I could hear him again, but he hung in there.

"You got your win."

Phil was crying so hard he could barely get the words out, "I never felt so good, Len. I'm so happy for you guys."

We talked for a few minutes more about the details of us getting down to Florida to greet Brit and the others when they arrived.

Not long after I got a text from Joe at my office—he'd worked for me for fourteen years, and I'd known him since he was fifteen. He said there was a picture from the Reuters news agency of Brit lying on a stretcher.

The rest of the night was a bit of blur. We were so jubilant that the explosion of noise we let out must have alerted the media people to come on in, because at some point I found myself in a giddy embrace with Ron Sanders, and he was crying in my arms.

For the next hour or so, it was a Gengel blowout. We cranked the music. People danced. I don't know if you've ever seen a celebration on the field or in the clubhouse after a World Series win or Super Bowl victory, but that was what it was like, minus the champagne being sprayed around. It was that loud and that joyful at the Gengel house.

At some point the four of us managed to separate ourselves from the pack. I looked at my kids and my wife and I shook my head. "I have to tell you, the last few days I barely recognized us. We all looked so old and so tired. Now you're all back. Brit's back." I couldn't get the rest out. I just stood there, my throat aching from crying, laughing, and shouting.

God bless him, Bernie managed to reset us to normal. "All in all, I'd say the day has started out to be pretty fabulous."

CHERYLANN

All things considered, our family has been really blessed. Yes, it's true that Len had lost his mother and father—his dad far too young of a heart attack—and my father had passed. Still, things could have been much worse. We're grateful that even though the kids all struggled with learning disabilities to a degree and that Brit was sometimes a handful who liked to party a little too much sometimes, we'd never had to deal with any major issues with the kids and the law or accidents or illness.

Maybe it's a Catholic thing, but sometimes you wonder if maybe you've been too fortunate, or that if some minor thing goes wrong—you can't find your car keys or whatever—you go back over the last few days and wonder what you did wrong that you're now being punished for it. I have to admit that some of those thoughts had crept into my mind those first two nights when I lay in bed and my mind raced.

I know this sounds contradictory, but when I lay there with Len, neither of us sleeping, I felt Brit's absence. It was like her lack of presence in our bed was something crowding me, making me feel cramped and uncomfortable. It used to be the opposite. When I was growing up, my parent's bedroom was a private sanctuary—someplace I didn't think of going. From the time Brit was little to when she was in college, we didn't have that kind of barrier. I can't count the number of times that girl would come home with her friends. Len and I would be watching TV sitting on the bed, and those kids would come in and make themselves comfortable with us. At first, as she got older and these other kids were with her, I felt a bit odd about it, but that quickly changed. To have those kids be so much a part of every aspect of our lives was wonderful—dealing with the crumbs from their snacking wasn't so much fun, but even that was okay.

Those first two nights, I lay there wondering if I'd ever get to experience that again, listening to one of Brit's stories, feeling her laughing, leg-kicking presence shaking our bed, making me marvel at her energy.

All of that went out the window when I heard Len yelling his thanks about Brit being found. To that point, I hadn't bargained with God that much, you know, telling him that if he just let us get Brit back, I'd do X, Y, and Z. I also felt like no parent deserved to lose a child. When we'd settled down a bit, I asked Len if Phil had been able to tell him who was still missing. Among those was Christine Gianacaci. My heart went out to them, and I wanted to call them to let them know that we understood what they were going through, that they had to keep the faith, that it's still very early and all the rest. I'm kind of embarrassed to say this, but after I offered up a quick prayer for all the others not yet found, I put them out of my mind for a while. I just wanted to enjoy the moment, let that relief wash over me and refresh me.

And things did feel kind of normal again, like a switch had been thrown, and even though this was still by far the most disorienting and troubling experience of my life, I could see the pieces falling back into place. Still, something had been nagging at me.

Just before Len had gotten the call, we'd received a text telling us to look at our Facebook page, just as Phil had done later.

After we'd gotten the news from Phil, we finally got around to looking for the picture that Joe texted us about. We were standing around the computer, the four of us and Brit's nana and aunts, and I don't know who else. We were all looking at the picture. Bernie and Richie immediately started saying things, making that normal feeling seem like that's how we were supposed to be reacting.

"Oh yeah, that's Brit all right," Bernie said. "Look at her just lying there on that stretcher while four guys carry her."

"She's like Cleopatra or some other princess on one of those things," Richie said.

We all laughed.

"That's our girl," Len's sister, Joan, said. "Always having someone waiting on her like that, taking care of her."

The photo was a bit blurry. Not out of focus exactly, but like something had happened to its sharpness when it had been blown up. The girl on the stretcher was a brunette like Brit with hair about the same length and pulled back in a ponytail like Brit did a lot of the time. She was wearing a yellow T-shirt, the same color as the ones that the Journey of Hope people were wearing. I couldn't make out the lettering on it, but there was enough of a resemblance to Brit that everybody else seemed convinced. I wanted to believe it, but I didn't. Then I was so upset because I was thinking what kind of a mother doesn't know her own daughter? I never thought it was Brit on the stretcher, but I wanted it to be her in the worst way.

"I'm not so sure that's her. It doesn't really look like her," I said to Len.

"Sure it does," one of Len's sisters said, overhearing me. "Look at the shape of the nose."

A few other people chimed in with other comments about the length of the neck, the ears, the complexion, and a few other things.

"I don't know. I don't think the nose looks like Brit's, or the cheeks," I said.

"Well, look, the nails are done perfectly, that's got to be Brit," someone else piped up. Everybody laughed, and I started thinking that maybe they were right. I had this funny feeling, but it was offset by the elation of having gotten word from Phil that Brit was on a helicopter going to the airport and then back to Florida.

With all the chatter going on, people talking on their cell

phones, and all the rest, it was tough to know just what to think. I went with my heart.

Then, a funny thing happened. I saw Richie standing with his palms resting on the desktop, his face close to the monitor, his eyes squinting. A minute or so earlier, he was laughing and joking, but I saw his face crease into worry. He shook his head real slow and deliberate, barely moving it from side to side. He pushed himself back upright and said, his words barely audible above all the clamor, "That's not her. That's not Brit."

With everything going on, it was hard to believe what I was suspecting and what Richie was convinced of was true. You know, you stand in front of the cameras and the lights nearly blind you, you're running on pure adrenaline, and more and more people are pouring into the house. First one news crew and then another is holding a microphone up to you, and they're telling you that cars are honking their horns in celebration, the junior-high and high-school kids have all been informed over the public-address system that Britney Gengel has been rescued. I'm trying to think and talk and respond to the interviewers' questions and not sound like an idiot.

I could hear Len talking to Susan Wornick. This was going out live, and I could hear how happy he was. He was joking with Susan about the fact that the year before Brit had done a brief internship with Channel 5, the ABC affiliate, and he asked her if Brit could have the internship again when she came home for the summer. Then he let out that big laugh of his, a mixture of joy and relief, and it overtook the room. Everybody within earshot was laughing, and the difference between then and before was just mind-boggling. In the middle of all this I saw people coming in, family and friends, Len's eighty-four-year-old Aunt Dot with her daughter Karla, and our friend from Connecticut, Tony Terzi, was smiling and waving. I was trying to keep my focus on what I was being asked, but in my mind, I was thinking, "Oh my God, we've got to get on a plane in a few hours. Brit's going to be there at 11:00 p.m. I've got to get tickets. I've got to do the laundry. None of us have clean underwear. We've got to have clean underwear."

During TV interviews I've watched, whenever some great thing happens to someone, the interviewer always asks if it has sunk in yet. Most of the time people say no. For me, when my thoughts turned to the fact that we had to pack and I had to make sure we had clean underwear, that's when it sunk in. Len was right. God is great—but he wasn't going to wash, dry, and fold. He took care of the most important thing: getting Brit back for us. She was coming home. That was the only thing that mattered.

I was on the phone calling Brit's friends like Lizzy, who was her BFF since they were three years old, to say she was rescued. Then I was on the phone with her friend Joe from Maine when another call came in. I had gone outside because of all the noise (wonderful joyful noise) in the house, and I couldn't hear a thing. My phone rang, and I saw it was a Connecticut number. Thinking it was friends of ours, I answered.

On the other end of the line was a bunch of static and a man speaking in a foreign accent that I could barely make out. It was cold out on the deck, and I hugged my arms to my chest and cradled the phone with my neck. He was asking me about Brit and how I found out that she was going to be rescued.

That's when I realized that I was talking with a member of Red 24, a group that Lynn University's insurance company had sent into Haiti to assist in locating and rescuing the group. I didn't know much about them; I only knew that Phil said they'd managed to get into Haiti after landing in the Dominican Republic. That was back on Monday or Tuesday when Phil told us about their presence, but as far as I knew, because of how bad things were, they'd not even gotten to the capital by the time we'd gotten the call about Brit being rescued. At that point, it didn't really matter.

Still, the man was pressing me for details.

"Have you spoken with her?"

"No, but the school told us she was in a helicopter on the way to the airport."

"We've lost contact with her." In retrospect this should have alarmed me, but I thought it was more a loss of contact as in he lost cell-phone service because of the earthquake. We were all just so overjoyed, the house was filled with family and media, I didn't have the capacity to think anything negative at the time.

"Well, we haven't heard from her yet, but if we do, we'll let you know."

"Yes, do that. If we contact her, we'll let you know."

I hadn't spoken to Phil myself, so I didn't know the exact details of who'd rescued Brit or any details of how she'd been found. The only thing that mattered was that she'd been found. I assumed Red 24 had something to do with it, but maybe not. It didn't really matter anyway. I just figured they were calling because they lost contact with her—that something had been messed up with the communications systems and they weren't able to speak to her directly. In my mind, that meant they had been able to speak to her at some point. That meant that Brit was alive.

I walked back into the house and the joyful noise. Whatever doubts I'd had about the girl in the photo were now forgotten.

5

BAD INTEL

"Let's enjoy the peace and quiet while we can."

—RICHIE

LEN

There's an expression that states "hope floats." True, and whatever hope floats on produces a powerful current that carries you along. We weren't the only ones riding that wave of emotion and expectation. With all our friends and family going nuts along with us, we barely had time to think about the logistics of our re-union with Brit. All I wanted to do was wrap my arms around her and never let her go. Cherylann and I had talked about how we would feel if she was injured, and Phil had given us no indication that she was. Nonetheless, we still would have been ecstatic. All we wanted was for her to be alive, for her to come home.

Driving into Boston to catch our flight from Logan to West Palm Beach, we started to come down off our high a little bit. That was natural, but something began to eat at me. I didn't want to say anything to Cherylann in front of the boys, so I just drove along with that feeling twisting my insides. We parked the car in Central Parking and walked toward the terminal. I hung back a little bit, thinking no one in the family would notice, they'd just figure the old guy with the bum heart couldn't keep up with them. Once there was a bit of separation between us, I took the opportunity to call Phil Riordan. I had to talk to him, had to get some assurances from him that would ease my anxiety.

After we exchanged greetings, I said to Phil, "Listen, I haven't heard from my daughter. And as time goes on, I'm getting more concerned. I know my daughter, and if that was her on the stretcher, she'd have called us. Tell me again what the plan is."

Phil repeated what he'd told me before. "Last we heard, Brit was on a helicopter with two other girls. They were taking them to the airport in Port-au-Prince. Don't worry. We haven't heard anything from her yet either. She was probably in line at the embassy getting her papers processed. From the embassy, she'll go to the airport. Someone has donated a private jet for the school to use to get our people out of there. Last we heard, they were at the airport with the other eight we already knew about. Once they got clearance to take off, they'd fly into the Dominican Republic and then from there to Fort Lauderdale."

What didn't make sense to me, and what I shared with Phil, was that all of this sounded wonderful as a plan, but had all those things happened yet? Had anyone heard Brit's voice? Had anyone seen her with their own two eyes and definitely identified her?

Phil couldn't answer those questions the way I wanted him to. He also said they had lost contact with Red 24. They were going on the information they'd received hours earlier.

After I hung up with Phil just before we walked into the terminal, I indicated to Cherylann that she should stop for a second so we could talk.

"Listen, there's a problem. You have to prepare yourself."

She just looked at me in disbelief.

"They've got no one who has actually seen Brit and they lost contact with the group," I said, my mind racing a thousand thoughts a minute. "Phil's last words were, 'We lost contact, but we think it's because she's in the queue at the embassy. And they're processing her.' And I said to Phil, 'Tell me before I get on this plane. She's the eleventh of the twelve, and they are all flying home together.' And I added, 'That other plane has not left. Before I get on this plane, Phil, tell me, has that plane left Port-au-Prince?' He said, 'No. They're waiting for your girls.'"

Cherylann, I could tell, did not get it. I knew that I was rambling a bit and not making the most sense. We were walking to the terminal to get onto the flight that was supposed to reunite us with our daughter, but I had this sinking feeling in my gut that I could not get rid of.

I have a friend in the building industry who is a big believer in the Kolbe Index. It's an assessment that identifies your strengths and weaknesses, and the kind of work you're suited for. Much of it is based on how instinctive you are, how much you listen to your gut, and how frequently correct your gut is. My Kolbe indicated that I should be a town planner. I'm a planner anyway. That's what I do in every part of my life. I'm good at it. And Lynn University's plan for us that day and with the kids in Haiti was a sound plan. At such and such a time, we're going to be doing A, then B, then C, then D. That all made sense. But what I was having a hard time conveying to Cherylann, because she hadn't been in on all the phone calls personally and she had so many other things fighting for her attention was this: The plan was great, but so far very little of that plan to get Brit back to the U.S. had gone off as planned.

I'm a very optimistic person most of the time. In this case, because I didn't have firm proof to demonstrate the truth of what we'd been told, I was skeptical

Also, keep in mind that we basically had not slept for the past four days, at least not in the strictest terms. It was more like we were passing out from exhaustion at some point in the day or night, catching a few minutes of something approaching sleep, but just enough so that we'd bolt back upright and feel the squeeze in our chests, that shock of adrenaline running through our bodies. When you're feeling that way, it's tough to think clearly. I still needed to work out some of the details of my assessment of the situation, so I was still operating on a bit of a hunch. But my hunches had been very good in the past, and I was hoping Cherylann would get that, would rely on her trust in me to have faith in what my gut was telling me.

Cherylann sensed my uncertainties and she told me so. "We've been through a lot. I can understand your doubts, but you know what Phil said: 'They've got her.' They'd lost contact with her means just that. They can't speak with her just then. That's all."

Cherylann started walking into the terminal, and there waiting for us was a group of news people again. I knew I had to rally a bit and put on a good face for everyone. I tried to tell myself that what Cherylann was saying made sense. Communications lines were down, getting crossed, and all the rest of the chaos down there was making it hard for her to get through to us.

The other thought that pained me was that maybe they had Britney at one point and she had died on the way to the airport. We had that picture of her on the stretcher, and it wasn't like she was sitting up and smiling for the camera. She could have been gravely injured and not made it. I hated thinking that way, and I kept telling myself that we had to remain optimistic, and I had been completely overjoyed and overwhelmed when Phil had told us the good news. I don't know, maybe this was the natural comedown after the high, but before we pushed open those doors and faced the cameras again, I reminded Cherylann that we needed to be prepared.

She nodded and smiled, and with a pair of Logan airport security personnel ushering us through the crowds of media and other passengers, we moved to the ticket counter to check in. As fate would have it, the two Logan employees were Haitian-Americans, and they couldn't have been nicer to us, telling us how glad they were to meet us and that they were so happy that Brit was going to be okay. I loved listening to their voices, their joy was like a sothing antiseptic ointment applied to my wounds.

Walking over to the security check-in, I gave myself a bit of a pep talk. For Richie's and Bernie's sake, I was going to get myself together and not agitate them anymore than they had been by all the events of the past four days. They could have handled it, I think, but they didn't need me putting additional burdens on them. Without explaining why, as the line slowed and we stood in place for a minute, I put my arms around both of them and drew them in for a hug. I could feel their relief as they relaxed into me.

"Just a few more hours," Bernie said.

"Let's enjoy the peace and quiet while we can," Richie said and rolled his eyes.

I glanced at my watch. It was five o'clock. We'd take off in half an hour and land three hours later. I didn't know how I was going to do on the flight. I'm not afraid of flying, but I had so much nervous energy buzzing in me that I wasn't sure I could sit still for that long.

CHERYLANN

Like I said before, my husband and his family are incapable of keeping their feelings inside. You always know what they feel; they let it out. So, when Len approached me in the parking lot with his concerns about whether or not Lynn University really had Brit in Haiti, it was pretty easy to dismiss those thoughts as just a high level of anxiety getting the best of him. I'm a pretty trusting person, so when someone like Phil Riordan calls us and tells us they found Brit, she's on a helicopter, she's on her way to the airport, I believe him. And I believed that Phil understood that to be the status of Brit and some of the other girls. He was just basing his statements on what the people on the ground were telling him. Besides, I wanted to believe him. Who wouldn't?

This wasn't the worst case of hopeful thinking in history either. We'd seen the picture, and by that time I'd kind of gotten over my doubts about whether or not that was Brit in the photo. I told myself that just because the young woman in the picture didn't really look like Brit, that didn't mean it wasn't her. After all, she'd just been through an earthquake. I knew my daughter sometimes didn't look exactly like she usually did. That's true for all of us. And what did I have to compare post-earthquake Brit to? This was a first for all of us, and if she wasn't exactly looking herself, that could have been the fact that she was dirty, tired, hadn't showered for a while, and all the rest of those perfectly logical explanations for things.

As for Len, he's an excitable man. I understood why he was on his knees crying and thanking the Lord one minute and running around the house excited the next. So also I could explain his new response logically. The pendulum was swinging. Normally Len didn't have any kind of wild mood shifts, but this was the most extreme thing we'd faced in our lives together. So of course, the back and forth was going to cover a lot more ground.

A lot of media were on the plane, and everyone in the cabin was trying to figure out why. Once the crew completed the routine safety presentation, they announced that Britney Gengel's family was on board and we were going to pick her up. The plane erupted in cheers and applause. I was so happy yet so embarrassed. Len and the boys were across the aisle so no one knew I was with them. People had figured out that Len was Brit's dad based on the media coming up to him. He'd also been our family's representative during interviews. Some of the other passengers were congratulating him and the boys. I sat in my seat just grateful that Brit was coming home. The woman beside me was happy for Len and was saying how she had followed the story. I felt awkward but then told her I was Brit's mom.

She told me that she thought the news about Haiti was so horrendous that it broke her heart and she had to look away from it. I told her I understood. She added that she was praying for everybody involved and was glad that some good news was coming out of the country. She was a mother herself, and she said anytime any of her kids were traveling anywhere, she was a bit of wreck until they returned safe and sound.

Only later, after the two of us had settled into silence after the plane leveled off and pointed south did I think about that expression, "safe and sound." We were told that Brit was safe, and Len wasn't going to really fully embrace the truth of that until he heard the sound of his daughter's voice.

I was picturing how great it was going to be when Len finally got to see Brit again, how his joy and his relief was just going to come pouring out of him. It was going to be like the floodgates opening up for all of us. I was eager to see her as anybody, but with Len it was different somehow.

At one point I had to go to the bathroom. We were at the back of the plane, so I only had to walk back a few rows. When I did, a woman popped up out of her seat and identified herself as a reporter for the New England Cable News. She wanted to get my reaction, and I told her how thrilled we were and all of that. I have to admit I was pretty caught up in the whole thing. I had joked with Len that it was like we were Brad and Angelina, the way all these photographers were following us in the airport and taking our picture. I wanted to share my happiness with the world, scream it from the mountaintops. Wasn't an airplane cruising at thirty-seven-thousand feet even higher than that? Of course, I didn't scream, but I was amazed that this news organization had found out what flight we were on, had gotten a crew on board, and then, here they were, interviewing me. I wouldn't say I was giddy, but this news was too big to keep all wrapped up inside.

Over the woman's shoulder, I could see Len twisting in his seat to check on us. I smiled and waved at him, and that didn't seem to go over too well. After I returned to my seat, I didn't think a whole lot else about it and how what I was saying to the media mattered in any way. Later that night, Brit was going to be in a car with us, driving to wherever we were being put up for the night, and the next day, we'd be back in Boston for the biggest welcome-home party in history.

I was in a state of semi-sleep when something caught my attention. I don't know why, but I sensed that something was up. I looked over at Len. He was seated on the aisle, and his head was turned away from the boys. He had a look on his face. The best way I can describe it is that he had the same look someone has when they are on the verge of vomiting. His complexion was alternating between pale and flushed, and he kept swallowing hard. I could see his Adam's apple rising and falling. At first I thought it might be his heart, and I strained against my seat belt trying to get up and go to him. He saw me, and he put his hand up to stop me and shook his head, gesturing toward the boys.

That's when I knew there was something to what Len had been saying about being prepared and that something was wrong. Len's a strong man, and I could understand his momentary bit of panic and doubt about what we'd been told and his suspicions that it wasn't correct. But if he had been sitting there for a couple of hours in that seat and hadn't been able to get over that bad feeling, hadn't been able to convince himself that things were okay, then there must have been something to it.

You know how when a plane hits a pocket of turbulence and the aircraft drops, and you feel as if your stomach and other organs stayed up there? That's the sensation that I experienced with the realization that maybe I'd built all of this up in my mind. Maybe I'd too willingly believed what I hoped was true and not what were proven facts. Call that denial, call it whatever, but I just didn't want to have to face any possibility other than that our daughter was coming home with us.

I mouthed to Len, "What's wrong?"

He ran his finger across his jugular and said, just loud enough so that I could hear him, "No more. No more interviews."

The rest of what he said I wasn't able to hear.

He got up, and we walked back toward the lavatories.

Len repeated what he said about interviews and reminded me that if there were all those people at Logan treating us like we were celebrities worthy of paparazzi treatment, it was probably going to be same once we landed in Florida. We needed to present a unified front.

"'We're cautiously optimistic.' That's what we have to tell them."

I agreed with Len completely. We didn't want to express our doubts. We couldn't let the people searching for our daughter, from the very top level to the people on the ground, think we'd lost any of our hope, any of our belief in them. The truth was that we hadn't. In those horribly chaotic days and nights, we were in a kind of freefall, reaching for and hoping to hang on to whatever we could to stop us from crashing to the ground.

We took our seats and settled in for the rest of flight into West Palm. After we landed, the pilot of our Jet Blue flight got on the P.A. and said he was glad to be able to wish Len and Cherylann Gengel and their sons good luck in reuniting with their daughter, Britney. He briefly explained her story, and the rest of the passengers burst into applause when he got to the point about her being rescued.

All along people had been so kind to us. All I could do was hope that God would continue to be kind to us as well.

We were prepared for the media reception we got, and we hustled along, following the signs for Ground Transportation and Rental Cars, all the while answering a few questions as politely as we could. Susan Wornick from ABC Channel 5 in Boston was the first person I saw. She flew with us from Boston and continued to stay with us for as long as the station allowed her. She'd been a godsend. We had no way of knowing this then, but she'd continue to be there for a long time to come.

I could tell Len was in full-on "bull" mode, meaning that you better get out of his way, you better not hold him up, or he was going to run you over. And these poor camera guys were having to walk backward with those cameras on their shoulders, and the on-air reporters were doing the same, only they had on heels and some wore tight skirts that made them have to do that little short-step shuffle. And I could hear Len's breathing, not because it was labored from walking, but because he was getting close to the goal: the counter of our rental-car agency. And I could see him sag and hear him mutter under his breath. "C'mon. C'mon."

LEN

At that point, I had no patience for anything or anybody. There were three people ahead of us in line. The woman behind the counter had her head down, and she was clacking at her keyboard, giving no indication whatsoever that anyone was standing in front of her. I felt like I was in a commercial.

"We don't have time for this," I said, louder than I thought based on Cherylann's behave-yourself look. It seemed like minutes were going by and no one was moving, no one was being helped, and still that woman stood there typing out what seemed to be the Great American Novel.

God love her, Cherylann took a more proactive approach than my increasingly tense grousing. At first I thought she just wanted to get away from me to avoid the raised eyebrows and stares of the other customers in our line. She just walked over to another rental-car company and got in line. Of course, God favors the patient, and Cherylann got to the counter and rented a car before I even moved one bit and before my systolic blood pressure reached 212, and my red cells boiled over.

I was still pissing and moaning a bit as we rushed to find our car in the lot. Finally, we loaded up in the vehicle and exited. I let out another groan and slapped my forehead. "Not this. Not this. Not now. Not this."

The rental-car employee at the check-out gate was an older man, black as it so happened, and wasn't the speediest of individuals. He was kind of stooped and slow in his gait, and it seemed to take him forever to get to us. I already had the window lowered and the paperwork he had to check hanging out the window, rustling in the ocean air. I was glad of that, at least. Coming from a Boston winter to a Florida tropical balminess was a bit of a relief.

Finally the man took the papers from me, and I just couldn't let this go on any longer, "Listen, we're down here to get our daughter. We're in a big rush, so if you could hurry through this I'd appreciate it. She was down in Haiti, the earthquake hit... "

I left the rest unsaid.

The man pulled his reading glasses back off his nose and leaned in. "I'm from Haiti myself. Terrible thing down there. I've got a few family members we don't know what happened to. God bless you."

That hit me hard. Here I was so, so wrapped up in myself and our troubles, and here was another man whose family was affected just like ours. I thanked him for his kind words and I wished him and his family well.

I also offered a little prayer up to God right on the spot, thanking him for reminding me that this whole incident was larger than just my family and I. I knew that on one level, but here I was being less than charitable and kind and incredibly impatient, and God sent me that lesson.

The half-hour drive down Interstate 95 was blessedly free of traffic. I spoke with Phil Riordan and asked him where we were supposed to meet. The plan hadn't spelled that out, and I wasn't sure if we were supposed to meet at the school, check ourselves into a hotel and wait for the other families to arrive, or what. Phil said the plan was to meet at the school. He didn't add anything else, and given that we were in the car with the boys, I didn't want to press him for any more details.

Pulling into the gated entry of the campus helped calm me a bit. I always liked the idea that unless you had proper identification or were cleared at the entrance, you weren't allowed on the campus. The gate also reminded me of the entrance to the Hotel Montana and how after seeing that photo of it, I was more certain that Brit would be okay in Haiti if they were staying in some place that took those kinds of security measures. Sure, nothing could prevent an earthquake, but short of that, I felt like I'd done as much as I could to keep our daughter safe.

Maybe part of my growing agitation was connected with my natural feelings of guilt. I'd okayed the trip and look what had happened. Logic dictated that I couldn't hold myself responsible, but still I was upset with myself. That's part of being a parent. You want to protect your kid, you do all you can to do so, and if something happens, you still lay some of the blame on yourself for the decision you made. Of course, I understood that hindsight was twenty-twenty, but I couldn't put a fence with a guarded entry around all my feelings.

It didn't help that even at that hour, even though school was not fully in session, the celebratory atmosphere that the wishful part of me was expecting to see didn't materialize. As we wound our way around the campus drive, there was no evidence that anyone was in a partying mood. The campus was mostly deserted, and as we pulled up in front of the Schmidt College Center, first one security guard and then another two approached the car. This was not something that settled my nerves. They asked what we were doing there, and we explained we were there to see Dr. Cynthia Patterson, the vice president of Academic Affairs. We were name dropping a bit, hoping that would explain our presence at that time of night.

In another sense, we weren't name dropping at all. Dr. Patterson had been one of Cherylann's most loyal customers when she ran her restaurant. She'd left our area to take the position at Lynn during Brit's junior year. We knew her well, and we liked the idea that Brit was at a school where we had some personal connection. The security guards didn't seem impressed or anything by that. They were polite and curious, but we were expecting more of a "Hey how are you doing? So glad to hear about your daughter!" type of greeting. To that point, nothing that had taken place, not my conversation with Phil, nor our first encounter with anyone at Lynn, had dispelled the sense of foreboding I'd had for the past four or five hours.

When we walked into the building, the routine was the same. A security guard was in the lobby area, and he told us that the president, Kevin Ross, and his cabinet—what they called the other chief administrators—were in a meeting upstairs. We could take a seat and then someone would come down to escort us to the meeting room. Cherylann and I exchanged a quick glance. Now both of us were really on edge. Why weren't these people running down the stairs to greet us? Why weren't we whooping it up? There could only be one answer, but a dozen possible other responses were ricocheting around in my brain. I couldn't sit down. I didn't want to sit down. No one was going to make me sit down. So I walked around the lobby, looked at a few of the portraits there, some other informational stuff behind glass-encased boards, and generally tried to work off the nervous energy that was rampaging through me.

I figured maybe a couple of minutes' wait might be understandable, but we were there to learn about the fate of our daughter. We'd been told she'd been rescued. That was short and sweet, so why couldn't we just cut to the chase? Bernie and Richie were sitting on a low bench or couch, or something in between, both of them resting their chins in their hands. They were as exhausted as Cherylann and I, and the flight had dislocated us as much as it had refreshed us. I don't think my nervous energy infected them; they could sense something was not right. Pretty soon, they were upset and talking about how all of this was bullshit, and why couldn't we just find out where we were going to meet and see Brit and screw the rest of whatever it was that was going on.

Even if I'd wanted to, I couldn't have told them to just hang on and be patient. By the time fifteen minutes had passed, and then twenty, all of us were even jumpier and growing angry. We also wondered why we were the only ones there. Five other families still had missing loved ones. Cherylann offered an explanation for why they might not be here—different travel arrangements, etc.—and as logical as that all was, I was beyond being rational.

A few times, the staff asked us if we would like coffee or

something to drink. Cherylann and I were very cordial, keeping our composure, but inside I was thinking, just give me my daughter so I can get the hell out of here. I also asked a couple of times if we could see the president.

"He's on the phone right now."

"He's gathering information."

All I could think was that they knew we were coming down here, shouldn't they have had all their ducks in a row? I knew the situation in Haiti was chaotic and things were constantly evolving, but why not include us in those conversations and fact-finding? At worst, just tell us. "Yes." "No." "We don't know."

A few moments later, we heard footsteps echoing from the top of the spiral staircase and its black marble steps. Cherylann and I looked up and saw the president of the college, Kevin Ross, in the center with Cynthia on one side, a man who I presumed was our contact, Phil Riordan, on the other, and another man I didn't know from Adam. Our hearts fell. Even from a distance it was clear that Cynthia and Kevin had been crying. Their eyes were red-rimmed and bloodshot. Kevin was only thirty-five years old, the university's second president in its history, and he was the son of the school's founding president. I don't know if Phil Riordan was crying or not because he dropped his eyes as soon as he saw us. The poor guy was oozing disappointment out of his pores.

We exchanged greetings and introductions, and we learned the identity of the fourth member of the Lynn team, Matt Shalou. Just as before, this was all kind of stiffly formal and awkward, and Matt couldn't look me in the eye, which got my radar sounding off.

From the start, when my suspicions were first raised and I sensed that something was wrong, I wasn't thinking that Brit was dead. I said something about her having died in the helicopter on the way, but that was just something I didn't believe and was using as an example. We walked down the hall to a small office; they shut the door and I sensed again that I needed to prepare myself.

"I'm sorry to tell you this, but we had bad intel. We don't

have your daughter," Kevin Ross said.

A wave of relief washed over me. That was not good news, but it certainly wasn't bad news like it might have been.

I took a moment to digest that information and looked Kevin square in the eye. "Please tell me that you had a satellite phone with them," I said.

Kevin blinked a couple of times, clearly thrown off by my question. I had been hearing for a while about "losing contact" with the people on the ground, and I wanted to know exactly what that meant.

Kevin looked at Matt, whose exact title I didn't catch but it had something to do with student security or some such. Matt looked at me and said, "No, but they did have international phones."

Ignoring the idiocy of his response, I looked at Kevin again. "You mean to tell me you sent our daughter into Haiti, a place with notoriously bad communications infrastructure, without a satellite phone?"

He didn't respond.

I went on. "So what you're really saying is that you have no communication going on with people on the ground in Haiti. You don't have bad intel; you have no intel."

Kevin immediately cut me off. "No. That's not what I'm saying at all." He explained that in addition to the group known as Red 24, the school had hired an additional search-and-rescue type organization called The Crucibles. They are both on the ground and reporting to us."

"So you have contact with someone there, but you don't have contact with our daughter."

"That's correct."

"Now, I'm going to ask you something else. You have to look me in the eye, and you have to promise me that you are doing everything in your power to make certain that, one way or another, you get my daughter back from there."

"We're doing everything we can for everyone from Lynn who is there."

I didn't get my promise, but Cherylann and I got to unload all our questions. It was clear what we were seeing and hearing on television and in the newspapers was true. Everything was so chaotic. And the Red 24 group wasn't reporting directly to Lynn but to their headquarters in the UK and then relaying messages to Connecticut and back down to Florida. Everything was tangled and broken and disjointed.

Finally, they told us they had booked rooms for us, and we left. After some confusion, we finally were able to locate the place. It was one of those old Florida resort hotels that had seen better days. It smelled of mold and the lush vegetation that grew around a tiny algae-choked pool.

"This is the place that bad news comes to stay when it's looking for some disappointment of its own," I said to Cherylann.

We weren't the only ones, it seemed, who were getting bad news that night. We saw Phil Riordan with another couple, escorting them either into or out of the hotel. We knew we weren't alone in our uncertainty and fright. That was no comfort at all. We were back to square one. With the cable news networks on the television, we lay there all night as the room's window air conditioner rattled like an old man's coughing chest.

For the second time in just a few short days, I'd heard news that my daughter was among the missing, among the hundreds of thousands of displaced, dead, and injured in that country that had had more than its share of bad news. We weren't experiencing devastation on that level, but it was cold comfort to know that the best news you'd gotten that day was that your daughter wasn't confirmed to be among the casualties.

CHERYLANN

Len and I agreed that night that we weren't angry about what had happened with the miscommunication. We didn't really blame anybody; we just figured they were as happy to believe something good as we had been. I can see now that maybe they should have waited a bit longer to get better verification before contacting us. Then, they would have run the risk of us being angry that they had waited so long to tell us something they already knew. I guess it was a classic no-win situation, even for those parents whose kids had already been rescued and account-ed for. I guess that's why they call these things tragedies. Barely anyone escapes unhurt and unchanged by the experience.

And as Len said, we were still hopeful. When Len had warned me to be prepared, I hadn't let my mind go to the darkest place and think about Brit being dead. I couldn't and wouldn't. The worst-case scenario for me was that she was injured, in some field hospital somewhere, not getting the best of care and in some pain. I just wanted to know what we were dealing with, but that wasn't going to be possible for at least another day. I felt pretty much like I'd been dragged under the bus already. How could things go on like this? For how much longer? And could things possibly get worse?

As we lay in bed that night, we had to consider our next steps. First on the agenda was what to do about notifying every-one back home about this most recent development. We knew that everyone was waiting to hear from us; undoubtedly, some parties were already in the planning stages as a welcome home for Brit. Everyone else had been riding the same high that we had been, and to feel their balloon being deflated along with ours was almost too much for us to think about. We also didn't want to send out an email that late at night. The best way for us to handle the situation was to let them go to sleep thinking those good thoughts. Bernie was so worked up that he wasn't able to stay in the room. The combined anxiety of all of us was too much for him. He went for a walk and came back smelling of cigarettes. I knew that wasn't the best idea, but if that was the worst thing that he was doing to deal with his stress, then I figured it best to just let it go. He also came back with the news that the hotel was essentially deserted except for a couple of rooms next door to ours. We figured that we were there with a few other families of the missing girls from Lynn. Knowing that there were other people who could commiserate with us and offer us support and we could do the same for them was a good thing. The fact that we had to be supported and commiserated with in the first place was a bad thing.

It seemed as if everything was either a mixed bag or a mixed blessing. We tossed and turned all night, and from 4:30 a.m. we lay there debating about whether or not we should get out of bed. But what were we going to do at that hour? The minutes just seemed to crawl by. Finally at about 7:00, we put the *Today* show on television. We were like addicts; we craved a fix of news all the time. Matt Lauer came on, and we both gasped a bit when we heard our names mentioned. Then a moment later, there was video from our house of all of us celebrating the news that Brit had been rescued. I felt like I was going to throw up. Now everyone in the country watching that show would think that Brit was found and safe. I knew that our family and friends were already under that assumption, but now the news—the incorrect news—was out there for everybody.

I couldn't stand that thought or having to relive those moments when our anxiety and worry proved to be legitimate. I got out of bed and walked into the bathroom. I shut my eyes and turned on the water in the shower, ignoring all the funky smells and whatever else made that hotel so depressing. I got in, pulled the curtain shut, and let the hot water work on easing some of the tension in my neck and shoulders. I tried to focus on my breathing. I felt as if my whole body was a clenched fist. After a while, I plugged my ears with my fingers and listened to the water tapping against my skull. At least the shower's stream was warm and powerful, and I even may have fallen asleep for a minute leaning against the tile with my head resting on my arm.

I was on automatic pilot and, without thinking, just went about my business of washing my hair and then drying it and changing clothes. Len was on the bed, and I could tell he was deep in thought. He had on his don't-bother-me-now face, so after I was dressed, I sat on the edge of the bed, trying not to think. I heard Matt Lauer's voice saying that they wanted to apologize to us. He said they learned that Brit was not among the Lynn kids who'd been rescued and accounted for. He said they'd gotten bad information from the people at the university. Join the club, I thought. At least we got the apology.

Len and I didn't speculate too much about the source of the bad information the networks had gotten. Susan Wornick had come down to Florida with us and so had reporters from two other local affiliates. Susan was really helpful to us, and she would continue to be a great friend and valuable resource. We hadn't really thought about what to say to them. We'd been told that Lynn University was conducting a news conference later that morning; we assumed they would explain the miscommunication and we wouldn't have to.

"At least they apologized," Len said.

"Who?"

"The *Today* show."

I shrugged my shoulders, thinking that none of this stuff mattered all that much.

"Do you trust me?" Len asked.

"Of course, I do."

"Good. Some of this is going to be painful, but it's got to be done."

"You have to do what you think is best."

"Well, the *Today* show gave out some bad information, but that may be a good thing. I mean, at least they're talking about us. Now that they have a thread of our story, I'm going to have to make sure that isn't the end of it. The more those kids are in the news, the better. Like the saying goes, 'The only bad publicity is when they spell your name wrong.'"

"That's true." I'd thought about the bad part of word getting out, but I hadn't considered there could be a benefit.

"I've got a plan," Len said. Normally that's cause for excitement, but this time I noted Len's voice didn't have its usual this-is-going-to-be-great enthusiasm. Instead, he sounded like a man on a mission he didn't want to undertake.

The next thing I knew, he was on the phone with Susan Wornick, and we were heading to one of Brit's favorite places, Palm Beach Bagel, to meet with our media tutor to discuss our strategy.

LEN

As I lay in bed while Cherylann showered, the pieces of the plan were falling into place. We needed to use the media to get exposure for our daughter's story. Now that the folks at NBC had opened the door, I was going to barge right through it. When I saw how ashen Matt Lauer's face was when he had to apologize for giving out that incorrect news, and I heard Meredith Vieira audibly gasp, I knew they were feeling a bit of our pain. I will do anything for my kids, so call it exploiting their emotions, call it whatever, in that instant I knew what I had to do.

Susan Wornick was devastated to hear what had happened. She echoed a lot of our thoughts. How could you have been told something so joyous and then have it snatched away from you? That was beyond cruel. But Susan was terrific, and she was right there with me moving beyond that and trying to keep focus on our main goal: getting more people into Haiti to assist with rescue operations. So, she agreed to help with my plan.

I'd written a few notes, and I've seen the video of the message I delivered to our president. Even today, three years after the fact, I'm still stunned by how drawn and haggard I looked, how anguished my quavering voice was as I delivered words carefully and deliberately planed to provoke some kind of response: "We are praying that our daughter, Britney, be one of the rescued today and brought home safe and sound. And I am pleading, I am pleading to President Obama to please send more troops to Haiti to rescue. As a father, President Obama, you must feel our pain and what we are going through. We were told our children were safe and rescued. Now, we are told they are not. We need your help. We know you can do it. Father to father, I am pleading with you to please, please get help and rescue those folks in the Hotel Montana in Haiti."

Anyone watching that would know they were witnessing raw emotion. I felt like the words were being torn out of my throat. As much as I'd planned those remarks and prepared to deliver them, and as calculated as they were, the emotion was not planned, faked, or anything like that. I was a man in growing despair as time went on and on and my little girl wasn't back with us. My goal was clear: The squeaky wheel gets the grease and moves to another level. By calling out the man who served as the highest official in the land, I was opening myself up to criticism and second-guessing. I didn't care. What mattered was that Brit's name get out in the media so she and the rest of the missing students and professors could be found. I'd pay whatever price necessary to ensure that happened.

I had Cherylann's support in doing what I did. That meant the world to me. As for the boys, I didn't let them know ahead of time what I had planned. I could sense Richie and Bernie were in shock. We all were, but theirs was a different kind. I could show that kind of emotion, but the boys seemed numb, dazed; they were sleepwalking through much of those first few days, unable to process what was happening. Cherylann and I were concerned about the toll this was taking. If the circumstances had been different, if we didn't think we were traveling to Florida to meet Brit, we would have considered alternate plans and likely not brought them with us. The atmosphere at Lynn and in Boca Raton was too emotionally charged for them.

If I did another good thing that day it was this: I called my sister, Chrissy, and asked her to join us in Florida. She also brought her son, Joshua, with her for support. Chrissy is a licensed and practicing child psychologist, and I wanted her to be around to monitor Bernie and Richie. I could only do or say so much. I needed someone with her level of expertise. Cherylann was doing a great job of caring for the boys, but I didn't want to tax her too much. I couldn't predict what the next few seconds were going to bring, let alone the next few days, but I needed to look as far down the line as possible and make sure that I did everything I could for my boys, as well as for Brit.

Later that morning, we all gathered in Kevin Ross's office. Oddly, he wasn't there, but the rest of the people we'd met with the night before were. So were the parents of the other missing students: Stephanie Crispinelli, Christine Gianacaci, and Courtney Hayes. Family members of the faculty members still unaccounted for, professors Richard Bruno and Patrick Hartwick, were also there. None of us really reached out in any significant way to the others. We all had that same laser focus—our daughter mattered, we wanted our daughter back. Completely understandable at the time, but later on, we started to work together.

Thirty people gathered in that room, and the combined frustration, anger, and anxiety was through the roof. The room basically vibrated at a high frequency. Not all of us were able to keep our emotions in check, which was completely understandable, but it was difficult to have that many people in such a high state of emotion gathered in one place.

Mostly, the meeting was a rehash of what we'd heard the night before with a couple of exceptions. First, the other eight kids were back in Boca Raton and had been reunited with their families. That was good but painful news. Second, Lynn University had pretty substantial resources and connections they were willing to use. They had a team ready to fly to Santo Domingo in the Dominican Republic to start a hospital-by-hospital, refugee-center-by-refugee-center, search to find our kids. That was terrific to hear, but when they offered to let any family members go there with them, I had to hesitate. Was that the best use of my time? Angie Hayes and Franklin Hayes immediately said they were going.

We all had our choices to make, and I was thinking the plan that I'd put in motion with Susan Wornick was more important. We needed to be all over the media with constant reminders about these missing American kids, these students who'd gone there to do good works. These kids were not very different from the viewers' and the readers' own.

Susan Wornick told us about the news cycle and how fresh angles were always needed, and how quickly a front-page story can move back and out of a newspaper or a newscast. If there were other people going there to check on the identities of patients brought there, then that base was covered. It was a good one to cover, since the last we heard the girls were on a helicopter. No one knew anything beyond that, so it was conceivable that they had been airlifted out of there. That was part of our frustration. If they were in flight somewhere, that expanded the number of places that would have the searched, more agencies consulted, and all that. That meant more man-power was needed. As far as I was concerned, not enough resources were being allocated at that point.

For us, there was an enormous sense of urgency. If Brit wasn't on the helicopter, then she could have been buried alive in a pile of rubble. This was Friday, four days after the quake, and stories were still coming out of Haiti that people were being found alive in collapsed buildings. Time was of the essence, and I sat there in that meeting for nearly two hours feeling like less talk and a lot more action was needed. That is with one exception: I had to do some more talking in hopes of stirring up more action.

6

WORKING ALL THE ANGLES

"For as much as we needed to stay on point in those media messages, I had to look beyond Brit to the boys and their needs. That's always a delicate balance for parents to strike. How much time and attention to spend on each kid."

—CHERYLANN

LEN

Tragedy can bring out either the best or the worst in people. Once I made that plea to President Obama, it was as if the floodgates opened. I wasn't proud of myself for having to ask for help, but I was going to do anything I could to bring Brit home. We'd lost her once and then a second time, and I was damn sure not going to let that happen again. By that Friday, January 15, the media had already been seeking us out. The local media knew Brit had been "rescued," and soon the national media got onto the story. I don't mean to sound too cynical, but in the weeks to come, I started to pick up on a few things about how news works. I'm a street kid and pretty savvy, but I don't know if even I was fully prepared for some of the shenanigans that went on when the various networks and shows began competing to be the first to tell our story.

I will say this. They wanted something. I needed something. I had what they wanted, and when they came across with what I wanted, I gave them what they were asking for. The thing is, though, they wanted ratings and advertising dollars. I wanted my daughter back.

I don't want to paint with too broad of a brush here, because even on that Friday, we heard from someone who wanted nothing but to help us out. Karen D'Uva was a freelance journalist living in Florida. She picked up on our story and contacted my office. Doreen, our office manager, fielded Karen's call along with several others. When I spoke with Doreen, a woman I've worked with for years and trust implicitly, I asked her what she thought about the people she'd talked to.

"Karen D'Uva came across as the most sincere," Doreen said, "She knows what you guys are going through. She lost her husband a year ago. She gets it."

My initial conversation with Karen confirmed what Doreen had said. As a freelancer, Karen made her living by covering stories on assignment from a network or show or by bringing the stories to them. To her credit, Karen didn't earn a dollar as a result of her interviewing us and getting us onto *CBS This Morning*. We had a lot of choices about who to go with, but we chose Karen and CBS because I negotiated with her for one thing: images from the Hotel Montana. To that point, at least as far as we knew, and someone in our circle was watching the coverage on all the networks nonstop, no images from the Hotel Montana had been broadcast. We knew, after talking with Lindsay, that they had been staying in Room 300 in the back right corner of the building. Not only did I want photos of the site of the hotel, I wanted photos or video of that exact spot.

Karen said she would do that for us. As a result, we agreed to go on with her first. Those first interviews were conducted in our hotel. We'd checked out of the one that Lynn had provided, and we sat there doing our few minutes with one crew, took a break, and then geared up for the next. It's disconcerting staring into a camera while listening to some voice from far away asking you questions. I'm sure we had that deer-in-the-headlights look on our faces, but none of that mattered. We kept hammering home one point over and over again: the Hotel Montana. American kids in that location. Get someone there. Send troops. Do whatever it takes, but get people to the Hotel Montana.

The images that Karen secured for us added to our urgency. Coupled with what the survivors had told us about what they'd experienced, we realized that our only hope was that Brit was in one of those pockets that honeycombed many debris piles. We were still hearing stories of people in various parts of Port-au-Prince being pulled from the rubble of collapsed buildings. We were especially anxious to get people out there immediately because of the horrific images and descriptions that began to emerge. Because of the potential health crisis that decaying bodies posed, corpses were being bulldozed into mass graves.

Whether we were Catholics or not, as parents the idea that our daughter's body might not be recovered crushed our souls. We still held out hope that she was alive, but just knowing that the situation had devolved to such a degree that the authorities were doing this saddened and sickened us. We couldn't imagine what the survivors were experiencing in knowing that some of their loved ones were lost to them in such a visceral way, that the scope of this tragedy was so great that their individual mourning and remembrance were literally being swept aside, providing no real closure for them or dignity for those lost.

I've worked in construction most of my adult life, and I know the sounds and vibrations a heavy piece of earth-moving equipment produces. I've heard the high-pitched beeping tones of its back-up warnings, and just thinking of those sensations chilled me, ate at my guts, and forced me to shut my eyes to chase those sights and sounds away. It was like those beeps were the sounds of a timer counting down, and for those few minutes when the bright lights were on us and the questions needed to be answered, from a dark corner of my mind those sounds intoned a reminder that time was running out. We couldn't afford a single minute's delay.

Lenny is the one with the big personality in our marriage. He's never been afraid to get up in front of a group of people and talk. Having to deal with the media put me way outside my comfort zone. I prefer to stay in the background, and that's what has made my marriage with Len work so well. We complement each other and make up for areas of weakness.

In this case, though, we needed to show a unified front, and that meant I had to step up and deliver in ways that I wasn't used to. I was willing to do anything to get my only daughter home. It was hard at first, but Brit provided all the motivation I needed to look into those cameras, block out all the crew people milling around, and stick to the message. Karen D'Uva was an enormous help with this. She told us that the media was going to try to spin things the way they wanted by asking questions and dirtying things up. We couldn't let them do that. If they wanted to ask about our feelings about Lynn University and if they were in any way negligent or whatever, we had to keep to our program: We want our daughters, our fathers, our husbands, home. If they told us that they had us slotted for a two-minute segment and we didn't feel like that was sufficient time to get our point across, then we kept talking. They might have wanted to interrupt, but how could they? How could they come across as anything but heartless if they cut off a family member of a missing person who was pleading for their loved one to be found? Karen told us all that and more, and we were enormously grateful to her then and today for all she did to help us.

I couldn't help but sit there between interviews and think of how much Brit would have loved to have been a part of this.

Before she told us that she wanted to switch to a social services emphasis, she'd always talked about being a broadcaster. Like her dad, she was comfortable in the spotlight. I found those moments in front of the camera agonizing at first, but then I relaxed into it a bit. You do what you have to do, and even though there were times throughout this ordeal that I just wanted to run away, when I just wanted to wake up from this nightmare, I knew I couldn't. I also knew I couldn't break down in front of the boys.

Like Len, Richie wears his heart on his sleeve. Bernie is more like me, more reserved, less likely to bare his emotions. Just because we don't show them doesn't mean we don't feel as deeply as someone who displays them more easily. I was worried about Richie because he was a few years younger than Bernie, some crucial years in terms of his maturity. Also, Richie and Brit had a different kind of relationship than Bernie and Brit. Because Richie was five years younger, when he was a little guy, Brit was old enough to be in that caretaking phase. Bernie and Brit are much closer in age, so there was a little more competition for attention between them, a little more of that sibling tension. Despite their occasional dustups, Bernie loved Brit and he worked on trying to get the word out through the social-media networks to gain as much information as possible. Being able to immerse himself in this task also gave him purpose and kept his mind focused. Richie didn't have a job like that, leaving lots of time and space in his mind for worry and anxiety to come in and take up residence.

When Richie was a toddler and even after that, Brit and her girlfriends lavished all kinds of attention on him. He was the cute little guy, and Brit and her friends also had a lot of fun with Bernie. I always liked and appreciated that all the kids got along. And later Brit seemed to relish her big-sister role in a way that she didn't with Bernie. He didn't really need her in the way that Richie did. At the approach of each school year, and as they got older, Brit was the one who took her youngest brother to get his school supplies and clothes.

It broke my heart toward the end of that first week when Richie broke down crying and said, "If Brit doesn't come back, who's going to take me back-to-school shopping?"

As a mother, as a parent, you often have to face things that you're not prepared for. You try to draw from your experiences, but this was so far out of the realm of what I would have ever thought I'd have to deal with, that for a few moments I couldn't think of what to say that might make any sense to our youngest, might offer him any kind of comfort. Of course, I told him Brit would be coming back, but saying those words unsettled me a bit. We were now five days removed from the earthquake hitting. We were in Florida and away from anything familiar that might help Richie and Bernie and us, and for that matter feel any kind of stability.

I wasn't giving up hope—you never do that—but you do have to think beyond the hope to the heartache. I knew that no matter what, whether Brit was rescued or recovered, our boys had their lives to live. So, for as much as we needed to stay on point in those media messages, I had to look beyond Brit to the boys and their needs. That's always a delicate balance for parents to strike. How much time and attention to spend on each kid. I was always particularly sensitive to that. I knew it couldn't have been easy for the boys to follow behind on the trail that Brit had blazed. She was such a vivacious kid, so full of energy and sparkle. It would have been easy for them to have disappeared in that kind of glare. I always hoped that teachers wouldn't do the comparison thing, though I understand that's a natural and inevitable but irritating part of life in a family.

I knew they understood that given what was happening, they had to step aside and let the focus be where it had to be. I had to let go to a small extent that desire to make sure that things were equal among the three of them. Something told me also, that no matter the outcome, this experience was critical to us all, a defining moment, a marker we would use to measure every other event from that point forward. Even though that was all true, I didn't want the boys, or us for that matter, to get stuck in that time and place. I was eager to get the interviews done, deal with the people at Lynn University in whatever ways necessary, and then get out of there, away from Florida and all the reminders of that place. Brit's birthday was looming, another one of those markers and memories.

Would the pain of any of this ever stop? The only way it would was if we could throw our arms around her, feel her solid and alive, her hands gripping our flesh as fiercely, a reminder that we would never, ever, let one another go.

LEN

As much as we were trying to get information out to the American public and to our government officials, at times it felt like the people at Lynn University were trying to keep us from learning anything additional. I can see now why they had to do that, to prevent another "bad intel" calamity, but it was hugely frustrating to take time away from our efforts to attend those twice-daily sessions.

If there was one good thing about them, it was the fact that the six families could get together and compare notes. Who talked to which congressman from where? How could we coordinate our media efforts to ensure we were all on the same page?

Somewhat miraculously, the Hayes family had a relative by the name of Zip who managed to get into the country. At each of those meetings, we would learn from Courtney's boyfriend, Matt Sears, what hospitals they had visited. They'd brought down pictures of all the girls and were posting them all over, asking if anyone had seen any of them. Through this connection, we also learned the rescue efforts were being hampered by a lack of tools and supplies, and especially by a lack of electricity. They couldn't run power tools, so that meant they needed generators. With my background, you can only imagine how helpless I felt. I knew what it took to dismantle and put up buildings, and here, these poor people were trying to do this incredibly hard physical labor with whatever hand tools they had available. Sure, there was some heavy equipment on site, and yes, each day more search-and-rescue teams were flying in, but there were also the survivors to consider, the refugee camps to be set up, the food and water to be distributed.

It was mind-boggling and overwhelming to say the least. And a few times I did let some guilt creep in. What did the lives of these six people matter in comparison to the scale of devastation and loss the entire country of Haiti was experiencing? We were only beginning to learn how many other Americans were in the country, and how many of them were among the dead and the missing. In time we'd learn that more Americans died in that earthquake than in the September 11 terrorists attacks on New York, Pennsylvania, and Washington, D.C. Those moments of contemplation were brief. They had to be. I was like a dog shaking water off itself, shedding those other concerns to keep my focus on our daughter and the other Lynn University people who were missing. Whether that meant this tragedy was bringing out the best or the worst in me wasn't something I could take the time to consider. I had to keep digging, keep working every possible angle.

We all shared one feeling: if only we could get to Haiti somehow. If only we could be there on the ground and actively searching ourselves, somehow everything would be okay.

FORTIFIED BY FAITH, HOPE, AND LOVE

"Before we could go back to Boston, I had to do one other thing: I had to pack up Britney's dorm room."

—CHERYLANN

CHERYLANN

Nearly every moment of this ordeal had a quality of unreality about it. When you spend so much of your time and energy trying not to think about a very real possibility, I guess that bleeds over into what actually was taking place. Even after a week in Florida, I still wasn't used to stepping out into sunshine and warm breezes. Where was the New England snow and cold? Why was I wrapped in warmth instead of a wool overcoat?

As much as I'd been trying not to think about Brit trapped in that rubble lying there hurt and suffering, as much as I tried not to think about her being buried in one of the mass graves I'd heard everyone talking about, as much as I tried to shut my mind to the horrible image of her being bulldozed like so many others, her body being treated like just so much debris, I especially didn't want to think about her birthday.

Nine days in, January 21, I had to face the reality of that day and what it meant for all of us. Silly, in a way, when you think about everything else going on, but knowing that we'd be spending her birthday without her was heart wrenching! My kids are everything to me, and the fact that she wasn't there was more than I could handle. Brit LOVED her birthday. The day after Christmas the focus shifted to Brit's birthday. It was a big joke among us how the countdown would begin. But now this was no joke at all. I couldn't even allow myself to think of past birthday celebrations. Doing that just hurt way too much!

Len had been kidding me post-Christmas and post-New Year that year about not wanting to have another party for Brit. I always threw big parties for all our kids, especially Brit. We had big extended families, so even a low-key party still would include a crowd. I didn't want people to feel obligated to bring gifts, and no matter if I told them that, they'd still do it. The girl had as much as she needed. It would have been fun to have another family bash, but I knew Britney would have hated being the center of attention. Ha! Ha! Ironic given that in those days following the earthquake, I spent so much time distracting myself by feeding the crew that came to the house to show their support. Not exactly a festive atmosphere, but Britney was still in the spotlight for a reason none of us could have imagined before.

As usual, Len and I woke up before dawn from our brief nightly collapse. We looked at each other and neither of us had to say a word. I could tell Len was awake and already in get-things-done mode. I'd heard him tapping away at the laptop a half hour earlier, bathed in the eerie blue light of the screen. I let him be. When he saw that I was awake, he shut down the computer and crawled into bed next to me. I lay my head in the crook of his arm. The hotel room's air conditioner clicked on, and I wrestled with the still tucked-in sheets.

"I'm thinking I should be home. Richie's there," I said. He had flown home earlier than the rest of us. "He needs me."

Len heaved a big sigh, and I rose and fell with it. I *knew* he knew that what I'd said was true, but it wasn't foremost on my mind.

"We should get there early today." Len's voice was raspier than usual—from the sleep deprivation and lack of water. I wanted to constantly remind him to take care of himself, but I knew he had enough on his mind.

"Okay."

"We could go to the chapel before the first meeting."

"That'd be nice. I like that idea. Just the two of us. Bernie can stay here?"

* * *

Walking through the center of campus toward the chapel, I was struck again by how different this all was from home. When we'd left Rutland, there was still snow on the ground, the trees were bare, and you had to squint your eyes against the face-stinging wind. In Boca, the wind carried the scent of jasmine and citrus. With classes not yet in session, the campus was deserted, and as we walked along the blindingly white concrete walkways, all we could hear was the hiss of the sprinklers and the faint sound of a lawn mower.

Len took my hand and it was warm and moist. Somehow that familiar sensation gave me comfort.

We were surprised that the door was unlocked. The chapel was cave-like, small and dark, and I couldn't help but think of what space Brit might be in. A small altar with two candles stood in the center of the room, their flames flickering and wavering in the just disturbed air. Len and I stood there, and I couldn't help but think this was not where I wanted to be saying Happy Birthday to my daughter.

We took a moment to say a few prayers and to wish her Happy Birthday, neither of us saying a word out loud, but both knowing what the other was thinking. It had been nine days, but we still had our faith, we were there praying for our little girl, letting her know we weren't giving up on her. We aren't ever going to stop until we find you.

We broke the silence by singing Happy Birthday, both our voices wavering like the candlelight. Tears streamed down my face. In my mind I was asking: Am I really singing Happy Birthday to my daughter without her being here? Please, God, let me sing to her again. Please, God!

Of course, the moment when a husband and wife conceive a child are about as intimate and private as any two people could share, but there was something about standing there with my husband of twenty-two years that brought back that same sense of communion, that same sense that you were there with the only person you wanted to share that with. We knew we were going to have to leave Florida soon, but like I told Brit in that chapel, we were not in any way shape or form saying good-bye.

LEN

If the Lord moves in mysterious ways, then the federal government moves in ways unknowable to man and God. That Thursday, though, it moved in ways I was grateful for. It was as if Brit had blown out the candles and made a wish, and it instantly had come true. Cheryl Mills, Secretary of State Clinton's chief of staff, notified me at 11:00 A.M. that we were going to be allowed into Haiti. U.S. Congressman McGovern and Senator Kerry had worked their magic on our behalf. In exchange for this extraordinary breach of standard operating procedure and protocol, we were sworn to secrecy. At that point, only the military, search-and-rescue crews, and medical personnel were being allowed into the country through official channels.

Had I known this when we were in the chapel, I would have offered a prayer of thanks that our congressman had served as Hillary Clinton's New England campaign manager. He was on good terms with Hillary and Bill Clinton, and the fact that they both had a special attachment to Haiti also served our cause. The Lord and Washington, D.C., were moving in synchronous orbit on this one. In less than four days, Jim McGovern had moved mountains on our behalf. I don't know if that also proves the power of the F-bombs that he was dropping (which seemed completely out of character for him) in our initial conversations about the government's response to the crisis, but no matter. One family member of each of the missing Lynn group would be allowed into the country and be taken to the Hotel Montana.

At Thursday's update meeting, I finally was able to tell the Gianacacis, Crispinellis, Hayeses and the others that we'd be allowed to go. We didn't have a lot of details, but when we met again on Friday, the logistics were finalized. We would depart from Fort Lauderdale the next day, fly to the Dominican Republic, and be taken by bus into Haiti and eventually to the Hotel Montana.

It's hard even for me to fathom this, but I was happy to learn the combined efforts of a lot of people had paid off. I had to get my passport, so that meant flying back to Boston, packing a few things, and then hightailing it back down to Florida to make my flight the next morning.

CHERYLANN

Before we could go back to Boston, I had to do one other thing: I had to pack up Britney's dorm room. There was no way she was going to attend classes that spring semester. We wanted our girl back home with us, after everything we'd all been through. I'd talked it over with Len, and though we had made every attempt to keep all our thoughts and statements positive, he knew there was another reason for my wanting to pack things up.

"I don't think I can do that. I don't think I can be there to help you." Len sat cradling his head in his hands.

"That's okay. I want to do this. I need to do this. It's now or not at all. I couldn't possibly let anyone else touch her stuff. This is something I have to do. I'm her mother. This is what a mother does to take care of her daughter."

He held one palm up to stop me like a crossing guard. Next, he stood up and hugged me, telling me how brave I was. I shut my eyes and buried my face in his chest. Tears leaked past my closed lids, and I took a few snuffling breaths.

Len held me tighter and kissed the top of my head. Finally, feeling strong enough again, I pulled his arms down. I stood there looking at my mess of a husband knowing I didn't look any better. I shook my head a few times and then shrugged, "I don't want to, but I have to."

He drew me in again, and we hugged for I don't know how long. Dazed by lack of sleep and feeling slightly nauseated, I said, "I'll be back. I love you."

"I'll be here after I do the Bill O'Reilly thing. I love you."

* * *

I had been in touch with the residence director to help facilitate the move. I was so concerned about the young woman who was going to be Britney's roommate that coming semester. I couldn't imagine what Cat was going through and what she would think if she saw the mother of her missing friend and future roommate packing up all of her daughter's things. I'd made arrangements with the resident advisor to be sure that Cat was out of the room so I could work in isolation. Like many of the students on campus, Cat was taking advantage of the counseling sessions the school offered. A lot of the kids were struggling with the news about their classmates.

I was glad they had that opportunity, but a part of me got defensive—almost possessive—when I heard and saw other people's reaction to our situation. I appreciated the support that Len's and my families were showing, but still, there was something different about what we were going through and what they were experiencing. As sympathetic as they could be, as full of sadness, they couldn't go to the places that Len and I and the boys were traveling to. We'd crossed a line, and in my head it was almost as if we'd put one of those crime-scene tapes around certain aspects of our lives. We were the only ones with the credentials that allowed us access to those places. Len and I had also been vigilant about how much and how far we let Bernie and Richie in, so it was only natural that someone who was virtually a stranger would be scrutinized by our screening process.

It wasn't that I didn't like Cat—quite the opposite. This was just something I needed to do alone. When I walked in the room, I saw that they'd taken a load of Britney's dirty clothes home and had washed, dried, and folded them. A little thing, but at a time when everyone said, "If there is anything I can do. . ." to have someone do something helpful without asking was wonderful.

A couple of RAs were stationed in the hallway in case Cat or another one of Britney's friends came by, and they smiled and nodded at me, but I could see in their eyes what I came to think of as "the look": a quick meeting of the eyes and then the inspection of the floor, the far wall, anywhere but on me. I understood. In some ways that look was better than the one I got from the other parents when I told them I was emptying Brit's room. Everyone viewed that as a sign that I'd given up, that I'd admitted to myself that Brit was gone. I tried to explain to them, and to myself, that wasn't the case. Truth is, as I then put it to myself, things weren't looking so good. I couldn't bring myself to say any of those words of finality. Like Len kept saying in various interviews, "We're hoping for the best, but preparing for the worst."

I knew myself. I knew that if we did get the final word that Brit hadn't made it out alive, there was no way I could go back to that dorm room to retrieve her stuff. This way I could tell myself that we were just packing her up to take her home so that she could spend the time she needed to recuperate, to separate herself from the horror of that experience. There were plenty of good schools back near Boston. We'd keep her closer to home after this, be able to pop in on her or have her pop home on weekends. After what she'd been through, she'd need that.

We still had the plastic bins that we'd used to help her move in. A couple of the kids who saw me in the hallway offered to help me, but I shook my head and said, "No, thanks. I want to do this myself." I wasn't ready to admit to anyone but Len that I needed help of any kind. It was also true that I wanted and needed to do this myself. Brit was my daughter, and I didn't want anyone else to touch her things. This was extremely personal to me; I needed to protect Brit and her things. I wasn't sure how composed I'd be able to stay, despite walking around like an overly polite zombie, answering, "Yes, please" and "No, thank you," and "My pleasure" all polished and at the ready. Truth was, that last one was the biggest lie—there was no pleasure in my world, only duty and obligation. The only real yes answers would have been to questions like these: Do I miss my daughter? Do I feel like someone has ripped my guts out? Would I rather be sitting at the Cheesecake Factory in Boca with my daughter giggling with her gaggle of girlfriends than here?

I put my hand on the doorknob and took a deep breath. "C'mon, Cherylann. You're an adult. Do this thing and be done with it." A twist and a shoulder thrust and I was in there.

With the exception of a pair of large walk-in closets and a private bathroom, the dorm was pretty much your standard-issue cinder-block room. Except the cinder blocks were there to help protect my daughter against a hurricane and not because it was a cheap building material. Precautions had been taken, but who knew what could happen, how far a distance danger could travel.

Brit hadn't spent a whole lot of time or effort on decorating the place. She had used large cutout letters to spell her name on the wall alongside her bed, and on the window she also had hung the word "Love," in letters that were like the ones used on the cover of the book *Love Story*.

I lay on her bed knowing she had slept there—trying to feel her and smell her. As I looked at her comforter, I started laughing because I thought back to when she was a freshman picking out all her stuff. Her roommate, Meghan, was setting up her side of the room: bright yellow, pink, teal, all these happy, cheery colors; and across the room was Brit: black sheets, black comforter and tiger-stripe pillows. I remember looking at her new roommate's face and seeing that she was horrified. She probably was wondering, Is my roommate a Goth? No way was Brit into all that, but by looking at her stuff, you couldn't tell!

After that uncertain start, Meg and Brit became best of friends and to this day Meg and I laugh about the first time they met.

The rooms were fairly large and part of a quad, so she hadn't wanted or needed to build bunk beds or a deck underneath which her desk could sit. Instead, her bed and furniture were spread out along a side wall and the back wall. I imagined her sitting on her bed, legs crossed, tapping away on her laptop, surrounded by photos of family and friends. Loyal to a fault, there were three-by-five pictures of her old friends from junior high, from high school, and her new friends from college—young women posing for the camera, their perfect white teeth nearly blinding against their deep salon- and sand-earned tans. Other photos: her Mustang; Brit and her cousin, Shelly, posing outside their fabulous trailer in Maine; her brothers, aunts, and uncles—a whole timeline of her joyful exuberance. No matter who else was in the picture, your eye was drawn to Brit and her smile.

Every one of those pictures brought back a flood of memories I had to dam up.

Out of respect for Cat, I wasn't going to take everything. I left the decorations and Brit's bedspread so the room wouldn't look completely empty. I was more interested in her personal things. The first thing I wanted to find was a silver necklace and cross we'd gotten her for her Confirmation. She wore that all the time and it was so much a part of her. We told her not to take it to Haiti, that something like that (though it had more sentimental than real value to us) easily could get stolen.

I looked in her desk drawer and couldn't find it. Her little wooden jewelry box was empty as well. A couple of other necklaces dangled from a small wooden jewelry tree, but not her cross.

What the hell, Brit? Where'd you keep it? Or did you defy us and wear the thing?

Then it dawned on me that if she knew she was going to be gone for three weeks, she probably hid her most valuable things. I tore through her clothes drawers, more annoyed that this was taking more time than I wanted it to than angry with her. Eventually I gave up.

I sat on the bed and pressed my palms to my eyes, futilely trying to keep the tears from coming. A couple of hiccoughing bleats shuddered my shoulders. Aware of the student standing just outside the room, I faked a couple of coughs and blew my nose. Damn lingering colds. I wished.

There was more to do, and I tried not to think of the stories that went with each item—scarves with the tags still on them, that kind of thing. Brit and I loved to shop, and in a way you could mark the progression of our lives, not just by the things we bought together, but also by how much time we spent together in stores. As I sorted through her things, it was like I was time traveling. When Brit was young and first going back-to-school shopping with me, I really saw how strong minded and independent she was. From the beginning, I wanted to keep my suggestions to a minimum. As it turned out, we had similar tastes, and I was fortunate that I never had to wage any of those battles that other mothers do over how low was too low of a pair of low-rise jeans, or how much was too much of a deep V-neck.

Maybe I wasn't thrilled about hundred-plus-dollar jeans, but those were a rare treat, and she'd pair them with an inexpensive T-shirt anyway.

Our shopping trips since Brit had started college weren't quite like we were sisters or girlfriends, but weren't quite just mother/daughter either. She was as happy picking things out for me and showing me her suggestions as she was looking for herself. I was looking forward to that going on and getting even better.

Something about going through her underwear and packing that up stabbed at me. Same kind of time travel thing went on. It seemed like it was only a day or so earlier that I was picking out little-girl stuff for her—T-shirts and panties with stuffed animals and flowers on them. Brit and I were close, and as a mom you grow to have this odd kind of don't-ask-don't-tell thing going on. As she got older I'd buy more sophisticated kinds of things for her, and in doing her laundry and now packing up her stuff, I wasn't shocked by the thongs and cute and sexy bras and things. You just kind of grow used to those things being around as your daughter gets older.

Brit and I had our fair share of talks about sexuality, but I knew there was a line that neither she nor I had ever been either willing or able to cross. We had a joking agreement: Don't talk about your sex life, and I won't talk about mine. In some ways, I envied those girls and their freedom, and I also knew that along with that came a lot of confusion and pressure and just plain weirdness. I was comforted by the fact that Britney and her girlfriends made fun of the whole celebutante thing—that Paris Hilton and her kind were people they mocked, from the sex-tape scandals to the poofy dog in the purse thing. (Bruno the English bulldog is not exactly cute in that way!) But standing there packing away the latest lingerie from Victoria's Secret, I wondered if my daughter had ever felt the kind of love, the emotional bond, that Len and I shared in the chapel. Was that word just going to be for her something she pasted on a window, or was it going to be the thing that gave purpose to her life?

I knew she loved Haiti and what she was doing there and those kids, but that was different.

Looking back, as painful as those thoughts and memories might have seemed, they were a lot better than thinking about the reality of what I was doing, how unnatural it all seemed. Len had lost his parents, and my father had passed. We had gone through the process of sorting through belongings. As hard as that was for us, it seemed natural. Your parents grow old, they fall ill, they pass on.

This was different! I wasn't supposed to be there in that room. This was not natural; anybody who thought it was strange for me to be doing this before we had confirmation would never get it. What kind of protocol was I supposed to be following here? Who issues instructions when you leave the hospital with your baby daughter telling you that in case of a natural disaster (and don't think I didn't hate the idea of calling what happened to our daughter and the people of Haiti something "natural") and the premature death of your daughter, here's what to do.

From the beginning, Len and I had told ourselves and our families that we weren't going to judge. Dealing with loss and grieving was not an Olympic event. You didn't receive a score; there were no degrees of difficulty factored in—everything was difficult—and no deductions were taken for breaks in form. No medals were going to be awarded based on time, style, or distance.

That didn't mean that I didn't appreciate or understand the physics of mourning. We hadn't yet gotten to that place anyway, and even though I knew the bins, bags, and boxes I was packing up were going to be left behind, they were going to be shipped to us. And even though Len and I were about to board a plane for home, we couldn't fly far enough or fast enough to escape any of this.

I loaded Britney's things on a dolly cart and wheeled it into the hall. I looked at the RA and said, "Thank you so much for your help. I really appreciate it. I'm just going to go back in and make a final check." The word "final" felt funny coming out of my mouth, buzzing my lips like low voltage had been run through them.

I shut the door and leaned against it, not even pretending to search the room. As much as I didn't want to be there, I didn't want to leave either. I knew this was the last time I was ever going to be in that room.

I hated this!

I thought of Brit going to elementary school for the first time. She always had to pick out her own clothes, and that first day of first grade she wore pink leggings and a loose polka-dot top. The thing that got me, though, was that she insisted on doing her own hair as well. (God love her, Brit said "Me do" much earlier and with far greater frequency than Bernie or Richie.) When I stood at the front door to escort her to the bus, she proudly came marching up to me, the straps of her *Beauty and the Beast* backpack squeaking.

"Let's see," I said.

She spun around. I had to bite my cheek to keep from laughing then, and I had to do the same now to keep from crying. Britney had put her hair up in more than a dozen little ponytails, each held in place with a rubber band, a scrunchy, or a pin.

"How pretty," I told her and hugged her.

A moment after that, I was walking her down the sidewalk, my heart in my throat knowing this was phase one of who knew how many in the process of letting go and watching her grow. The funny thing was, she came back that day and reported that all the other little girls loved her hair. Later on, none of that really mattered to her, the fitting in, the trend following. Sure, she wanted her belly button pierced because that was one of the things to do, but that was an exception. Normally she was at the head of the line, not at the back playing catch-up. Most of the time she wasn't in line at all, really; she stood off on her own, and gradually people were drawn to her.

Standing in my missing daughter's dorm room that January afternoon, wondering if she was alive or dead, hoping that she wasn't feeling or hadn't ever felt any of the pain that was stabbing me, it was like I was the one in first grade. I was just starting to learn the ABCs of grief, standing at the board doing a simple problem to add up reality, feeling—and I mean really feeling—the agonizing subtraction of my daughter, my friend, from my life.

As much as I was hurting for her and hoping that she wasn't suffering, I selfishly felt sorry for myself. I wondered if I'd ever be able to walk into a Forever 21 store again during bathing suit season and not end up bawling. Would I ever be able to look at a restaurant menu and not want to puke when I see filet mignon, or not be able to think of the time we went to Angelino's with the Crones and Brit ate their high-school football linemen sons under the table?

The tears were flowing again, but this time I didn't care who knew or who saw me. That's how Brit would have handled it. She didn't care what strangers thought of how she looked. How important was that?

I wheeled the cart out into the parking lot, not even looking around to see who saw me. I walked as briskly as I could, my head down, praying that I wouldn't see anyone. I loaded all the bins into her car. The security guards asked me from a distance if I wanted help. I shook my head no thanks. I was doing everything in my power to keep it together. I stood there sobbing and packing, once again stabbed by a painful irony. Brit had worked her butt off to earn that car, and she loved her Mustang. Now most of her college life was packed inside it, but those were only things and not really who Brit was. It was all just stuff and not flesh-and-bone substance.

LEN

"Hey, Bern. There they are." I nudged Bernie's elbow and nodded toward the gathering of media at the end of the gate at Logan. "Good work, son."

Bernie nodded and managed what passed for a smile during those torturous days. "Thanks. It's something, but not what I really wanted. Brit's still not home."

I put my arm around his shoulder as we continued walking. "Look, all the work you've done in getting the word out about Britney and everyone else at Lynn has been huge. We probably wouldn't have all these opportunities to raise awareness if it weren't for you. We'll get her home. We will."

Bernie shrugged and shook his head. His tension and disappointment were a part of his being that I could feel. In profile, I could see the veins in his temples and jaw line pulsing. I hated this. Not only was my daughter lost in Haiti, but my sons were caught up in the whole unnatural order of these things. No little brother should have to worry so much about his big sister, let alone be caught up in all the cover-your-ass and have-your-ass-covered media/government/political games we were playing.

"I know that some of the people we've had to deal with at Lynn have been, as you said, idiots, but I can't say that. These people"—I nodded again in the direction of the cameramen who had fired up their lights then—"They're helping us out. You know that."

As tired and as frazzled as we were, we knew we'd been using the media to get our message out and they were just doing their jobs. Knowing that we would have to do this little tit-for-tat thing when we arrived, we'd written up a statement so we could get it done and move on.

We wanted to keep the message positive, especially because we knew the various government agencies were eager to turn their efforts from search and rescue to recovery. From the White House on down, from our perspective, they wanted this thing done and over with as soon as possible. Get the focus back on the economy, immigration, or whatever hot-button issues might help earn them votes.

We weren't ready for that, and we'd fought them off twice already, and we weren't about to give them any kind of ammunition to make that fateful call again.

With Cherylann and Bernie at my side, I reiterated our message: We remained hopeful, and we were fortified by faith, hope, and love. We were very concerned for our loved ones and for the health and safety of the Haitian people.

I knew that to keep the pressure on to make sure that our daughter was either rescued from that rubble, was found in some makeshift hospital, or kept from being bulldozed into a mass grave, we had to be on point with our words and actions. By making the story as all encompassing as possible, by reminding people it wasn't just about the four girls and the two faculty members, by repeating that a quarter of a million people had lost their lives, we'd keep that story on the front page and at the top of the newscast. We knew that as time went on, the story would fade to the back pages and later in the broadcast. Having Susan Wornick from our local ABC affiliate as an ally and later as a dear friend helped enormously.

As much as I tried to stay focused each time I got on camera, I could feel my emotions overwhelming me. In my mind's eye, I was being a stalwart, an upfront dad, clearly focusing his energies on a single task: getting his daughter home. Later, when I watched myself on television, I was struck that I wasn't as bulldog-like as our pet, Bruno. I heard a lot more quavering in my voice, and in my eyes and in my tone I could hear and see the anguish and the pain that I thought I'd managed to push aside in order to deliver my message. At times I looked like some enormous fish that had washed up on shore and was struggling for breath. The reality was that's how I felt. Every time I let my thoughts wander from the next task at hand, I felt beached—powerless and directionless.

I told the assembled media we were going home to regroup. We had some thinking to do.

For obvious reasons, I couldn't tell them about what the State Department had done for us. As I was speaking, I couldn't help but think that I would be back here at 5:00 a.m., and none of them would even know I was here or where I was going. It wasn't like I took great satisfaction in whatever level of deceit this was, but it was good to have some bit of privacy back after nine days of baring our souls for public consumption and comment.

I don't want to make it sound like the people in the news business were callous. We saw these people day after day for nine days, and we could tell they got it. We recognized that even when the cameras rolled and focused on them and they were on the air; they kept their composure and remained professional. Even in those moments, they felt some part of our pain. We'd be standing in front of them with the cameras trained on us as we made our statements and answered their questions, and we could see their faces. They were a mess. Men, women, reporters, sound guys, cameramen. Didn't matter. They were crying. Tears streaming down their faces as we were speaking. It wasn't easy for them. I thought of myself as one of the on-camera people, but they were much better at keeping it together on screen than I was.

Other people were equally great. Logan Airport's director of operations, Phil, would meet us at the gate and provide escort for us. They'd provide a state trooper to drive us to where we'd parked our car in the lot. At times, we were so tired and in so need of a laugh that being swarmed by reporters, having lights and flashes in our faces, being hustled through the bowels of an airport where just the A-listers usually go, went from being surreal to a running joke.

I also knew that Britney would have found certain aspects of this very strange pseudo-celebrity stuff hilarious. On our way back to the house, I said as much to Cherylann. I said I could hear Brit saying, "You know, Dad, if the camera puts ten pounds on most people . . ."

We laughed, not so much because that was funny, but because of how un-funny what we were about to face was going to be. Between fifty and sixty people were gathered at the house, and when we opened the door and walked in, we were greeted with sobs, tears, and hugs. Cherylann and I didn't linger. From the outset, we'd made a promise to one another that we were going to keep the boys in the loop. We wanted any news, any bit of information, to come from us and not from anyone else—friend or foe, family, or member of the media. I got everyone's attention and said, "Cherylann and I need to speak to Richie. We haven't been with him for a few days, and we want to see and talk to our son."

With that, we went upstairs.

I came back down a few minutes later to complete silence. Not everyone could fit in the great room, so they were lined up in the kitchen and down a couple of hallways. I scanned the crowd looking for my sisters, Ruth and Chrissy. Once I saw them, I was better able to compose myself. I took a deep breath and started in, explaining what they already knew—that Britney was still missing, that search-and-rescue crews were on site, but we hadn't gotten any news. Just as I was about to launch into my news about my trip to Haiti, my cell phone went off. Everybody in the room could hear it, and you'd have thought I'd just vomited on the carpet or something—they all went wide-eyed and kind of leaned away from me. I looked at the phone's screen and it read, "Incoming Call." I knew that meant it was from someone in the government: no caller ID.

"Excuse me, everybody, I have to take this." I didn't even look at them. Out on the back porch in the cold, I could breathe normally again.

"Len, it's Jim McGovern. House Ethics. House Ethics." I could tell Jim was agitated because when he's upset he repeats himself. "Bad news. Bad news. Don't worry, though. House Ethics ruled that I can't go with you on that flight tomorrow morning."

"What do you mean you can't go?"

"Don't worry. I'll be there. House rules about flights, and since this one is being funded by a private party, I can't go with you on the flight. But I'll be there. I'm at Logan. I'm taking a commercial flight to Santo Domingo. I'll meet you there."

I couldn't believe two things: first that the government would make a congressman pay on his own dime to help out a U.S. citizen, a taxpayer, in this time of crisis. Second, I couldn't believe Jim would go to the lengths that he did to be there with us. Talk about a man's character. Talk about stepping up to the plate and delivering. I knew that other members of the missing Lynn group were going to have family members going on the trip, but how many of them were going to have their senator or congressperson there? None of them. I thanked Jim and hung up.

I went back into the house and told everyone about the trip and about what Jim was doing for us. They exploded into cheers and applause.

I knew that I had two additional hurdles to face. As much as my going to Haiti was good news, in my mind I knew it was in a way bad news for some other people. First among them was Bernie. He was glad we were given the opportunity to go to Haiti, but he hated the idea that we could only send one representative per missing person. Even though Bernie knew as early as Thursday morning about the flight and the conditions the government had imposed on us, he kept saying to Cherylann and me, "Screw them. I'm going. I don't care. She's my sister. I have a right to be there. I've got to see that hotel. I'm going."

As much as I tried to explain things logically to Bernie—it was a small private jet, the government was concerned about security—I knew those efforts were futile. How do you apply logic to the heart and what it wants? As empathetic as I was to Bernie's cause, in the end, all I could say to him was that he had no other option. I was going. He was staying. At a time when it seemed like everything we faced was difficult, that one especially hurt.

As a second semester high-school senior, Bernie probably had witnessed enough hypocrisy and self-serving behavior in adults already. A really bright kid getting ready for college, he'd gotten some early coursework credits in Bad Information Dissemination 101 and Advanced Covering Your Ass by witnessing what was going on over at Lynn. In hindsight, I can see that some of what he experienced was a good introduction to the adult world, given the circumstances and the life and death nature of it all. All things considered, I wish he could have skipped this lesson entirely. Still, I wanted him to be involved with this, too. I wanted him to have a say in and be a part of our efforts to get Brit home. I knew that later in life he would question whether he had done enough. All of us went all out, and I prayed for his sake that he knew this.

The second hurdle was one that I knew I couldn't jump over. I was just going to have to trample over it. In 2001, I had two stents put in my heart because of a congenital defect. I was forty-one years old at the time, and my father had died of a heart attack in 1989. After a recall notice on my stents, I was back in the operating room having them bored out like you would a cylinder head in car's engine. Unfortunately, while on the table, an artery completely blew out, and as a result, I now have five stents in my heart. I'm also on eight medications for various heart and circulatory issues, and I'm a guy who carries around a lot of stress on my best days. The intensity of my emotions and my focus in the previous nine days were taking a toll on me, I was pretty sure, but I wasn't about to admit any of that to myself. I was going to Haiti. Period. End of sentence. Unfortunately, not the end of the discussion.

My sisters, Ruth and Chrissy, walked up to me, and I could see how disappointed Chrissy was. Chrissy originally was going to accompany me to Haiti, but when the limit was imposed on us, she couldn't. She let the issue drop with me, but I know she was worried. She had always protected me. I was the youngest of eight children, and she was ten years older than me. She raised me when my mother, who suffered from undiagnosed post-partum depression, was unable to. Now we comforted each other. I wrapped her in my arms and let her sob for a minute. I tousled her hair and said, "Hang in there, kid." I knew that imitating our father's typical gruff response would get her to laugh.

She looked up at me as she wiped her eyes, "I know I'm supposed to just rub some dirt on it and get back in there, but that's the thing." Her whole body started quaking again, and I held her tight again.

I buried my face in her hair and kissed her head. "I know.

I know. I wish it could be otherwise. I wish you were going." Chris was waiting to have knee surgery and physically couldn't go, even though she wanted to so badly.

"I'm sorry, Len. I know it's selfish of me, but I'm just . . . I don't know what I am but I know that I'm also worried about you." She stepped back from me and lightly punched me in the chest. "I know it's big and it's hurt . . ." Her words trailed off, but then Ruth picked up where Chris had left off.

"I know you've got to do this. I know you need to be there, but we're worried about you. What about Cherylann and the kids? They need you. And not just now."

I looked into Ruth's steel-gray eyes and saw the look of determination—the same one I knew I had.

"Please don't play that card, Ruth. Cherylann has come to terms with my condition. We both know the reality. I wouldn't want to live anyway, knowing that I didn't do everything I could."

I could see my words had hurt them both. "Remember you guys, faith, hope, and love. That's what we've been talking about all along. I'm going to be fine, just letting you know that worst-case scenario, I'm good with it."

The three of us stood in a locked embrace saying we loved each other. Ruth stepped back and said, "If you climb that tree and fall and break your neck, don't come crying to me." We heard the echo of one of my mother's famous warnings and laughed.

Later that night as we lay in bed, sleepless again, Cherylann told me that everyone was bombarding her with questions about my heart and my condition. Cherylann has had to live with the reality of my condition for a long time, and as she said, "I know you have to do this. I know you won't be able to live with yourself if you don't go." She reassured everyone that I would be okay, and she believed that herself.

I did a lot of praying that night. I asked that God let them find Brit alive. He could take me, but Brit had to live. That wasn't the first time I'd made that deal with God, and I know that I'm not the first parent who ever had that thought. This prayer had an "urgent" stamp on it. That night I'd gotten an email from Susan Grantham at the State Department letting me know that the next day, the government was moving from search and rescue to recovery. That news scared the shit out of me. Once again the image of those bulldozers shoved their way into my consciousness. They already had tried to move to recovery, but we had stopped it by going on camera. The media was our leverage to keep pressure on the government. I felt like I was in a chess game, staying two to three moves ahead. It was a precarious position, and I had to use all of my strength and my will to stay ahead.

By 4:00 a.m. prayer time was over. My body pumped full of adrenaline, my mind overflowing with contingency plans, I got out bed not really having slept. I showered and kissed Cherylann good-bye, grateful she was getting some hard-earned rest.

I was immediately grateful for one thing: The New England weather cooperated, and it was a gorgeous mid-winter morning. As I drove toward Boston, the sunlight bled across the horizon and stained the few clouds as it climbed. As I drove, I had some real thinking to do. I didn't trust the government. Yes, they made the arrangements for this trip, but I wasn't convinced I was going to be able to get to the Hotel Montana and that they would continue operations until she was rescued or her body was recovered. They'd been keeping us informed, but just like we'd been informed that Britney had been rescued and was on a helicopter, we continued to receive bad intel. They were moving to recovery, and I'd never received assurance—and even if I had, could I believe it?—that they'd remain on site until all the bodies were located and returned to the U.S.

Even though the trip was to be a secret, I had to do what I had to do to assure my daughter wouldn't be left there. Almost from the beginning, Karen D'Uva had been one of our guiding lights. She was more than just a freelance producer for CBS. She'd suffered her own loss, having buried her husband just a year earlier, and we knew she empathized with us. For that reason, we trusted her, and it was her guidance that helped us navigate the world of the television news media. Susan Wornick, a thirty-year veteran of the broadcasting business in New England, also was enormously helpful. A few years before, Brit had shadowed her at the news station because I had met Colleen Marren, who was the station's general manager, on a trip to Fort Myers to watch the Red Sox during spring training. I'd mentioned I had a daughter who was interested in broadcasting, and she graciously offered to let Brit see things from the inside. Now Susan was taking us under her wing as well.

Susan reminded us of what another New Englander, John Irving, once wrote about television and news: It gives good disaster. For some in the media, particularly the producers who compete with the other morning shows for exclusives, our personal tragedy was more about ratings than how heartbroken we were. Fortunately, those few people were an exception. Susan made it clear to us from the beginning that a lot of the "relationships" we would develop with these people would be all about power. We had something they wanted. They had something we wanted: to keep the attention focused on the Hotel Montana and our kids and their professors.

I sensed that after a time, the government was going to lose patience and not want to continue to expend resources—dollars and people power—to keep the recovery efforts going at the Hotel Montana. I knew I'd have to violate some trust and do what I'd been instructed not to do. I needed to do this as a father who has a commitment to his kids, and I was going to see that through.

I texted a message to contacts I had at CNN, ABC, CBS, NBC, and Fox News: "Heading to the Hotel Montana today. Need reporters there at 5:00 p.m. tonight." I gave up no additional details, revealed nothing of the State Department's involvement, or anything else. We weren't alone in desperately trying to get to Haiti. I had been on the news, we'd been on Facebook, and made ourselves and our ordeal as public as possible, we had hundreds of people asking us for help to get them into Haiti to locate a loved one. All over the country, people were trying to get to Haiti and they couldn't. No one was being allowed in as private citizens like we all were. Now I was going to be let in for a few hours. I knew I was running the risk of having one of those contacts get in touch with the government to verify my story. That would have, in all likelihood, forced the government's hand, and they could have cancelled the trip. I weighed carefully all the options and consequences and knew I had to send that message. I needed the media to be there at the Hotel Montana. Once those images—of parents and children of the missing on site—hit the airwaves, we would put additional pressure on the government to not leave any of them behind.

I know our military has a longstanding position of not ever leaving its wounded or the dead behind. I wanted to be sure the same treatment was given to our group. As far as I was concerned, Britney and the others were there as ambassadors of the U.S. They were there as soldiers fighting poverty. The risk was worth it. Even if it meant I wasn't going to be able to go see my daughter, if the government pulled the plug on the trip, I'd have just one more arrow in my quiver to go to the media with.

As it turned out, I had nothing to worry about except for the fact that the one-person-per-family rule wasn't necessary. As other parents or children declined to go, other seats opened up. Frank and Angie Hayes were on the plane (which a Lynn University alum generously provided for us) as well as Patrick Hartwick's brother and his son. Other than that, the plane was empty. Either Chrissy or Bernie, or maybe both, could have joined us. I didn't have long to think about that. Shortly after I took my seat we were in the air heading to the Dominican Republic.

CHERYLANN

As a mom, you try to do your best for your family. Sometimes your kid kicks you in the gut to make you realize you haven't done your best after all—and then you want to kick yourself. That's the only way I can describe how it felt when we saw Richie the night we got back from Florida.

Len and I sensed that Florida was too much for him. Too many meetings, too many other parents around, too much uncertainty. He was only fourteen, just a boy, and he idolized his big sister. The intensity of emotions from everyone around him was overwhelming. We could hardly handle it—how could he?

Len and I brought both boys into the room. We needed them to know that Len was leaving, and if and when we received information about Brit—good or bad—we would tell them first before the rest of the family. When Richie stepped into our room and we told him we needed to talk to him, he turned and sat on the couch opposite our bed. When he faced us, my heart was at my ankles. It was like Richie's face was a candle that had been burning for a long time; the collapse began at his forehead where it was creased with wrinkles and made its way down to his nose and mouth and quivering jaw. After we'd told him that Len was going to Haiti, the tears and the words came pouring out of his nearly unrecognizable face. "I thought you were going to tell me she was dead," he said, with a few F words spit out along with his heaving exhalations.

Even after Bernie and Len went downstairs, Richie just sat there sobbing. Even at that moment when he was hurting more than I'd ever seen him, I'd try to wrap him in my arms, and he'd push me away in one second and then next he was reaching out for me. I felt about as helpless as I ever have. No words seemed to soothe him, no touch could calm him.

"Richie, honey," I said, "like Daddy and I told you, we made an agreement that we would tell you. And I'm sorry if you thought we were going to tell you that Britney is dead. We're praying that she's alive, Richie. We, we're still hopeful. We're never giving up, Richie. We're Gengels. We don't give up. But Daddy needs to go down there. He's going to go and look, and I'm going to stay here. We're hoping he's going to go find

Brit and bring her home. And we're going to be here and I'm not going to leave you again." It felt like there was this giant hole in my kid's life, and I was trying to stuff it full with anything I could.

"You were down there and I was up here, and I got sick. You weren't here to take care of me. YOU WEREN'T HERE!"

"Richie, I'm sorry I wasn't here. But I wasn't leaving you. I just, I had to get Brit home. I wanted to get Britney home. I wanted to be there when she walked off the plane." Richie was wracked by a sob so strong I thought we were both going to tumble off the couch. "It was time for us to come home. I wanted us to be together."

"Mom, I just want to kill myself. I can't stand this."

I knew how Richie was feeling, and worse, I knew why. When Brit left on that Tuesday morning, Richie never said good-bye to her because he was sleeping. He was sleeping when she came home Monday night, and then she was sleeping when he left for school at 7:30. So here this poor kid was feeling so upset that he never got to say good-bye. He never got to hug her good-bye. And he just kept crying and swearing, and he was partly in my lap, and I felt like if I let go he was going to literally fall to pieces.

I held him and squeezed him and said, "Listen. You and me. We've got to make a pact here. You just can't do what you said, Richie. It's okay to say that, but you just can't do that. We've got to stick together, and when you're feeling like this, you've got to come to me. You can trust Dad. We're going to take care of you, like we always have. You hear me?"

I felt like somebody had just reached into my chest to grab my heart and was squeezing it for all they were worth. My mind was running at a thousand thoughts a second, waiting and waiting for him to respond. Finally, I could feel him nodding his head. I said a quick thank you and brushed my lips against my son's head, my baby boy smelling of sweat and sleep and sadness.

Like most times in a family, Len and I had been trying to do the right thing. When there are five of you, sometimes what you do for one doesn't always work for all. I had to know that Richie was back on board with us, and it was going to be a long, long time before I could forgive myself for having blindsided him.

CONFIRMATION

"I knew I was only hours away from having some of my questions answered, and that push-pull of desire and dread gnawed at my heart."

—LEN

LEN

As a lifelong Red Sox fan, about the only thing I knew about the Dominican Republic was that it was the birthplace of David "Big Papi" Ortiz, their great and generous slugger. I knew that it shared an island with Haiti, but that was about it. We were flying into Santa Cruz de Barahona and Aeropuerto Internacional María Montez. I'd never heard of the airport's namesake but was told she was a famous film actress who was born nearby in the province of Barahona. Later, I learned she starred in a bunch of adventure films in the 1940s, always playing a Latin seductress. That was appropriate: When I'd left Boston it was in the icy grip of Old Man Winter; here the tropical warmth and humidity smacked me in the face the minute I got off the plane. I squinted against the bright sunlight, even though I was wearing sunglasses, and marveled at the difference between what I'd left and where I now was. We'd been having a tougher than normal New England winter, and the snow was piled high and leafless trees had been strafed by the wind. In the D.R., as so many refer to it, the warm breeze carried the scent of tropical flowers, and the only word I can think of to describe the area was lush.

The airstrip had been carved out of the jungle. The small terminal building was flanked by the tower, both a bright-green stucco that seemed to glow the mid-afternoon sun. Compared to the airports in the U.S., this was a real throwback to the early days of flight. It felt like I had stepped back in time.

I was on a mission with an unknown outcome. To this point everything had gone smoothly. I'd made every flight, they'd all been on time, and now I was on the ground just hours away from achieving the goal that had been my focus for the last week: getting to the Hotel Montana and seeing for myself where my little girl was.

To be honest, my heart was in my throat. Of course, I wanted to be here, but by the same token I also didn't want to be here. I didn't want Britney to have been in the situation she was in. I accepted that reality, but that didn't mean I liked it.

Seeing Congressman McGovern walking up to us along with several government officials helped settle me down. It was hot as hell on the tarmac, and sweat rolled down my forehead and into my eyes. Despite the temperature, Jim walked up wearing a blue sport coat and Red Sox hat. He looked exhausted. We shook hands, and I wrapped my arm around him and told him he was my hero. He'd done so much, along with Senator Kerry, to make the trip possible.

Jim led us into the terminal and introduced us to Selena Nelson-Salcedo, a vice consul at the U.S. Embassy in Santo Domingo, and to a gentleman whose name none of us caught over the sound of a public-address announcement. Throughout the trip, he remained silent and let Selena do all the talking. As we walked along with her, she did her best to fill us in on what to expect. The problem was, not even she could say exactly how long any of this would take.

"Look, even during the best of times, border crossings can take an hour to two or three hours. With what's been going on lately and the influx of people crossing over from the D.R., we just can't say." I was surprised to hear her speaking with a Midwestern accent, expecting to hear a Latin one instead. When I talked to her later, I found out she had graduated from the University of Wisconsin and spent time in Minnesota as well.

When we walked out of the terminal and into the parking lot to the bus we were told would be waiting for us, I almost burst out laughing. Here we were, on a hush-hush trip to Port-au-Prince, essentially sneaking into the country under the radar, and we were going to be doing it in a large Greyhound-type motor coach painted the gaudiest, brightest banana yellow you could ever see. I thought maybe they were going to issue us fake noses and glasses to complete the camouflage.

Jim and I took a seat across from one another, and the Hayes family sat just in front of us. Shortly after the bus had pulled away, Angie Hayes walked up to Jim and said, in her thick Southern accent, "Congressman, I had this man come to my hotel at 11:00 last night and give me a map to where my daughter is." She unfolded the eight-and-a-half-by-eleven-inch sheet of paper and pointed at it. "We're going right here."

I felt bad for Angie and Franklin. They are wonderful people, but like all of us, they were frazzled and on edge. Franklin's ramblings about terrorist involvement, and now Angie being taken advantage of by some stranger preying on her vulnerability had my heart going out to both of them. They were grasping at straws, trying to make sense of the unthinkable and unknowable.

I'm sure this caught Congressman McGovern by surprise. He asked her to repeat what she just said—either because he couldn't understand because of her accent, or because he was trying to take in what she had just told him. Knowing what we were all going through, having been jerked around so much already, he wanted to be respectful but also firm in what we could and could not do, and who we should trust in this situation. He reminded her we had to adhere to the itinerary that the State Department had approved. They weren't to go off on their own. Angie shook her head and under her breath muttered, "We're going. We're going."

I had to laugh about these things—Jim's struggles with understanding the Hayeses' Southern drawl, the goofy bus—to keep my sanity. We all had been drawn into this tragedy—and this brief but important part of the whole drama—from very different backgrounds. We all had our personality quirks and ways of coping, and I'm sure on more than one occasion I rubbed people the wrong way. In my business, if there's a problem, you solve it. You don't spend a lot of time and energy on the whys and wherefores of things—you just assess, plan, and execute. I didn't have time for distractions and, in public, I tried to hold my emotions in check. Private time with family was when I let those feelings out.

Maybe it was because Jim McGovern and I are the same age and both originally from Worcester, that the two of us bonded in a way that was different from the ties I developed with the other victims' family members. I'd only met Jim a couple of times before the Britney situation arose, but felt an immediate connection with him. The fact that Jim hadn't lost someone was obviously a factor in the nature of our relationship, but I would come to learn how much the two of us did have in common. We sat alongside one another and talked about matters of faith for quite a while. I could see etched in his face a concern and compassion for our group, but also more generally for all the victims of the quake.

When we weren't talking, I just sat there watching the thick vegetation go by. The D.R. was so lush and tropical that every turn in the road revealed another postcard-worthy vista. Along with all the green, I spotted flocks of yellow birds darting around, seemingly intent on diving like kamikazes into our windshield before pulling out in tight formation just in the nick of time.

I also could see the few SUVs behind us that made up

our little caravan. Members of the U.S. 82nd Airborne Division were accompanying us to provide security. So as not to arouse too much suspicion or potential hostility, they were traveling in coveralls, but we could still see brief flashes of their uniforms and weapons hidden beneath.

The closer we got to Haiti's border, the more the roads deteriorated and eventually became rutted dirt tracks. I was also surprised by how the amount of trees decreased. The hillsides were stripped bare and scarred with a few pitiful patches of ground vegetation rising haphazardly on their surface. Once we arrived at border control, it was as if we'd entered into a swamp. Bare trees stuck up out of the flooded lowlands. Their trunks were scaly and flaky. When the bus came to a stop, I realized I had been clenching my jaw practically since the moment we left Boston.

What was it about this place that had so inspired our daughter? It certainly couldn't have been that she saw this as a tropical paradise, a place where she could get the ultimate tan. There had to be something deeper that drew her in and embraced her. I knew I was only hours away from having some of my questions answered, and that push-pull of desire and dread gnawed at my heart.

I twisted the top off my water bottle and took a long draw on it. I was glad for my sunglasses and my sweat. It would be easier to explain my tears and red-rimmed eyes.

I watched as our military escort got out of the vehicles and stripped off their jumpsuits. Whether it was their presence, decked out in full military regalia and weapons in plain sight or some other arrangements, those one to three hours that Selena had mentioned were reduced to minutes. They waved us through. I heaved a deep sigh, and some of my fears and anxiety were expelled along with my breath. This was what I'd pushed for, and I was more eager than ever to bear personal witness to what my daughter had experienced—both the hell and the happiness.

I was in Haiti and I wasn't alone in being excited. The bus came alive with a kind of energy that I remember from my days playing ball and we were approaching the other team's school.

According to our timetable, we were supposed to be at the embassy building in Port-au-Prince at 4:00 p.m. We were on schedule for that, as well as our arrival at the Hotel Montana at 5:00 p.m. Obviously, I hadn't said a word to anyone else about my earlier text message to the media. Privately, I took a great deal of satisfaction in knowing that we'd held up our end of the bargain. We'd be there, but would they?

That buzz in the bus didn't last long. As we continued to motor along, the scenery was an uncomfortable mix of the beautiful and the ugly. As a home builder, I take great joy in transforming a piece of land into a safe and comfortable place for people to live. What I saw troubled me. Nearly all that lush vegetation we saw in the D.R. was gone—it had been stripped away, and I saw angry gashes of dark brown and black on the hillsides.

By this point, Selena had insisted we call her by her first name, so I asked her, "Selena, what's with the scarring of the landscape? Where are all the trees?"

"I'm not an expert on Haiti in particular, but in underdeveloped countries like this, as well as the D.R., people want to have their own homes just like we Americans do. They take a great deal of pride in building their structures. Even closer in to the capital, people come out here to take down trees to use as roofing material."

"What are the exterior walls made of then?"

"Cinder block and cement. You'll see very soon." I liked hearing about their pride in craftsmanship and ownership, and I flashed back to a memory of Brit, Bernie, and Richie when they were little—about five, three and one. We were building our house and the foundation had been poured, and after the concrete set for a bit, I took the kids and had them press their handprints into it while it was still wet. Brit turned to me with her blueberry eyes even wider, and her expression said it all, "That was cool!"

I was grateful the bus was air-conditioned, and Selena had thoughtfully supplied sandwiches. I had let my mind wander a bit, thinking about the kids and making those impressions. Then I was drawn back into the present. As much as we were devastated by our daughter being missing, there were hundreds of thousands of others—men, women, children—who were dead and missing, and even more relatives and friends who were going through what we were.

Jim, Selena, and I talked a bit about Haiti.

"I'm having a hard time here," I said. "I'm looking out these windows knowing that this country was hit with an enormous earthquake, and all these people were killed, but I don't see any damage at all."

"I know." Jim paused and shrugged. "I don't get it."

"Just wait," said the armed guard at the front of the bus.

"In some ways I wish I didn't have to see any of this. Why did this have to happen to the poorest country in the Americas?" Jim asked.

"But lots of money is pouring in, right? The U.S., other countries?" someone asked.

"What you have to understand is that money is going to help, but there's been a larger problem and a longer history here. The U.S. has been a huge supporter of Haiti, but we've had to cut off aid because of problems with corruption. The money doesn't always get to the people who need it," Jim said.

Despite my ambivalence about what our government was doing for its own citizens and our daughters, knowing the American military had taken control of the airport, and had begun delivering relief supplies systematically made me feel safer. That didn't quite offset my anger about no one really paying attention to the Hotel Montana, but I had to look at the bigger picture, especially now that I was on the ground in Haiti.

"Mr. Gengel, what you have to understand is that what Congressman McGovern is saying is very true and has been for a long time. The U.S. has been generous, but those millions of dollars weren't enough before, and now with this . . . " Selena shrugged and held her palms up. "Governments can only do so much. It's up to private citizens, NGOs, to do their part. They have, but it took this earthquake to make the American people really see and think about Haiti again."

I heard our security guard say, "Five minutes to the embassy. Five minutes."

I was shocked. I looked out the window, and the landscape had gone from countryside to city, but all the buildings—a series of low-slung commercial buildings, all stucco, all with brightly painted signs in Creole and French—were intact. But no debris, no evidence of structural damage.

Jim and I looked at one another and shook our heads.

"What a crapshoot the whole thing must have been—who lived and who died, who got wrecked and ruined, and who didn't," I said.

I didn't want to think anymore about that harsh but accurate assessment. I was focused on the people in the streets. To be honest, I didn't know what to expect. A part of me hoped in some strange way that I'd see people walking around all dazed and, if not bloodied, showing some outward sign of my inner upset. I saw a number of women wearing what my mother would have called a housedress or housecoat walking down the street barefoot, baskets on their head, moseying along. What hit me were all the kids—too many to count—not a one of them looking like he or she had ever had too much to eat. An image of Britney came back to me. When she was young and I'd give her a big hug, it almost always took my breath away just how fragile a child's body was, how easily someone or something could crush her.

I had to push that thought aside as well.

Regrettably and gratefully, I had something else to occupy my mind. We came around a ninety-degree turn, and there was the U.S. Embassy building. It reminded me of the Pentagon and other government buildings in Washington and elsewhere, except its roof was dotted with old satellite dishes and a rat's nest of antennae. Lined up along the fence, armed guards, members of the 82nd Airborne, spread out about every fifty feet or so. They waved us through, and as we made our way onto the grounds of the embassy, I could see hundreds of tents spread out. As we drove a bit farther, I could see a phalanx of people lining either side of this driveway—military people, civilians, half of them wearing surgical masks and the other half not.

As soon as I stepped off the bus, I knew what the masks

were for. I've been in the building trades for a lot of years, so I'm used to the smell of raw sewage from pipes and septic tanks, but I'd never smelled anything like this—a savage mixture of human waste and the stomach-churning smell of decaying corpses. It was like this odor was a living thing, and it came up to you and wrapped itself around you and slithered up your nostrils and nasal passages. Someone walked up to us with a jar of Vicks VapoRub.

"Put this under your nose and then apply the mask."

I did as instructed and was immediately brought back to my childhood and my sisters, Ruth and Chrissy, slathering that stuff on my chest and under my nose whenever I had a cold. I was glad and sad that neither of them, nor the rest of my family, was here with me.

Despite that horrific start, I was struck by the impression that we were visiting dignitaries there on official government business. A kind of receiving line was formed, and I was introduced to a whole host of people who shook my head, handed me a card, expressed their concern, and moved along. Among those there were Paul Cantrell, consul from Haiti, Gary Rex, deputy political counselor, and Kenneth Durkin, first secretary and consul. We were told that they were there on behalf of Virginia Millhouse, the director of the U.S. Department of State in Haiti. She was understandably not there, attending to other matters.

One of the other staffers gave us the rundown on the agenda. The ambassador, Kenneth Merten, was going to meet us there. I was a little taken aback by that. While on Wolf Blitzer's show, Cherylann and I had laid into him pretty good. The majority of the Americans who were missing in the Hotel Montana were our kids and U.N. people. We couldn't understand why a guy in his position, who only lived a mile from there, couldn't have at least made an appearance on-site in those early days to help draw attention and rescuers to that location.

I was even more taken aback when Jim McGovern walked up to me and said quietly, "Len, I just got a text. CNN is asking me if I'm in Haiti." The mask hid his face, but his eyes were wide in what I hoped was confusion and not anger.

"Really?"

"Yeah."

"Well, that's a good thing, right? We're going to need them there to videotape our arrival. Our visit."

"Oh, okay. But I'm not going to confirm or deny any of this."

"Whatever you think is best."

I didn't like not responding fully to Jim, but I was just doing what I thought was best. I needed that protection. I had no idea if when we got to the Hotel Montana, we were going to see bulldozers burying our kids. This was the same day the efforts had been switched from rescue to recovery. To my understanding, that meant those heavy-equipment operators were going to go about their business of moving rubble, and if one of the spotters saw a body, they'd recover it. If they didn't see it, it was like it didn't exist. It went into the pile of debris. I couldn't let that happen to my daughter or anyone else's loved one.

If I'd been struck before by how little damage I'd seen in Haiti, I was blasted in the eyes by hell on Earth when we left the embassy grounds and made our way to the Hotel Montana and Petionville. I burst into tears when I saw the thousands of people in the streets, the tent cities, the collapsed Presidential Palace. If in the faces of those women on their way to or from the market I'd seen a kind of indifference, on the faces of these people I only saw pain, suffering, and indignity.

What really made me sad was that I saw little of the vibrant hope and unsinkable spirit that Britney had mentioned in her messages to us. I understood why that was the case, and that deepened my sadness. I'd brought my camera with me, but it stayed in my bag. No way did I want my family to see any of this.

It's not like I shut my eyes and tried to deny that any of what I was seeing was real, but I didn't see the point of capturing those digital images. If we say that we burn CDs or DVDs, then I don't know what word to use for the searing sensation I felt in my eyes, my brain, my gut, and my heart. After 9/11 I'd seen the images of people wandering out of that billowing dust cloud of collapsed concrete, fire and smoke, but this was a week and a half after the earthquake, and I still watched people walking unsteadily, literally and figuratively trying to keep their balance as they walked among the endless, and mostly still, line of traffic.

Words failed me.

If it was like this here, what were we going to see at the Hotel Montana?

I was sitting in the back seat, and I leaned forward and tapped the driver of the vehicle, a member of the 82nd Airborne.

"How much longer to the hotel?"

"He shrugged. I've only been there once, sir."

"Really? How long did it take you?"

"I was on a scooter heading up there to rescue these eight kids who were trying to get to the embassy."

I felt my stomach drop. I couldn't believe that of all the soldiers to be with us, for me to have picked to ride in this SUV out of the others, I was there with the guy who'd done so much to help those other Lynn University kids. I'd heard about him, and now I was there with him. He was the soldier with the M16A2 rifle and the scooter escorting the survivors to the embassy. I grasped his shoulder and rubbed it. "I just want to say thank you. Those are our friends. My daughter's friends. You're a real hero."

He didn't say anything; he just kept looking ahead, trying to find his way through that tangled mass of vehicles and pedestrians.

Gary Rex was in the Suburban along with me, and he was relating bits of information about the quake, the city, and generally acting like a tour guide through this hell. Instead of the usual smiling tour guide, he was very dour. At times he would say something, purse his lips, exhale, and tilt his head back as if he was trying to keep tears from running down his face. I asked him if he was okay, and he told me he was fine. I pressed him further and he said, "There's been a lot of loss here."

He paused, and I let that linger. And then Gary Rex shared his story with me.

"On January 12, I wasn't feeling very good. I stayed home from work. I called my wife and told her she should take me to the doctor. So she closed up her work and sent her employees home, except for the security guard. While we were at the doctor's office, the earthquake hit. My wife's building collapsed, killing the guard."

He chewed at his lips and swallowed. "I'm so grateful that my wife is with me, that we're both okay. But today at another hotel in Port-au-Prince, a colleague of mine, a guy who I started in this service with thirty years ago and who was my best friend, was found dead."

He looked down at his lap and his folded hands. He unfolded them in a quiet gesture of grief and overwhelm.

"I'm really sorry for your loss. Thank you for helping all of us today, especially considering the circumstances."

We turned our heads and looked out the window, my words crumbling into a pile at my feet.

Approaching the Hotel Montana, after nearly an hour in traffic, put us a half-hour behind our schedule. We climbed a series of hills, and the road narrowed until we were on what must have been a driveway. Lining it was a stone wall, still intact, and vines and creepers cascaded down it. I didn't know what to expect of a five-star hotel in Haiti, some kind of grand entranceway, a gate, a porte cochère, something to mark the difference between there and outside there. After all, this is the place where presumably my little girl is. Finally, that gate came into sight. It was still intact, brilliant white stucco pillars standing sentry flanked by palm trees.

The vehicles stopped and my heart was pounding. I swallowed hard and eased the door open, wondering if I was going to be met with a blast of that horrible stench; and there it was. Not as bad as before, but still the masks and the VapoRub were needed. Daylight was beginning to fade, and everything was bathed in a kind of golden light. I wanted to have my photo taken with the Marine who helped rescue the other kids, and as we were standing there posing, I saw a cameraman and a reporter heading toward us. The reporter identified himself by saying, "ABC News." At least one had made it.

All of a sudden, this older man, sixty-ish, wearing a floppy fishing hat, just flew over to the reporter. He pulled aside his jacket, looking to me like he was showing his weapon, because the reporter immediately threw his hands in the air and said, "Diane Sawyer, Diane Sawyer." I knew I had to get into this, so I jogged over there, yelling as I went, "Hey! Hey! It's okay, he's with me." My text message had produced the results I'd wanted. Someone from ABC was on the premises—unwelcomed and unwanted—but still there to document what I wanted.

The security man—I didn't know for sure, but in my mind he was CIA—turned around and said to me, "What do you mean he's with you?"

"If I get to the top of the hill and don't like what I'm seeing, I want somebody there to report on that immediately." What I meant was that if this had all just become a clearing operation, then I was going to raise unholy hell.

"He can't go up there. He stays here."

I looked at the reporter and the cameraman. Their gear didn't have any ABC logos on it, so I figured they had to be freelancers. More important, they both looked petrified.

"Look, guys, no one is going to hurt you. You stay right here. When I come back down that hill," I pointed up toward the Hotel Montana, "I'm going to give you all a statement."

They both nodded. I had to make that promise. I had to keep those media guys around. I needed to keep the pressure on the government, even if that meant letting the cat out of the bag regarding this secret trip. In my mind, the government was trying to keep not just our trip, but also the whole truth about the Hotel Montana and the number of American casualties quiet. As far as I knew, the only TV footage of the Hotel Montana had been about a two-second clip on CBS. Why weren't they showing what was going on there? Why wasn't my daughter and the story of the other missing Lynn group really being told in full?

I just couldn't get out of my head the words that I heard on that Thursday: "Your daughter is on a helicopter heading to Port-au-Prince airport with two other girls." Once I found out that wasn't true, I had to call everything else into question and only trust what I could see and hear with my own eyes and ears. In addition, a Florida-based reporter had put out the news several days earlier that Brit's body had been found and that she had photographic evidence that Britney had been declared dead. We were horrified by that and added it to our list of bad intel.

About halfway up we stopped again, this time to meet some of the dignitaries who had gathered. The first part of the driveway led to a paved circle centered around an out-of-service fountain. We always kidded people that we were a budget-hotel family, I wondered what Britney would have thought coming up this same approach to the opulent hotel. Was she feeling the same kind of gut-teasing sensation of fear and excitement that I was?

Just as before, we walked along a receiving line shaking hands, hearing expressions of condolences, all of that. I was polite when talking with the ambassador, and then I was introduced to Colonel Norberto Cintron. The colonel was several inches shorter than me, slighter of build, wearing glasses that in the fading light hid his eyes. He stood ramrod straight and was all proper military with me when he gripped my hand and gave me that direct-in-the-eyes look that only a well-trained soldier can give you.

"Pleased to meet you, sir," he said in a clipped but strong baritone.

From that point forward, Colonel Cintron served as my personal escort. I was eager to get all of the preliminaries out of the way. I wanted to get up that hill. Jim McGovern and the ambassador walked together, a representative of USAID led Franklin and Angie, and the others were similarly guided past the temporary morgue. There we saw a signboard that clearly listed our daughters as still among the missing and not confirmed dead.

My mouth was dry, and walking up that steep slope had me breathing hard, but it was my hearing that seemed most affected by what was going on. I felt like I was underwater and could just barely make out what was being said through the distortion. This wasn't the usual kind of movie slow-motion sound effect, but something different, like the pressure of all the thoughts inside my head was somehow audible.

As we crested the hill, I saw a thing that made my jaw drop. Seeing an elevator shaft stabbing the sky on a horizontal plane startled me. What the hell kind of forces could be at work to do that to a building? To the right, I saw the main section of the roof still in a very large slab. It had slid down from the backside of the hotel to the front, like some cool dude pushing the back brim of his hat to the top of his head to cover his eyes. I fought the impulse to do the same. I saw someone walking along that slab and could see that he and some others had been working to break apart that concrete. The slab was pockmarked with holes, and the rusted re-bar in that light looked like a tangle of veins.

The contrast with the photos I'd seen when Brit had first spoken to us about the trip was astounding. Gone were the graceful arches of the windows. The wrought-iron railings that surrounded the balconies that ran the perimeter of the structure had been twisted into gnarled skeletal shapes, warped by a geometry of forces unimaginable to me. The striped awnings, eerily like the bedspread Brit and her mother had bought for her dorm room, lay in dusty tatters, their colors muted. The sprawling complex that had been carved out of the hillside and gracefully followed its natural curves and contours was now a jumble of obtuse and acute angles. What had once been a realistic landscape had been reduced into some kind of horrific work of modern art, but still it told a powerful but horrible story.

The rest of the structure had pancaked each of the five floors on top of one another into a pile a few feet thick. I'm no structural engineer, and it wouldn't have taken one to know what I concluded immediately. My Britney was gone. There was no way she could have survived that. I suppose I had suspected that was true for a time, had prepared myself for that moment, but nothing I could have done would have eased the pain. There had been points during the past week and a half when I just wanted my heart to stop beating, to be done with all the struggle. Those thoughts always passed. I knew Brit would not have wanted me to reach that level of despair, and I knew as I stood there dealing with the reality of my daughter's death, that Cherylann and the boys still needed me to be around. I knew that Brit needed me, too. Someone had to fight in her place to make sure that she got back home.

In the center of all that destruction, an enormous tree, at least one-hundred feet tall still stood. Its branches, arcing like the hotel's windows once had, fanned out from a trunk several feet in diameter and nearly touched the ground. I couldn't believe it. How the hell could that tree still be standing and my daughter was in that rubble? If she'd only stayed in her room, she would have had a better chance to survive. Why God, why? My chin fell to my chest, and I pinched the bridge of my nose hoping to stem my tears and quiet my anger—not at God—but at the cruelty of fate.

I stood there in the gathering dark, listening to the birds and from the distance one pick beating against the concrete and a shovel shushing it into silence—taps and shush, taps and shush, another kind of heartbeat.

I remember reading in a Nike ad that the heart is the strongest muscle and also the stupidest. It doesn't know when to quit, and as beat up and damaged as my ticker was, I knew that it was going to keep doing its thing. I pressed the flat of my hand into my eyes, watched the light show, and was reminded of how Brit loved the fireworks displays on the Fourth of July. We'd have a huge party at our restaurant. When she was very little, she'd stand there with her fingers pressed against her ears, her smile an eruption of joy, her eyes sparklers. She'd stomp her feet and jump up and down and point to the sky and shriek. I wanted to do all those things right then and there myself but for other reasons having nothing to do with celebrations or independence.

Cherylann and I had had to gradually let go of our little girl step by step from her first training wheel-free bicycle ride, to her first cell phone, to her first date, to her first trip to a third-world nation to offer aid and comfort. My guts were in a knot thinking that somehow I'd failed her, that I'd not done the one thing that I'd devoted so much of life to: keeping her safe from any harm. How do you do both those things—let them go and keep them safe? And at the end, at a time like this, how do you fold your daughter in your arms, tell her everything is going to be all right, let her know that Daddy is right there with her, when she lies beneath a mound of cement and sand, ceramic tile and cinder block? How do you shore up the thin walls of our belief that we have some control against a mountainside of evidence that tells us that no matter how much we plan, no matter how many suitability studies we undertake, life can sometimes just come crashing down around us?

I didn't want to fall apart right there in front of Colonel Cintron. Call it male ego or whatever, but I wanted and needed to hold it together a bit longer. I dabbed at a couple of tears and took a deep breath. I noticed that my jaw and teeth were aching and a knot of tension was choking my neck and throat.

I continued my inspection, telling myself this was just a job site, not the place where my daughter had lost her life.

Most of the trees were still intact, so it wasn't as if the ground had risen up and uprooted and swallowed everything. I was grateful that only a couple of backhoes were on site; they weren't going to bulldoze the site just yet. I kept scanning the building, and to my right and toward the back, I could see through the trees, a part of the outdoor balcony that encircled the building was still in place and attached to what looked like a complete room. From that window, I saw a blanket draped like a flag fluttering in the breeze.

Colonel Cintron stepped up to me, he had removed his hat and his mask. "That's Room 300," he said.

I nodded and swallowed an acrid bit of bile. "I figured."

Following Colonel Cintron's lead, I took off my mask. I'd taken off my ball cap as soon as I'd stepped onto what to me was sacred ground. Instead of the stench of decay from the sixty-eight people who'd lost their lives there, the scent of orchids, citrus trees, and the cool breeze off the now visible ocean had scrubbed the air. The two of us were essentially alone. I figured the other escorts had taken the family members to the spots where they presumed the bodies were. We walked farther along the perimeter closer to Britney's room. A couple of welded iron pipe railings, like heavy-duty croquet wickets, one two feet high and another three feet high, were sticking out of the ground. Colonel Cintron and I stood there, each with a foot up. He, a career Army man who worked with the Corps of Engineers, me a successful home builder. Just two guys looking at a wasted pile of a lot of wasted man-hours and materials.

Except it wasn't that at all.

From the rubble, a man came walking toward us. I was about to lose it completely. I kept biting the inside of my cheek and swallowing big gulps of air. I couldn't control my head, and it just kept nodding on its known, forcing my eyes to focus on that room, the destruction, the verdant hillside and the orange and lemon trees.

The man introduced himself to me, "Captain Bob Zoldos. Fairfax, Virginia, Search and Rescue."

That snapped me out of it. How common of a name was that. Britney's best friend in junior high was Ally Zoldos. I told him that.

"Where's she from?"

"Pennsylvania."

Bob shook his head and wiped the back of his neck with a bandana. "Unbelievable. My whole family's from there."

I had no idea what to say, and before I could respond, Bob said, "Senator Kerry called last week. Asked me to come down here. I searched Brit's room on Thursday. When I heard you were coming down here today and that you thought she might have been in the shower, I checked the room again, and sir, she wasn't in the main room, and she wasn't in the bathroom."

I nodded, grateful for the information and the confirmation that what we'd been told was true. There had been people on-site looking for our daughters.

"It's my belief, sir, that when the earthquake hit, they had fifteen seconds and she ran outside the room. Everything collapsed in the hallways. I believe that's where she's at, and with the aftershocks and the instability of the structure, we just can't get to her at this point."

I couldn't speak and I knew the muscles in my face were working, but I had no control of them. I just stood there and tried to take it all in. I was in Haiti, and I could hear my daughter telling my wife how beautiful this place was, and I could hear the excitement in her voice when she showed me on the computer before she left that it was a five-star hotel that was guarded with gates. And that she was going to be safe. All those things went through my mind as I stood looking at the devastation of Mother Nature—the danger that no gates or walls or guards could have protected her from.

I asked the colonel and Bob Zoldos if I could have a minute, and I walked over as close as I could get to her room, and I just prayed. I asked God to let them recover her and to take care of her—to help me bring her home for a proper Christian burial.

And I had peace. I had peace in my heart. And I had peace in my soul. And as crazy as it sounds, it was okay. At that moment, it was okay. And so I walked back up to that railing, and the colonel said, "Len, the chaplain would like to meet you."

I looked up and there was this man, probably five-foot-six and two-hundred pounds, all muscle, standing there with this warm smile. He looked like a guy I knew from work by the name of Billy Ward.

I was a mess. Looking at me he said, "You did everything right."

I turned to him and said, "What are you talking about?"

"My buddy at home," he said, "fellow chaplain, we talk about you every day."

"What?"

"Yep. He calls me about the news stories. About you calling out Obama. About getting people here. About getting your daughter's face all over. Funny thing is, this morning when I talked to my friend, he said, 'He's done everything but show up.'"

He smiled at me, and he said, "And here you are."

We wrapped our arms around one another, and he asked if we could pray together. We said the Lord's Prayer, our heads bowed, one arm draped over the other's shoulder. When we were done, I thanked him and he walked off.

Colonel Cintron was still standing there, toeing the ground with his boot. Then he looked up at me and nodded, and a thin smile spread across his lips like barbed wire.

"Colonel, do you have any children?

"Yes, I have a son and two daughters." His expression brightened and that smile widened into a grin.

"Well, I have two sons and a daughter, and that's my daughter in that pile." I reached into my pocket and took out a beautiful photo of Brit from her high-school graduation and showed it to him. "This is Britney. This is who you're searching for, Colonel. Please, please bring my Britney home." I knew he was my only hope to recover Brit's body. He connected with me as a father. Simply put, he got it!

Colonel Cintron took out his wallet, and he showed me the pictures of his two daughters, wearing Army fatigues.

"Sir," he said, "one daughter's in Afghanistan and the other's in Iraq. I wouldn't presume to know your pain, but I know your angst. I understand. I promise you." I could see him fighting back tears and watched as his Adam's apple bobbed up an down, and his eyes brimmed with tears. "I promise you that we will find your daughter and bring her home."

We collapsed into each other's arms. Two grown men, two fathers, just crying in front of everybody, holding each other up, supported by that strongest muscle, one that neither of us could have designed or built, putting to its best use the only thing I know of that could have survived those forces that are beyond our reckoning.

In the full-on dark, Colonel Cintron and I made our way down the hill. I left him at the gate, confident that he would do as he'd promised.

I had a few moments alone, and I stood and gazed back up the hill where the ghastly glow of the work lights still couldn't dim the beauty of the place. I scanned the ruins and the mountainside behind it and the vista beyond. Such beauty and destruction.

How appropriate. I took the opportunity to say a few words to my daughter.

"*Beauty and the Beast* was one of your favorites, Brit. You could be both those things, and no matter which you were, I still loved you the same. That time you came home from a party so stinking drunk you couldn't make it up the stairs (and thank you for honoring our agreement that you would always call home for a ride, no questions asked), I was so disappointed, but I loved you, maybe not quite as much as I had before you left that night but almost. And I knew that your slurred beer-smelling "I'm sorry" meant that you loved me too.

I couldn't admit it to you then, but a part of me admired you when I'd say, "Hand it over," and you'd slap your cell phone in my palm and turn away before I locked it in the safe. I heard but didn't feel and didn't believe your, "I hate you." You were such a feisty kid. And, Brit, I'm telling you that right then, I wanted nothing more than for you and I to be singing our favorite song, "Oh Happy Day," from the movie *Sister Act II.* I even might have let you sing lead.

But what really got me was how you'd tell us over and over again that you knew what you did was wrong and accepted the punishments as the price of admission to whatever club it was you were hoping to join.

You and me, we had our battles, Brit. The thing is, I didn't realize until I stood looking at all that ruined paradise was that we were on the same side, both of us fighting for the same thing—to see that you'd mature into the young woman you were becoming, the young woman who sent those messages to her mother, letting us know that we'd done the right things most of the time. I will be back to honor your last wish someday, Brit, even though you didn't know that's what it was when you sent that text to Mom. I promise you!

* * *

The other members of our party straggled in while I was thumbing a text to Cherylann, letting her know that I was okay, really sad, but okay. There was no signal on our service, but I knew because of the connection between us, all that we'd shared, the message would get through anyway. I could feel her arms around me, kneading the knots in my shoulder, whispering in my ear that she loved me, trusted me, that I needed to take care of myself, and that I was needed and missed. I let her know that I was bruised but not broken, devastated but determined.

Once the group was assembled, we headed toward the scattered lights and smoldering ruins of the besieged city, the place where my daughter learned the strength of her own heart, the place where she was determined to put that strength to the test.

Brit, you will not fail. We will bring you home, and you will bring us back here.

I had one more thing to do that night. The ABC news cameraman and the reporter were waiting for Jim and I just outside the gate to the once luxurious hotel. I was at peace. I'd found what I came searching for. It was clear the ruins were being taken apart layer by layer. Our missing daughters would be recovered, but I had to continue to keep the American people aware of their plight. The lights came on, and I played my role as a grateful father and spokesman on behalf of all our daughters and the other missing Americans. I knew that my voice was just one of the thousands who'd cried out in pain during those darkest of hours, and I was determined that a light would always shine on this and other corners of this jumbled, violated, but now sacred ground.

9

BRINGING BRIT HOME

"A father's duty to his children is never done, and sometimes you have to take on unpleasant tasks."

—LEN

CHERYLANN

Len and I have said that we belong to a club that no one wants to earn admittance to: parents who have lost a child. While Len was away in Haiti, I thought of this family, the Bish family from Warren, Massachusetts. Back in 2000, their sixteen-year-old daughter, Molly, went missing. She worked as a lifeguard at Comins Pond in her hometown. She left to go to work one morning in June and never returned. The story was all over the newspapers, and the largest and most expensive search in the history of the state for her produced nothing. Then three years later, her remains were found five miles from her family's home. She had been murdered. At the time of her disappearance, I remember Len and I talking about how awful the story was, and as it went on and on, after all the attention settled down, we still thought of her, still thought about how horrible it must be for her parents, the not knowing.

In our part of the country, Molly's story was as well known as JonBenet Ramsey's and, like hers, a murderer has never been arrested and tried. When we first learned about the earthquake and Brit's being missing, in those sleepless hours in bed, Len and I had talked about so many things. One of them was Molly Bish and the agony her parents had endured for those three years, and how, finding out that she hadn't run off, wasn't living someplace else whether because she wanted to or was forced to like that other little girl who was kidnapped in Utah, Elizabeth Smart, we figured that the not knowing was better. We'd say to each other that we didn't want the Molly Bish ending. We wanted the Elizabeth Smart ending. She'd been held for nine months and then rescued. That's what we wanted. Our thoughts and prayers were for the Bish family and their beloved daughter, Molly.

Of course, we knew the circumstances were different, especially after Len went to Haiti and saw the Hotel Montana with his own eyes. I made sure the boys weren't home when Len returned. We needed to be alone, and as soon as he walked in the door, we wrapped each other in our arms and sobbed and sobbed. We'd been telling people for a few days, from just before Len's departure, that we were preparing for the worst but hoping for the best. As I stood there in his arms, feeling him shaking and heaving, both of us bearing up the other to keep from collapsing, we knew. We couldn't bring ourselves to say it, and in the days leading up to Len's return, I had understood that with each passing hour, the chances of her being found alive diminished.

Finally, Len stood tall and held me at arm's length, and looked in my eyes and said, "We need to . . ." He ran his tongue over his cracked lips and dabbed at his tears. "She's gone."

I melted into him again and nodded over and over, feeling the rough fabric of his shirt against my cheek.

"It's too soon," I said. I could feel Len nodding in agreement.

He knew what I was saying, that we couldn't share these thoughts with the boys and the rest of the family just yet. We needed more time ourselves.

What helped me was that despite our tears and our shared enormous outpouring of grief, I could tell that Len was at peace. He had needed to go to Haiti, had to be there himself, to accept this reality. I understood that, and I was glad he got the opportunity to go. The thing that is so funny is that Lenny said he couldn't have done what I did in Florida. He couldn't have gone down there and cleared out her room. I don't think that I could have done what he did in going to the Hotel Montana, at least not then. I could have done it, but I didn't feel the same need that he did. My boys needed me and I needed them!

I was glad that we now had assurance, at least in our minds, that Brit wasn't in one of those mass graves, that she was at the Hotel Montana, and now it was just a question of time before her body would be found and she would be returned to us.

At the start of the New Year, Len and I had talked about picking out cemetery plots for ourselves. With our usual dark humor, I'd teased him that it was because of him and his heart that we needed them; I was planning on being around for a good long time. Given his and his family's track history, though, this was something we needed to do. The kids may not have appreciated what we were doing, but later when they wouldn't have to deal with all the details, they'd be glad we did.

We agreed as we entered the last week of January, that we had to go on with that plan, with the variation that now we were to be burying our daughter in the near future. Death had been more a part of Len's life, with his parents going so young. Len's dad was sixty-five, and his mom was about seventy-four. Death was part of our life because of Len's heart issues and what we had already gone through but we agreed this was an important step in our moving forward with our lives and coming to terms with this excruciating new reality. And in some odd way, we were still playing tricks with ourselves. We could say that because this was on our to-do list anyway, and we had to do it for us, we may as well go ahead.

And then as the days went on and the bodies of the other Lynn University group were being recovered and Brit's wasn't, hope kept sticking its head up and looking around and nudging us, making us think that maybe she had been on a stretcher and then flown out of there somewhere. She was gone, but not gone, missing but not . . . We couldn't use the word, still don't. We found ourselves in a place that you never want to be as a parent, somewhere in the nether world—existing, moving forward because you have to for the sake of your other children, but not really living.

We hadn't known the families of the other Lynn University students lost in the earthquake. I don't know that it made it any easier knowing there were others going through this with us, but we felt a strong kinship with them, feelings that last and unite us to this day. Because of the very nature of who those lost were, students versus faculty members, we were more drawn to the families of the other students who were not among the survivors. Losing a child is different from losing a husband or a father. Not any easier certainly, but because we had more of a point of commonality among the four students who were in the Hotel Montana and didn't get out.

In a way, we were doing what the girls had done. As time went on and each family talked to each of the girl's friends, we learned the group had gone out partying the weekend before and that they had bonded. It was comforting in a weird way. One day Jean Gianacaci went back to Christine's apartment and turned on Christine's computer to do some work. The screen wallpaper image that loaded was a picture of Christine and Britney! Knowing they were together gave me some kind of peace.

The surviving students from the Lynn group are also very

dear to us, and some of them have become like family members. Many of them reached out to Bernie and, to a lesser degree, Richie, and were great shoulders for them to cry on and laugh along with in sharing stories of Brit, allowing them to gain more insight into who she was.

This book is primarily about what Len and I and our family experienced. We respect the privacy of the other families too much to go into detail about what was said or done back then or since—just as I don't feel comfortable relating how we told the boys about the fact that their sister hadn't survived the collapse of the Hotel Montana. If I thought that what we did or how we handled it would benefit families in a similar situation, I might reveal those quiet and agonizing moments.

All I can say is that every family is different, every family member is unique, and we prepared Richie and Bernie as gently as we could, but it was still a very, very difficult fact that they had to accept. They mourned her loss privately and publicly and in their own ways. All we could do was let them know that grieving was not a sport. No one keeps score. No one judges your performance. There are no degrees of difficulty assigned to certain moves. You just do what makes sense to you at the time and know that what feels right to you at any time may not necessarily be what's best for you in hindsight, so don't look back and don't judge.

As January transitioned to February, I was getting concerned about the timing of Brit's recovery. Even without the tragedy of Haiti and when it occurred, February is a tricky month for us emotionally. I lost my father on February 12, and with Bernie's birthday on the 13th and Valentine's Day immediately following, we had had to be careful to not let our loss overshadow Bernie's day. I was hoping that Brit's recovery wouldn't coincide with either my father's anniversary or with Bernie's birthday as well. I guess it's unrealistic to think that any day can be free and clear of negative associations, but still we hoped and prayed that our kids could be spared another bit of agony.

We knew that nothing could be the same, but still we wanted there to be limits to the damage done to the other parts of our lives. What helped is that we knew Brit and how she would have wanted us to behave. She didn't live long, but she lived large, and that offered us some comfort. Sure, there were parts of life that we wished she could have experienced, but as far as what she packed into her limited time with us, I don't think that any of us thought she had wasted much, if any, of it. That's why I wanted to return from Florida and why I didn't travel with Len to Haiti, and why I knew that he needed to take the lead in continuing to get updates about the progress at the Hotel Montana. Besides hoping the dates wouldn't overlap, I didn't concern myself much with when she was going to be recovered and brought back home to us. Sooner or later it would happen.

At the same time, I knew things needed to be done in the calm before the storm. I had experienced this before, though the circumstances were far different, and knew what to expect. My father died of cancer. Knowing his time was running out, one of the smartest things my mom, sister, Jodi, and I did was make the arrangements with the Miles Funeral Home before he passed. Once he was gone, we knew we didn't want to be dealing with our grief at the same time we were making all the many decisions and arrangements for the funeral and the burial. Instead, we wanted to focus our energy on celebrating my father and what he had meant to us, and begin to heal.

Miles was the same place that would be in charge of Brit's funeral. As with my father, we wanted to get a cemetery plot and a headstone for Brit even before we had confirmation that her body was recovered. We didn't view doing that as a sign of disrespect or giving up or anything like that. We knew that what was important when Brit came home to us was our emotions and our memories and our being together as a family—not attending to all kinds of details.

So, I started thinking about and planning Brit's funeral. That's the word that most people use for it, but we didn't. We couldn't think of it that way. We were going to hold a celebration of our daughter's life, and wanted every last detail to be handled in advance of the time when we learned she was coming back to Massachusetts to be with us.

LEN

For Bernie's birthday, Cherylann arranged for us to go into Boston to the North End for a nice family meal. She knew how important it was not to lose sight of the boys and their needs, to try to keep our spirits up as much as possible.

I had been in touch with several members of the State Department who were keeping us apprised of what was going on at the Hotel Montana. When it became clear that Brit was the last of the six to be recovered, we—being Gengels and all—had to laugh. Of course, she was going to be fashionably late; of course she was going to be one to hold things up and make the grand entrance.

I was also in touch regularly with Colonel Cintron who was an absolute rock-solid presence in our lives. He called me on the 13th, Bernie's birthday, in the morning while we were still in Rutland. I was torn. I looked at the number on my cell phone and saw that nothing registered on caller ID, so I knew it had to be someone from the government. I decided to answer, and was glad to hear the colonel on the other end of the line. He told me that they'd reached the hallway that led to where Room 300 was. It was just a matter of time, likely hours at the most. I thanked him and told him, father to father, that I'd appreciate it if he didn't call me again that day. This was my son's birthday, and I didn't want anything to detract from that. He said he understood.

Dinner wasn't a laugh riot or anything like that, but we managed to enjoy some good food. Bernie and Richie seemed grateful for the fact that it was all of us together in the car ride, and then later walking from the North End on a nice late winter night to my nephew Josh's loft. For the first part of the day, it was just the four of us, no extended family, and me present in a way that I hadn't really been for them during that first month or so. A few other family members joined us for dinner, and it was good to have most of the conversation be about Bernie and Richie and what they were up to.

Early the next morning at about 12:07 a.m., the phone rang. I recognized Michelle Bernier-Toth's voice. She had been wonderful to work with, just a really sweet and compassionate woman who worked with the State Department.

"Len, they've recovered Brit. I'm so sorry for your loss. I have a daughter her age, and I can't imagine how you must be feeling right now."

It had taken a while to recover Brit's body so we'd experienced a few moments of panic—maybe she hadn't been in her room, maybe she was in one of those piles of bodies—so hearing confirmation that she was recovered came as a relief. I'd known since my trip to Haiti that she was gone. Now she was found. That was the best thing I could have asked for at that time. I was prepared to get on a plane and escort her back to the U.S., to make whatever identification of her was necessary. I'd even talked with our priest and dear friend, Father Robert Lord, who told me to just say the word and he would be on that plane with me. As it turned out, the State Department didn't want us to do that. Understandably, they were worried about more U.S. citizens traveling to a place that was a mess, and with the possibility of a cholera outbreak (which did become a reality), it wasn't worth the risk.

Michelle told me it would be three to four days before Brit would be back on American soil. One additional irony was that because of a series of severe snowstorms on the Eastern seaboard, the bodies of the recovered Lynn group were still in Haiti. They wouldn't have been able to land at Dover Air Force Base—the place where all the American military casualties from Iraq and Afghanistan were flown into—because of the snow. As a result, Brit would be flying back with the rest of them. That gave us some comfort, knowing that she wouldn't be by herself, that she'd be with members of the group who were with her in Haiti and they would all come home to their families together.

While Cherylann and I had known this was the likely outcome, we knew some members of our extended family were still holding out for a miracle. I do believe in God's miraculous powers, but I also knew that reality was reality. How some of our family was going to take this news, this final and absolute confirmation of the worst being true, troubled me. I didn't like seeing and hearing some of the things that had been said, and I'd tolerated a lot of it, but now was the time to draw the line in the sand. We set up a meeting for that night, Valentine's Day evening, at our house where we would address our concerns and our plans for how we were going to memorialize Brit.

We'd had some things in motion for a while, but we needed to get everybody on the same page with us in terms of logistics and in some way emotional responses. Before we could do that, we also had to address the media. Four network trucks were outside on the street that Valentine's Day. Instead of going through the ordeal of addressing each of them individually, we decided to host an impromptu press conference just outside the house. In a show of family solidarity, about forty of us gathered around the front steps. We informed the media that Brit had been recovered, stated we were enormously grateful for the outpouring of support, spoke of how much we loved her, and gave a brief outline of how we had planned to honor her in the next few days.

Next came the hard part. I love my daughter more than anything. But I was bothered by a few people making statements—and granted this was a very emotional time—about how she should be put up for sainthood or some such nonsense. I couldn't deal with that. I know that the temptation anytime someone passes on is to gloss over the bad. That's understandable and makes it easier on everybody, but you know as well as I do that those words about what a great guy so and so was are coming out of one side of your mouth while you're also thinking about what a crotchety bastard he was. That's okay, but to really believe that Brit was saintly was just such a distortion of the truth, that I had to let people know that Brit was a great kid, a real kid, a kid who struggled academically, who often didn't apply herself completely to her studies, who tested every limit placed in her way to protect her and to teach her, who sometimes tried my patience, who, like every other fourteen- or fifteen-year-old girl, would tell me that she hated me when I took her phone away and popped it into our safe as a way to discipline her.

That she was all that, as well as a kind and generous spirit, made her special. I didn't want to see that specialness wiped out. You can't know if things are good if you think that everything is good. You need contrast to know what's sweet because you've experienced sour. I didn't want Brit's life, all the different aspects of it, whitewashed into a blank canvas. Brit, with all her faults and her fabulousness, was a human being, and I wanted to be sure we recognized the fullness of her humanity. To treat her as if she was angelic and saint-like would diminish her, and I couldn't have that. Having her taken from us was punishment enough. We knew the real Brit and all those different parts of her—the saintly and the not so saintly—were what together made her our shining star. We wanted other people to know her in that way too.

I've heard it said, and I believe, that one of the saddest things in the world is when a human being doesn't live up to his or her potential. Brit was loaded with potential, and what made me so sad was that she never got the opportunity to fully explore and expand on it. I can't say enough about how proud we all were of her for making the choice she did to go to Haiti, to give of herself, and even though she never got the chance to act out the dream that she had to work with those underprivileged kids, I knew that she would have done it. Her eyes sparkled in those photographs from Haiti, and they are evidence of her passion and commitment. I didn't want to see anyone mistake that light as being some supernatural agency taking over her spirit. God was working through Brit as he had been her whole life, but she had free will—and in lots of frustrating ways she was willful—and it was Brit who was taking possession of the spirit within her, making a conscious and deliberate choice.

What also frustrated me, and quite frankly drove me to point of breaking for one of the few times during that thirty-three-day ordeal, was when well-meaning people outside the family would tell us that God had a plan for Brit. What I heard them saying was that God was the one who took her life from her. I never believed that for an instant. An earthquake took our daughter, not God. Maybe I was too sensitive and overreacted when I heard those words, and I heard them from more than one person, but the God I worship doesn't do those kinds of things. I didn't spend a whole lot of time contemplating the whys of what happened to our daughter, those sometimes unfathomable questions that we all ask whenever some tragedy occurs. Mine wasn't to question or to give motives or explanations for what took place. I had to learn to quietly accept the reality and to make as much good from a horrible bad as possible.

So, I had to say something to that effect to everyone gathered in the room. You could hear a pin drop, and I knew a few people were thinking they'd like to let me have it right then and there, but gratefully they didn't. I don't know if a father's grief can be bottled and used as a calming agent, but it sure seemed to work that day.

Cherylann spoke next, and the only thing you could hear when she was through was crying.

She told everyone that it is every mother's dream to help plan her daughter's wedding. She wasn't going to get that opportunity, but she was going to be able to, and had already begun to, plan the celebration to mark the passing of her daughter from this world onto the next. I was losing it as she spoke, sitting in the chair while she stood beside me, and I felt her hand on my shoulder, steadying me. She went on to go over some of the details for the private and public events we had planned. She made it clear, even without saying it, that what she and I decided was final. There would be no unofficial "committees" formed, no other opinions needed unless asked for, and that we should conduct ourselves in the manner of a celebration. This wasn't going to be a joyous moment in our lives, but it would be a way to honor the best of Brit, the lover of parties and gatherings, and we would really be letting her down if we were down.

These moments were going to be about Brit and not about us. Anything we did to draw attention to ourselves would detract from our appreciation for what she meant to us all.

We spent the next few days working with the people at Union Station, an old train depot converted into a restaurant and party space. We were also being kept apprised of what was going on as far as Brit's body being shipped to us. We were given a target date of Wednesday, and so we based our plans around that date. On Thursday we were going to have a private gathering for family and friends and then on Friday two visitations open to the public, with a funeral Mass, burial, and then a celebration meal at Union Station on Saturday.

On Sunday, the afternoon after we'd been notified that Brit had been recovered, I got a call from Senator Kerry. He expressed his condolences and said he was calling from Pakistan where he was going to be for another day, then in California for a few days, and that he was hoping that the funeral would be on Saturday so he could attend. We were all touched that he would make that effort, and he sounded genuinely glad the scheduling would work out. Throughout our ordeal, he was someone we could call on, and he and his chief of staff in Boston, Drew O'Brien, were always responsive and gracious.

We were informed that Brit would arrive in Boston at 7:00 p.m. that Wednesday. We were given two options, but there was only one that we even considered. The funeral director convinced us that we shouldn't drive to the airport; instead they would provide a limousine for us. We'd be allowed on the tarmac to watch as Brit's body was taken from the plane. Of course, we were going to do that, and Cherylann and I were joined by Bernie.

I know that it probably gets tiresome to read this, but the whole scene was surreal. You never imagine yourself sitting at your house waiting from a limo to take you to the airport so that you can see your daughter's casket being offloaded from a jet. In a lot of ways you're numb the whole time, but some things just jump out at you and burn themselves in your memory.

We fly out of Boston on quite a few occasions, and it normally takes us an hour and fifteen minutes to an hour and a half to get there on a good day. So, we were ready between five o'clock and five fifteen, and then sat there until almost six wondering what was going on. It didn't take too long to find out. The limo pulled up, and three Massachusetts State Police cars pulled in as well. When we got onto Interstate 90, we understood better why the limo had showed up so late. At every exit and on-ramp, another trooper was parked blocking other traffic. Of course, we had to laugh about it, zipping along like we were the King and Queen of England or some other dignitaries being escorted to the airport. It felt good to laugh, to break up some of the tension. This was so hard to believe, that we were actually in a car going to get our daughter, Bernie and Richie's sister, only we hadn't needed to make a plan to meet her at baggage claim or on the departure's level or whatever. We weren't going to be greeted by Brit and her radiant smile (or her sullen sneer if we'd been late or if the flight had been delayed), and we weren't going to be able to wrap our arms around her and ask her how her flight was. None of that. So, we drove along, and I had this sensation that my chest was hollow, that it had been scooped out, and I was just this shell being driven along, not quite against my will but with no action needed on my part, just sitting there trying not to think and trying not to feel.

CHERYLANN

When we arrived at the airport and the limo wound around to get us near some arrival gates so that we could escort Brit, I tried to prepare myself for it as best I could. I didn't need to know every single detail, but I figured everybody involved had crossed all the T's and dotted all the I's. We parked, and the funeral home people got out of the car and told us to wait. I assumed it was going to be just a matter of minutes before this next bit of unreality took place. Each step of this intensely painful journey was difficult, but I put one foot in front of the other and move along. Having had so much difficulty and confusion through this long ordeal, I hoped things would now move ahead smoothly. I just didn't have the energy for it to be otherwise.

So, when we were told well after seven o'clock that Brit wasn't on the plane, I was flabbergasted. Len made some calls to tell people that the State Department had told us she would be there at seven, and now we were being told she would not; she would be there at 11. Len told the State Department that if she wasn't on that plane, then they'd better find a helicopter because they WERE going to bring our daughter home—THAT NIGHT! If they did not, he said, "Heads will roll!"

What was going on? We tried to laugh it off a bit, thinking, "Of course, we were told again that Brit was flying on something and now we're being told she isn't." This was the bad-intel thing all over again.

I tried to make the best of a bad situation. One of Brit's roommates lived nearby, and several of her college friends from around the country were coming in for the funeral. Bernie had been in contact with them via text and phone on the drive in, letting them know when we'd have her body and what not, so we decided that instead of sitting on the tarmac with the sound of jet engines and the smell of aviation fuel making us woozy and cranky and nauseous, we'd head to Nina's (the roommate's house) to pass some of the time.

That was the right decision. We got to see the kids outside the environment of a funeral home, so none of the stiff awkward stuff passed between us. We knew that some of the survivors felt horrible, that guilt that came along with not being one of the six, and as much as we tried to tell them not to, you can't tell anybody how they should feel. We hugged and cried and laughed about the fact that, of course, Brit was making another delayed grand entrance. We chatted for an hour and got to meet Nina's parents, who were just incredibly gracious. It meant so much that so many of the kids were going to be coming up, and that others from the Lynn group were going to join us over the next few days.

We got back to airport, and the same routine took place. We were told to wait in the car. Contrary to what I thought had been agreed, for safety reasons we were told we could get out of the car, but we couldn't approach the plane when it taxied and parked. Len had learned that when the bodies had been removed from the site of the Hotel Montana, it was just like at Ground Zero. We also knew the bodies were draped with American flags, as were the caskets, and the dignity of all those actions really helped soothe me in a way that's difficult to explain.

When the plane pulled in, we could see inside the cabin. People stood when the plane landed and were on their feet looking out the windows at us. I imagined those people wondering what the heck we were doing standing outside a limo looking up at them looking out at us. After a few minutes, some men from the airline came out and opened the cargo hatch that was facing us.

I knew what I'd been told about staying back, but I could feel this nervous energy coursing through me. My Brit was home, and though it wasn't the way we wanted it to be, it was the best we could now hope for. As her casket came down the conveyor, I couldn't hold back anymore. I had to touch her, eliminate as much of the distance between us as was possible, given the limits of flesh and wood.

My stomach was in my throat, and as soon as they started wheeling her down, I broke loose and ran right over. The State Police were there along with a few other men as they said, "Ma'am" as if to stop me. I turned to them and gave a look that said, "Don't even think about keeping me away from my daughter . . . just don't!" No one said another word.

I was at the bottom of the ramp, there to welcome her home. As the casket went by I wanted to jump on it, as if to hug her. I wanted to open it...was that REALLY her? But all I could do was put my hand on the casket. This was the closest I was ever going to be to my daughter again.

Back in the car, driving toward Rutland and home, that

feeling that should have been familiar by now but still hit me at every turn washed over me. That hearse ahead of us? That has my daughter in it. What is she doing in there? Why isn't she sitting beside me fiddling with the radio? Shouldn't she be singing along with Lady Gaga or Beyonce? Shouldn't she be yacking on the phone with one of her girlfriends figuring out what party to go to, "Oh-my-God-ing" over what someone had said, done, or seen?

And yet, there were Bernie and Len sitting there in silence, their faces blank instead of registering some amusement, faint disgust, disbelief, or whatever with an eyebrow raising or an eye roll at something Brit had said or done.

We were all lost in our own private thoughts, and held together in our grief. I felt like screaming at the driver to stop the car, to let me out because this wasn't my life, this wasn't what I was supposed to be doing, this was all some very, very big mistake, some major case of "bad intel" gone mad.

We'd travelled that same route countless times, and I could probably name each of the exits on I-90 between Logan International and Rutland. But even though the mile-markers were the same and the landscape unchanged, none of it would ever be the same again.

LEN

We had laughed with Brit when the day before she left for Haiti she'd gotten a manicure and done some tanning. Eventually, we were very glad she'd chosen to do those things, specifically her nails.

It's tough to know that your daughter was killed in an earthquake or any other way. But, in addition to agonizing about so many other things, I worried she had suffered a painful injury only to lose her life hours or even days after the quake struck. Colonel Citron and I had developed such a strong bond that I could ask him questions without feeling like I was being judged. So, when Brit's body was discovered, I'd asked him to be truthful with me. Were there signs that Brit had struggled? She was found just outside her room in the hallway. She was a tough kid, and I'm sure that when the walls started to shake, she did what anyone would do—she tried to get the hell out of there, and fast.

I don't know if it really would have mattered if she'd been given earthquake survival instructions or not. I'd like to think that if she had, she would have stayed under a doorway, but given the type of devastation, the levels and levels of debris that Colonel Cintron described to me, it likely wouldn't have mattered. But what did matter was knowing that she didn't suffer too greatly. Strange how things evolve in your life and what you find comfort in.

I asked Colonel Cintron about her nails, if her manicure was still in good shape. I figured that if she had been struggling to get out from beneath the piles of rubble, her nails would have shown the effects of those efforts. He told me they were still in good condition.

While I trusted Colonel Cintron, so many aspects of the search and recovery were filled with wrong information that, as a father, I had to see with my own eyes that the body that was sent to us was indeed our daughter's. I asked Rick and the owner of Miles Funeral Home to cut open the cloth that they triple-wrapped Brit in and to take a photo of her hands. I knew what her nails had looked like, and I wanted to make certain that those dark-maroon filed nails were on the body identified as my daughter. Believe me, I didn't want to have to seek that kind of confirmation, but this was just one more item on my list of things I'd rather not do that had to be done. I experienced no relief, no joy, no anything other than sad resignation as Rick told me the photo showed her nails were fine.

A father's duty to his children is never done, and sometimes you have to take on unpleasant tasks. Though Brit was no longer with us, that didn't mean that our duty to her was done by any means. Just as we'd started thinking about and planning what to do for her celebration and her resting place, we had other ways to honor her already in mind. The work that she wanted to do would get done. We'd make certain of that, even if it meant having to get some dirt under our nails and sweat soak our clothes and tax our patience and test our resolve.

We'd done it all our lives, and Brit knew that was the Gengel way: you always gave it your best shot.

I don't know if numbers can translate to the amount of impact that one person's life can have on the world, but that Thursday more than four hundred people passed through the funeral home for the private wake and one thousand the next day. On Saturday at St. John's, more than one thousand people attended the Mass that preceded the celebration of Brit's life at Union Station. It's a good thing we are used to hosting events for large numbers of people. We knew that we could only accommodate five hundred at the celebration, and how we were going to manage to let people know who was in and who was out was a major discussion. We had so many details to attend to, from the flowers, to the linens, to the menu, and we were grateful that we had all that to think about because the other reality, the fact that we were celebrating Brit's life because her time on Earth had ended, was still nearly impossible to bear.

As an adult, as a parent, you know there are times when you have to flip that switch and go into autopilot to get through something, to not let your emotions get the best of you. I'm not very good at keeping my thoughts and feelings below the surface, so my goals were a bit more modest: to get through the day without losing it completely. I'd spent so many hours of my life in St. John's Church, celebrated so many special days on the church calendar—Easter and Christmas most especially, along with weddings, baptisms, First Communions, and so on, that the rush of memories of our times there with family and in particular Brit was not unexpected.

As we filed into the church behind the pallbearers and Brit's casket, I remembered the last time I'd seen Brit walking along that aisle. It was Christmas Eve Mass, and it was one of the moments that was pure Brit and what made her so special to me.

We've already talked about the Christmas charity project that Cherylann and Brit had worked on. Well, in 2009,

Brit helped out. Every year, the Sunday before Christmas, Father Madden includes in the church bulletin a story about the Christmas gifts for the poor and mentions the names of all the wonderful people who volunteer to do the work. On Christmas Eve we got to church, flew in our usual formation into our pew near the back—Cherylann always goes in first, then Bernie, then Richie, then me, then Brit.

I had the church bulletin and started scanning it. In there was another story, again written by Father Madden, about how he inadvertently left Brit's name off the list of volunteers. We already knew about the oversight, but we figured no big deal. Father Madden is a great guy, about fifty-two or fifty-three years old, and he gets us and how our family works. So, instead of just making a brief mention that he regretted the error, he did this over-the-top, very funny bit about how the whole Christmas charity program was a success only because of the efforts of Britney Gengel. I started reading this and laughed. When I showed the piece to Brit, she murmured, "Oh my God," and she started laughing. But I could see something else working behind those beautiful eyes of hers.

At the end of the Mass, Father Madden was leading the processional back down the aisle, and he was nodding and smiling and acknowledging the congregation. Brit, who was on the outside of our pew, leaned in and said, "I'm going to get him." Her mischievous grin let us know how much she was enjoying the moment. She stepped out into the aisle and made a beeline for Father Madden, walking like she was really upset with him or something, pumping her arms furiously. When she got to him, she opened her arms and the two of them embraced. She whispered something to him, and they both burst out laughing, walking arm in arm in front of twelve-hundred people.

When they got back to our pew, Brit peeled off and stood beside me.

I had to ask, "What did you say to him?"

"I told him that next year I wanted him to include my Facebook picture in the story—or else."

It was hard not think that there would be no next year's

Christmas volunteering for my daughter. But at least I had that moment and many others like it to keep me strong, to keep me happy, to remember for the rest of my days. No one could take away my memories.

CHERYLANN

The celebration of Brit's life went off as we'd envisioned. I was worried about Len, who had to start first. He began things at the funeral Mass by making it through his opening list of thank yous to the many people who helped in recovering Brit's body and assisting us during those thirty-three horrible days. He also paid tribute to the other girls who'd lost their lives, including Courtney, who was being laid to rest that same day.

When he rejoined me, I held his hand and he squeezed it, letting me know that he was going to do this thing, be as resolute in honoring her in a way that fit with our determination to make this a celebration. We took comfort in the familiar words and rhythms of the Mass as Father Lord and Father Madden officiated.

One of the more difficult moments for me was when the Wachusett Choir sang "We Are the World." We'd had to do a bit of work to get permission to use that song in a Catholic church because it is a secular one. Another group of performers had re-recorded the song in the aftermath of the earthquake and released it as a fund-raiser, and it really meant something to us; the message it put out there echoed what Brit had told us about the direction she was taking her life. I was glad we could bend the rules. The song was absolutely beautiful and absolutely the right touch to add to the celebration.

I didn't want to have to deliver a eulogy for my daughter. Not that I didn't want to honor her, but I didn't want to have to honor her in this way. I wanted to be at her wedding, standing at Disney's Wedding Pavilion with a glass of champagne in my hand, toasting her and offering her best wishes on the new adventure she and her husband were undertaking. We don't always get what we need, but we always did what we had to as parents, and this was no time to change that.

Here's what I had to say:

I really struggled on what to say about my Britney. No words can really adequately describe how I feel about her—it's that same feeling that I had when they put her in my arms for the first time . . . incredible! She was born a happy child and stayed that way! She had a lot to be happy about! She had her faith, her friends, and her family! I received a gift yesterday . . . this necklace I'm wearing today was Brit's. We gave it to her for her confirmation, and she wore it every day and never took it off—that was four years ago! Brit was wearing this when she died. It gives me peace knowing she had God with her in her greatest time of need.

Brit had great friends, but more importantly she was a great friend. You could always depend on her. Over the past thirty-nine days we've had the pleasure of hearing great stories about Brit. One story that was shared was from a student from Lynn. He came back from break and wasn't too happy to be back. He was feeling all alone, he was walking across campus, and he heard this voice from hundreds of feet away, "HEY, MICHAEL . . . HOW ARE YA?" He turned and saw Brit and her beautiful smile and a big wave. He said she made him feel like a million bucks, and he knew that it was going to be okay!

So many more stories like that. A girl came through the wake last night and told me that high school was awful for her and that everyone made fun of her . . . everyone except Brit. She said if it wasn't for Brit, she would never have made it through high school. Brit was always watching out for the underdog! That's one of the reasons she went to Haiti...to help those that needed it the most.

When Brit left for Haiti she was at a crossroad in her life.

She was debating whether or not to change her major to Human Services. Len and I sat with her at Christmas break and told her that when she came back from Haiti, she would know what she should do. Well, a few hours into the trip I received a message from Brit telling me she knew what she wanted to do with the rest of her life! She wanted to move to Haiti to start her own orphanage. When she called later that night the sound of her voice was pure happiness! It was a different happiness that I had never heard from her. She had truly found her calling! She fell in love with the people, but especially the children of Haiti! She was so impressed with their kindness and happiness and their appreciativeness for everything. They HAVE NOTHING! She told me that they have a tin roof over their head and dirt on the floor, but they are happy.

As a mom, I ache for the children of Haiti but am so proud of my daughter that she wanted to make a difference! I'm so grateful that I was able to hear the joy in her voice, and thankful that I know when she left this Earth she was at peace.

Don't get the wrong impression. Brit was not perfect! She was a typical teenager doing stupid teenage stuff!

Plenty of stories, so little time! A few examples of "my little angel" . . . I would drop her off at the movies with her girlfriend thinking they were going to WATCH the movie . . . only to find out that she was going out the back to meet some boys. Or the time she and her girlfriend "borrowed" my car to go get some ice cream . . . in another town twenty minutes away. Only one problem: they were fifteen, and in Massachusetts the driving age is sixteen and a half.

In between those "proud parent moments" I truly had proud parent moments. I loved watching Brit with all her friends. They always had so much fun; they just loved being together, just hanging out. This is true of her friends from elementary school through high school, her friends from Maine, and now more evident in her college friends, who I am so thankful have been here with us over the past few days! To all of you who were her friends . . . THANK YOU! THANK YOU FOR BEING THERE FOR HER. She loved you and so do WE!!

Brit loved God, she loved her friends, but nothing really compared to her family! She loved her nana, her godparents, her aunts, her uncles, and especially her cousins. You have all given Britney such great memories and have all played an important part of shaping who Britney is . . . thank you! Brit loved each one of you!

But at the end of the day, every day, Brit came home to the ones she loved the most and the ones that loved her the most! Her incredible brothers: Richie and Bernie who she so loved! Her father who gave her an amazing life, and me, who loved her more than words can say. We're a family! It was the five of us! We'd sit around the table at dinner, talk about our day, mostly Brit would look at her reflection in the window to check herself out, but when she was done we'd share, we'd fight, we'd love, but most of all we were enjoying just being together.

We won't be able to see our Brit at the table anymore.

We won't be on Wells Beach with our Brit anymore.

We won't be able to see her beautiful smile anymore.

We won't be able to wrap our arms around her anymore.

But we WILL KEEP HER MEMORY ALIVE and we WILL MAKE SURE SOMETHING GOOD COMES FROM THIS HORRIFIC TRAGEDY, AND WE WILL CONTINUE BRIT'S WORK TO HELP THE POOREST OF THE POOR!

Brit deserves this!

SHE WAS FABULOUS!

LEN

Cherylann's sister, Jodi, and I spent hours and hours putting together a video tribute to Brit that we played on a large screen at Union Station. We went through boxes and boxes of photographs and, with Bernie's computer assistance, added music to the slideshow. In nearly every one of the photographs that we looked at, those we included and those we didn't, Brit's bright smile dominated the frame. Cherylann had said in her eulogy that Brit was such a happy person, and there was evidence of that fact you could see from every corner of that space. And her smile lit up that old railway station, just as it had—and continues to—light up our lives.

I was touched that Senator John Kerry had called us all the way from Pakistan where he was engaged in high-level work trying to keep the peace and deal with the terrorist threat of the Taliban. He called because he had learned of Brit's recovery, and he wanted to be at the funeral if at all possible, and he made good on his word. People came from all over, and the ongoing outpouring of sentiment for Brit, for our family, made that difficult time less so.

I still watch that video of Brit. I don't really need to. The sound of her voice and her image are as clear to me today as if she was standing right next to me. Still, I find comfort in those captured moments, the places where time has stood still. She truly is the "It girl." And now the "it" that we focused our attention on, as it shifted from rescue to recovery and now to redemption, was to make sure her vision, the one she fashioned for herself during those days in Haiti was fully realized.

A NEW FOCUS

"My daughter has been in touch with me. Brit loved to talk
and to share, so that's no surprise to me—it's just a
different kind of communication."

—LEN

CHERYLANN

You know you're married to the right person when you both come up with the same idea independently of one another at the same time. That's basically how it happened with the decision to establish a foundation dedicated to building an orphanage in Haiti to fulfill Brit's dream. As soon as it became clear to us that Britney wasn't coming back to us alive, Len and I talked about making her last wish come true. Brit had left us with some homework to do, and we were going to do it.

We didn't know how, we just knew what. For the funeral, we asked that in lieu of flowers people send donations to what we'd decided we were going to call the Britney Gengel Poorest of the Poor Fund. The name for it came about because St. John's, where we attend church, had always included "Poorest of the Poor" as part of its mission, from the time of its establishment. Father Madden and St. John's were such a big part of Brit's life that we decided early on that this was a very fitting name for the charity. At that point, calling it a charity was being charitable toward us. There was no real organization then, just the four of us knowing that we had this goal of building an orphanage, but having no clue whatsoever about how we'd do it. Even before the funeral, we'd started to receive some donations, and were overwhelmed by people's generosity afterward.

Just like so much of what happened in the aftermath of Brit's trip to Haiti, we found ourselves on very unfamiliar ground. Len had his business, and I'd owned and operated a restaurant, so we weren't completely new to running an organization, but the nonprofit world has its own rules and regulations.

When we figured out that we had to start a foundation, we learned that having a board of directors was going to be the first real concrete step. While lots of people might want to be a part of it, we knew we had to be selective. Richie was too young legally to be a member of the board—he wasn't yet eighteen, so he was an unofficial board member and his eighteenth birthday marks the date he becomes an official one. In addition to Len, me, and Bernie, we asked one family member from each side to join us. My sister, Jodi Sweeney, was appointed clerk, and Len's sister, Chrissy (Christine) Steinwand, became our program director. In addition to being Brit's godmother, Jodi is a go-getter, as is Chrissy, even under normal circumstances.

We really had no idea how to go about this project, so we turned to the Internet, specifically to Facebook, a place where we'd kept people up to date about Brit's status, and where we'd received hundreds if not thousands of responses. Our research took the form of asking anyone who knew anything about the not-for-profit world to contact us. To our pleasure and surprise, we got many responses, were given names of people we could contact at agencies, and everyone was generous with their time, patient in answering what were probably the most basic of questions, and willing to point us in another direction if they weren't able to help. It's really impossible to thank all those countless people whose hearts were touched by Brit's story, and who in turn touched ours with their outpouring of support, encouragement, and information.

A couple of people do deserve special mention. If it weren't for the efforts of Len's attorney and friend, Paul Novak, we wouldn't have been able to find our way through the paper trail in establishing Britney Gengel's Poorest of the Poor Fund as an official U.S. non-profit organization 501(c)(3). Just the fact that all those numbers and that letter are there gives you some clue as to what's involved. Paul was great and got things moving for us early on, so that by mid-February 2010, even before Brit's body was recovered, the foundation was established. Paul didn't do all the work, though he did do it pro bono. Len's accountant, George Isaac, and the comptroller of C&S Builders, Deb Whittredge, also worked their way through the mountains of red tape and filed the necessary paperwork for us. His office manager, Doreen Dunn, who had a more than full-time job with Len before this, tracked all the donors with their addresses and the amount of donations, so that we could say thanks and issue receipts. She did an incredible job managing and taking care of the first donors.

We were so involved in so many other things, that being able to put our trust in other people knowing they were going to get the job done was an enormous relief. All four of them and many others—too many to count—contributed their time and expertise to help make the foundation happen.

As soon as the announcement was made that we'd established it, we got a lot of coverage in the media, and many other groups we'd been associated with put out the good word on our behalf. Len was a former president of the Home Builders Association of Massachusetts, and as soon as that organization learned of our foundation, Judy Jenkins, the president, and Mark Leff, a past president, posted a lovely message in tribute to Brit and in support of our organization.

We weren't fully prepared for everything that running a charitable organization would entail, but we knew we had to get started immediately. In a funny way, it was like starting a family. You know you want to have kids, so you do. But no one can really prepare you for how that's going to change your life and how to manage every detail of childrearing. Len is the kind of person who likes to jump into the deep end, and over the years. I've learned to just trust him. We could have spent all kinds of time researching and investigating and studying and deciding. We followed our hearts, actually Britney's heart, and when your daughter tells you that she wants to start an orphanage, that's what you do. You figure out the rest as you go along.

At one of our first board meetings in March 2010, we were tossing all kinds of ideas around about the orphanage; we all felt like we had a grasp of what we wanted to do, but we were still struggling mightily with how to do it within the framework of an actual registered charitable organization. Fortunately, P.J. McDonald, the headmaster at Eagle Hill School where Bernie and Richie attended, immediately came into our minds. Eagle Hill is a private school, so fund-raising is an important part of what they do. At that meeting, Len thought of P.J., who'd been a huge help to all of us during the ordeal and was a great asset to our kids. Len called and asked him if he could stop by to answer a few questions for us. Typical of us and typical of P.J., the half hour that he said he could spare turned into nearly three hours of questions and discussion.

At one point, we were talking about a mission statement for the orphanage. What was it we were hoping we could do for these kids? What effect did we hope our program would have on their lives? We talked about Brit and how we thought she would serve as a great model for these kids—her enthusiasm, her generosity, her tenacity. As that discussion was going on—with, of course, everyone talking over one another—P.J. cut to the chase. "You mean you'd like these kids to be like Brit."

All the commotion in the room stopped. Every eye turned toward P.J., who sat there looking like he was afraid we were going to gang up on him. It was one of those aha moments you hear about. We all started talking at one time, telling him some variation of this: You did it! That's exactly right. That's what we should call it.

We'd always felt that Britney Gengel's Poorest of the Poor Fund was a bit of a mouthful. So, Be Like Brit (BLB) was born.

From volunteering a half hour of his time before a son's baseball game, P.J. had solved our name issue and earned himself a place on the board of directors as our chair of the Development Committee. From the outset, though, we knew one thing: We weren't about to completely change the world, let alone Haiti entirely. Our goal was simple and also was formed because of what Britney had told us about her time there. The kids she saw were happy. They didn't have a lot, but they were happy. The goal of Be Like Brit was fairly modest in a lot of ways. We wanted the kids to have the basic necessities, many of things that we take for granted: food, shelter, clothes, and the chance to go to school. We knew that by helping them with those essentials, they'd have an opportunity to develop their potential. Believe me, we understood the kids in Haiti weren't playing on a level field. The historical record of devastation, political corruption, and everything that the people have endured is long and tragic.

We'd experienced this in our lives before with other charity work we'd done. It's easy to see a big problem, think you have to come up with a huge solution, and then shrug your shoulders and walk away saying, "Nothing I can do can really help solve this." I guess that what we were doing is a variation on that idea of "Think globally, but act locally." We took a look at what was a huge problem, and decided we could do our small part. As it turned out, we eventually decided we would have an orphanage that housed sixty-six children: thirty-three girls and thirty-three boys, one for each day that Brit was missing. Thirty-three is a symbolic but also a practical number. You might think that helping sixty-six kids out of the thousands and thousands of orphans is just a drop in the bucket. Well, these kids are not drops, and it's not a bucket but a human life, a future.

Contributions started to pour in, from kids saving pennies, nickels, and dimes, a young woman donating the money that she normally spent on her horseback-riding lessons, a seven-year-old boy who donated his birthday money, and so many other donations from people we didn't even know and about whom we had no idea how they learned about us and the foundation. To say those donations touched us and humbled us is an understatement. Sitting there at the dining-room table and opening up an envelope in which that little boy had put his birthday money and a nice note, had me in tears. It also had me in awe. When I was that age, I never would have thought of giving up my birthday money for anyone! That such great spirits lived in our world made us realize that what we were doing was the right thing. We wanted those orphans to have a chance to be like Brit, but also to be like those people who selflessly gave us more than dollars—they gave us hope.

So much of this was a blur at the beginning, but the rules governing not-for-profit organizations required us to keep books. Now, almost three years removed from the tragedy, I have to go back and review them to tell you that we received our first donation on January 26, 2010. By the time we received confirmation that Brit was gone, we had a total of $9,435.97 in the account. Our request for donations in lieu of flowers had an amazing impact on people. By the end of March that first year, we reached

the $100,000 mark. In April alone of that year, we took in an-
other $22,000 plus. We were still so busy trying to figure out
how to go about meeting all the requirements and regulations,
that we hadn't even started formal fund-raising. All of this was
the result of people opening their hearts and bank accounts to
us. We were humbled and enormously grateful.

Brit's high school sent us a check. The funeral home that
provided her burial services, the place where we frequently purchase furniture, friends, family, the colleges where Brit's friends
went to school, all contributed. How was this possible?

The only answer we could up with was a simple one: Brit.
She touched so many lives, and now people wanted to see her
legacy come to life. Seeing these funds grow was still more than
slightly uncomfortable for me. We never liked the spotlight, and
we were clearly on the minds of a lot of people. Making our first
public appearance after Brit's funeral was going to be hard. At
first, we didn't want to go, but we knew we had to out of respect
for those who wanted to help us.

Brit's high school, Wachusett, held a pasta dinner every
year as fund-raiser. In 2010, they decided the money they collected would go to Be Like Brit. Len and I showed up, and it
was hard to be back in the place where Brit had spent so much
of her time. We don't like being fussed over, so being the center of attention at the dinner wasn't easy. I would rather have
been serving pasta at home to those folks than being served, so
that's what we did—we served everyone. Acting as servers allowed us to say hi to everyone and thank them, yet keep us at
a distance so we didn't have to talk too much. All the people
there were connected to Brit in some way, and it was our first
time seeing people face to face. It was extremely difficult, yet
comforting knowing they cared enough for Brit to come. The
kids from Best Buddies and the Distributive Education Clubs
of America (DECA) worked with the National Honor Society
(NHS), which coordinated the event. We got a laugh about the
NHS being involved because that was one group Brit never fit

into—although we were really proud that she made the honor roll her last two years of high school!

The kids and the organizations' sponsors were wonderful, and the turnout was amazing. Receiving a check later for $6,000 had us all choked up.

I can't say it got any easier emotionally for Len; but I got a lot of comfort being out there and hearing from other people. Whatever pain I might have felt, I had to put aside my feelings and recognize that these wonderful people so wanted to help us and Brit's vision of her future. In April, we attended a local Red Cross breakfast and learned they were establishing an International Humanitarian Award that they were going to name after Brit.

It seemed as if every day something out of the blue happened to remind us that our mission had become other people's mission as well. We wanted to have a fund-raiser in Maine because Brit LOVED Maine, and she had a lot of great friends there.

Our friends, Mike and Sally, said they would have one and organized a Beach Bike Ride along the coast. They secured sponsors, and fifty riders participated and raised $8,000 for us. We attended and were touched by the generosity of the cyclists who were essentially strangers to us before. They held the event again in 2011, and raised another $11,000 and again in 2012, adding another $11,000.

Even more amazing was that the country was in the middle of a long and difficult recession. We knew people were losing jobs, taking pay cuts or receiving no raises, enduring foreclosures on their homes—but still the money kept coming in. Something about our story, Brit's loss and her desire to make a difference, had struck a chord with people. By the end of 2010, we'd received nearly $300,000. And to that point, we'd done no real fund-raising. This was a lesson in "ask and you shall receive," a validation of the words that Father John Madden had spoken to Len and me before our daughter's funeral, "Brit cannot die in vain."

LEN

For the longest time, from the minute we knew Brit wasn't coming back alive from Haiti, Cherylann and I were dedicated to making certain that whatever fears Father Madden had wouldn't be made real. Every parent wants to provide for their child, wants to do everything in their power to make their kids' hopes, dreams, and wishes come true. When Brit sent that text to us, telling us about how she saw a new path for her future opening up, in a very real way she was providing us with a blueprint for herself, and as it turned out for the two of us.

I've been in the building industry for three decades, and I know that a blueprint is only as good as the people who will execute that vision. But you've got to have one to start with. And even though as a builder I also understand that you have to start at the beginning, excavate the earth, and then pour a literal foundation before you can begin to erect walls and floors and a roof, to best tell you the story of our helping to bring Brit's dream into reality, I'm going to skip ahead a bit. I'm a person of faith, and I do believe that one day I will be reunited in heaven with my daughter. I also know that over the years, and it is hard to believe that as I sit here writing this, it has been three of them, that my daughter has been in touch with me. Brit loved to talk and to share, so that's no surprise to me—it's just a different kind of communication.

Losing Brit was hard, obviously, and after those thirty-three days in hell, it wasn't as if the hurting stopped. I know it never will. It will change, but even now out of the blue, I'll hear something, see something, taste something, experience something, and I'll be reminded of my daughter or I'll think, "I'll have to tell Brit about that." The fact that she's not here on Earth with us doesn't mean that I don't talk to her still, and the memories themselves aren't painful, but the fact that she's absent from our lives physically is painful. I can't tell you the number of times we're all sitting around as a family, and we'll be sharing stories, and I'm thinking of saying, "Hey, Brit, tell them about the time . . . ." And that thought goes unexpressed because she's not there to entertain us with one of her renditions of a great adventure.

Our house was loaded with memories. It was like the place was overcrowded with them. You know how it is when you just move in and you have storage boxes and furniture everywhere, and it's hard to move around and you bump into something and hurt yourself? That's how it was those months after we buried our little girl. We had been building a house closer to the boys' school in Hardwick, and we had planned, even before the earthquake, to move there later in 2010. After Brit died, we knew we couldn't stay in our house in Rutland, so we put it up for sale as soon as we could.

All the while we were making those beginning steps with Be Like Brit, we were preparing to move out of the house where she'd spent most of her life. I knew the holidays, especially, were going to be really tough, and being in a new place might make some of that easier for us all. In some ways I was kidding myself, but also having something to do, anything else, was a distraction. We moved into one of the model homes we'd built for the new development, the Highlands of Holden. Cherylann wanted some changes made to the new place, and that was a good distraction as well.

Packing up and moving is never a lot of fun, and of course, that meant going through things once again, catching yourself on some sharp and painful reminders of good times that couldn't be repeated. I procrastinated a bit on some things, so the day the movers were to arrive, I went upstairs to the bedroom closet that Cherylann and I share. I was doing a final sweep of the place, making sure I had gotten everything out. A few misshapen clothes hangers were still on the pole that supported the shelf. I was down on my hands and knees and stood up, clanking my head against those wire things, rattling them, and they sounded like an out-of-tune wind chime. I pushed them aside, and I noticed something on the pole, something wrapped around it, something sparkling in the fluorescent light in that confined space. I unwound a bit of string that was holding the object up there. I took it out into the room, and in the brighter light I could see what I had in my hand: a pair of angel's wings, a few feathers and wire, almost like a piece of jewelry, silvery and glinting.

I'd never seen these things before in my life, and I was stunned. I went to find Cherylann to ask her where they came from, if she had seen them before. She was downstairs in the kitchen doing a final cleanup of the sink. When I asked her, she turned. At first she shook her head, then shrugged her shoulders, and finally she said laughing, "Well, I guess Brit left you a present."

We laughed. That was funny to us because in that same closet where I found those wings, there was a secret compartment built in. A panel could be moved to give us access to the attic. That's where we always hid the kids' Christmas presents.

Sad as it was to be leaving that house, finding those wings made me happy. I really felt Brit's presence, her sending me a message in having me discover those wings. I wasn't sure what the sign was, but I took it as a reminder or as confirmation that we were doing the right thing in choosing to honor her memory and to make a difference in other people's lives through the Be Like Brit orphanage.

Also, my birthday was coming up, and those dates are always a chance to pause and reflect. It didn't take any real deep thinking for me to decide the wings were going to be my good-luck charm. In fact, I carried them with me on every trip I've taken to Haiti since then, more than thirty of them in the past three years, until July 2012 when we were pouring the concrete roof on the building. I'll share that story in a bit. Even when those wings suffered from the wear and tear of being in my pocket while we did all that work, I still felt Brit's presence.

The circumstances under which I found them that late in the process of moving, in that closet that meant so much to her and the boys, meant so much to all of us, was her way of saying that even though we were switching locations, she was going there with us. She wanted us to know that she was on top of things, still looking out for us, keeping an eye out to be sure that this mission we were on stayed on track. We were still very early in the process, and it could be overwhelming to think about the papers that had to be filed to establish the foundation, all the searching and the couple of near misses on properties in Haiti where we hoped to build the orphanage, all the fund-raising efforts, and everything else, and we could have lost sight of what was important. I'm proud to say that with the rarest of exceptions that was the case. We were all different people, and we had some variances in what we thought our agenda should be, but we agreed on that mission statement. I have to give Brit some credit for that.

Some people may say I make too much of these signs, that maybe we place too much emphasis on the symbolism of certain events. One of my catchphrases throughout our journey with Brit's passing and with our efforts to see her dream realized in full has been, "You can't make this stuff up." And I wouldn't report these things if they weren't true. It wasn't me who made the connection that Brit's ordeal, our ordeal in seeing her body be recovered and returned took thirty-three days—how long Jesus walked the Earth. I'm certainly not comparing Brit to our Savior, and maybe those numbers are just sheer coincidence, but they mean something to me.

When you lose a child, you cling to many things, often to bitterness and despair. I believe those wings were meant to symbolize the hope, the faith, that we will all be reunited one day in heaven. Since the earthquake, I've run into a number of people, many of them who professed their faith in God, who have said to me that it must be comforting to know that God had a plan for Brit. In a sense, what some of them have said to me is that God took Brit from us. I don't believe that, not one bit. God didn't kill my daughter and those thousands of other people. That's unfathomable. What happened was a natural disaster, and we all make choices and they have consequences. Just as I can't tell anyone how they should grieve the loss of their child, I can't tell anyone what to believe. All I know is that we've chosen to get up every day and put one foot in front of the other, and we choose to build this memorial to honor her, to fulfill her last wish, to help children in Haiti. That's why I carried those wings with me for so long, to serve as a reminder of what my focus should be.

I also believe that in a way Brit also helped to introduce us to a few other people who became angels in building the orphanage.

Paul Fallon is a senior planner at a very successful Boston design firm that works internationally, TRO Jung Brannen. They were celebrating their hundredth anniversary in 2010, and anybody who can be in business for that long must have been doing some things right. One of those right things they did was give their people, such as Paul Fallon, the freedom to pursue good works for free.

Paul had been involved in a charitable medical group doing work in Haiti. That had begun when he worked as the chief architect designing the two-story medical facility the organization had built. Paul worked with their staff and volunteers to design the clinic, and recently traveled to Haiti to make a site visit of the project, which is under construction as I write this. During his trip he also volunteered at the temporary clinic, running the intake process. Paul told us he specialized in hospital/health-care facilities, and he could bring his more than twenty years experience in designing them to our orphanage project. Among the many projects he worked on are hospitals and clinics in Albany, New York; Gardner, Massachusetts; at Yale University in New Haven, Connecticut; and the Maine Medical Center in Portland. However, credentials can only tell you so much; we needed face time with him to know if he was going to be our guy or not.

The first time I met Paul I liked him. I want my designers and architects to look like brainy people, and that was Paul. He kept his thinning brown hair closely cropped, and that, along with his wire-framed glasses and his Van Dyke beard, gave him a professorial look that inspired confidence. More than just that, his warm smile, firm handshake, and easy laughter let us know that if he was a professor-type, you'd never use the word stuffy to describe him. I initially met him in Gardner—Cherylann had met him before in Haiti and we thanked him for not making us trek into Boston.

"Least I can do. If we're going to do this thing, then there will plenty of time for that. Speaking of which, tell me how I can help," he said.

Cherylann and I made eye contact. We knew the fit was a good one. Paul was a let's-roll-up-our-shirtsleeves kind of guy. It didn't take much more convincing that Paul was going to be our man with the plan. Rather than dictate to us what his design ideas were, he collaborated with us. A few months after our initial meeting in Massachusetts on September 25, 2010, Paul and I stood underneath a mango tree on what was in the process of becoming the foundation's land.

Acquiring the land had been proceeding by fits and starts. I wasn't along on the initial trip because every year we hold a big family reunion for the Gengels, and it was also going to be Richie's fifteenth birthday celebration. So, while I was back home, Cherylann, Bernie, and Jodi were in Haiti visiting orphanages, talking to other members of various charitable organizations, and also visiting the Hotel Montana. Obviously, this was another of those bittersweet moments, but something very, very good came out of it.

Our three-person scouting team, was guided by another one of those angels who came to our aid. Through the same organization that introduced us to Paul Fallon, we also met Lex Edme. A Haitian pastor who tends a flock of nine hundred, he also owns a school of six hundred students. The man is about as charismatic and passionate as they come. I'm told I've got a large personality and I wear my stent-repaired heart on my sleeve. Well, except for the stent part, the same is true of Lex. The guy just doesn't light up every room he walks into, he also lights up the great outdoors in Haiti and elsewhere. Lex was one of the first people to offer his assistance when he heard about what we were doing. Fluent in French, Creole, and English, he was the ideal translator, guide, and broker for us whenever we made our trip to his home country.

As a home builder, I've lived a lot of my life based on schedules and itineraries, and I've been frustrated by how often those man-made plans don't quite work out. I know there's the cliché, "Man plans and God laughs." Well, to me that means he's laughing with pleasure, anticipating how we're going to feel when a surprise turns out to be a really pleasant one. That July, Cherylann and the others were scheduled to make a visit to

Haiti, but an impending hurricane delayed the trip so long that it had to be pushed back another month. As a result, along with some other logistical issues and pure moments of serendipity—which Cherylann will tell you about—she, her sister, Jodi, and Bernie ended up going to see Lex's facility in Grand Goâve.

The day after the earthquake, Brit and the other members of the Journey of Hope group had been scheduled to visit a small fishing village just outside of Grand Goâve. They never made it. We were going to make certain that they did, that Brit would finally complete the journey she began in January 2010. With Lex's help, we were able to secure the purchase of land on a hillside overlooking a bay.

Several weeks later, we were all gathered at our house looking at a computer screen. Using Google Earth, Lex was able to show us the exact property his contacts had identified. On it, we could see a large mango tree. At first I thought that the tree might be an obstacle, making it difficult for us to properly site the building on the plot of land. It was something that we'd have to work around. I wondered briefly if maybe it would be better to be taken down. Lex went on to explain how, essentially, the mango tree plays a similar kind of role in Haitian culture that the apple tree (and its fruit) does in ours. Knowing that it had such symbolic importance, as well as practical importance as a source of nutrients and that it contributes a lot to the Haitian economy as a primary export, we knew we'd have to build around it.

Eventually, that proved to be a very wise choice because we went with our hearts when it came to the building's design. When Paul Fallon and I stood under that very same mango tree, he was discussing some possible designs. While all his ideas sounded good, I stopped him and said, "We're going with Plan B."

He looked puzzled for a moment, but after I explained that we'd decided that the building would be constructed in the shape of the letter B for Britney, he understood. One of the great things about Paul and his design team was that they had no ego invested in this. Eventually, the narrow part of the B, the waist you might call it, would be the entrance to the building, and the mango tree would stand there as a kind of sentry/welcome party.

Cherylann and I had made some other decisions that we all related to Brit and had symbolic importance to us. We wanted the orphanage to house one boy and one girl for each of the thirty-three days that Brit was separated from us following the earthquake, for a total of sixty-six kids. When it came time to decide how large of a building to construct, we had several options, but ultimately Cherylann decided that it need to be nineteen thousand square feet. The nineteen was important because that was Brit's age at the time of the earthquake.

We all try to find meaning, and in some cases we make meaning out of the events that can seem so random, so out of our control. I've heard people say that control is an illusion, but I still believe that we make our choices, and in this case at least, we knew what the consequences were going to be. We were going to be able to help complete Brit's Journey of Hope, we were going to be able to help those poor children of Haiti.

Another one of those angels is someone I've already talked about, and ironically, he's married to a woman named Mercy. Prior to meeting Paul Fallon under that mango tree to discuss our vision for the orphanage, Bernie and I flew into Fort Lauderdale. Colonel Cintron was at the airport to pick us up and then have dinner with us. It had been nine months since the quake. I'd been back to that airport before, and a flood of memories always came back to me. Even then, long after most news organizations had abandoned Haiti for other stories, the Florida media was still actively covering our story. As I walked through the terminal, I saw a news crew and a reporter. I flashed back to that dreadful time when we came to Florida thinking that we were going to meet Brit and that whole plan went south.

I felt a pang of guilt as I walked toward Colonel Cintron. I was feeling pleased to be there, to see my new friend again, to soon be boarding an airliner that would take us to the site of the orphanage—my first time seeing it. Was it too early for me to start enjoying some pleasures? At that point, I didn't have those angel's wings.

The reporter, a younger woman, saw me walking toward

a man wearing a military uniform. She nodded, but her smile said it all. Down in Florida, Colonel Cintron is recognized for what he is—a true American hero. The man oversaw the recovery of sixty-eight bodies, including Brit's, and he and I are forever devoted to one another. The colonel led us out of the airport and to our hotel. Later on, we were going to go to dinner with the colonel and his wife, Mercy, at one of their favorite spots. I suppose I've been looking for signs from above my whole life, but even more so since we lost Brit. Bernie's the one who spotted this one for me, though.

"Hey, Dad. Look at that. On the right."

I saw a sign like an old movie marquee lit with round bulbs, Tropical Acres.

"That's what we're going to be looking for, Bernie."

"No, Dad. You don't understand. We've been here before. Last year. Easter. We were down visiting Brit."

On that trip we'd also seen my good friend from college, Vinnie Pugliese, his wife, Linda, and daughters, Megan and Rachel, who was my goddaughter.

"You're right," I said.

Colonel Cintron smiled as he pulled into the parking lot. "Sometimes coincidences need an assist."

Stepping into Tropical Acres was like going back in time to late 1940s Florida. We'd stumbled across this place—a longtime favorite for steak lovers in South Florida—and thought it was a hoot. For a long time I wondered what it would be like to go back and visit some of the places where we'd all spent time together. I wondered and I worried. But somehow this was okay. Brit loved the place and its cheesy charm. We took a ton of pictures that day, and among them are some of my favorites of Brit all decked out in her best clothes, while in the background it was Wranglers and gingham shirts like out of the Old West.

I could feel Brit's spirit all around the place. Bernie had arranged for Lindsay and Nina to come down for dinner with a few of other of Brit's friends, Harris, Brian, and Victoria. Seeing Brit's friends was like a soothing balm on my nerves. We sat at opposite ends of the long table, the young to the right and the wise oldsters to the left. I sat next to the colonel and Lex, and

Paul sat across from us. I rather enjoyed the grilling that Colonel Cintron gave Lex about how if we were buying this land we had to make sure it had a clear title! The colonel liked Lex, he told me later, and trusted the way he was proposing to do things. He said we were in good hands, and I had to agree.

It was also wonderful to see my new friend again. Who could have imagined that two men from such different backgrounds—the engineer and the builder—would share the bond that Colonel Cintron and I did. Back in late January when the two of us stood near that pile of rubble and ruin that was the Hotel Montana and hugged one another and cried, I don't think either of us could have envisioned this and the other moments we've enjoyed together since.

When it came time to shake his hand and pull him close, I could feel myself choking up a bit—not from sadness but from immeasurable gratitude. He wrapped his hand around the back of my neck and said, "Thank you."

At first this took me aback, but then I realized why he said what he did. He was feeling the same kind of gratitude that I was. We'd all been through a life-changing experience, and we were emerging on the other side better and stronger for having endured it all.

I looked him square in the eye and said, "And you too, my friend."

* * *

The next day, I was glad we could fly right into Port-au-Prince instead of the D.R. like we had in January. With all the relief flights back then and the U.S. military in charge, no commercial flights were going in or out at that time. I was also grateful that the air-conditioning was functioning. Didn't seem to matter what time of year, the hour, or the day, the one thing that never seemed to change about Haiti was the heat and the humidity. Colonel Cintron had arranged for a military escort for us. Lieutenant Pierre was a very solid-looking black man who at first seemed all businesslike.

As we walked toward the luggage area, I had a moment

alone with him. I didn't want Bernie to hear me.

"So, you can tell me honestly. What's the situation like here? I've been reading and hearing about a lot of kidnappings."

He shrugged and said, "Just like any big city. Same thing could go in L.A. or New York." He paused for a second. "Well, I guess I'm not as much as a target as you are, being black and all."

We laughed. "It's kind of hard to blend in here when you're as big and pasty as I am," I said.

"So true. So true."

It felt so good to be laughing in a place that held so many negative associations for me.

It seemed as if Colonel Cintron wasn't the only one who wanted to ensure our safety. As we were making our way through customs, another man joined our group.

"Len, this is Mr. Big," Lex said.

I held my hand out to the short but heavy guy.

"I'm very serious, Len." Lex went on, "In the future if I am not here with you, Mr. Big will escort you to Grand Goâve. You can trust him."

Mr. Big nodded solemnly and extended his hand. I shook it and ducked into the car, thinking about, and grateful for, all the new Mr. Big's in my life and the role they were going to continue to play throughout the construction of the orphanage.

CHERYLANN

I was committed to joining forces with Len to do this good thing. I knew that only Len, only a father as deeply committed to his kids as he is, would take on this task of making sure his daughter's last wish came true. Len has the ability to focus and to take on enormous challenges, and he'd done that all his life. I couldn't really say this to him, but I was concerned about one thing. Building the orphanage in Haiti, running the foundation, keeping the business running, all would take up an enormous amount of his time and energy. His health issues aside, I was afraid what effect Len's absence would have on the boys. I don't mean just his trips to Haiti and his absence, but how present he would be in the lives of his sons. I knew he was going to make every effort he could to be there for Richie and Bernie, but when you've been married to someone in construction as long as I have, you know that it can be a twenty-four seven deal when a major project is under way.

Our family members took on different tasks during the creation of Be Like Brit (BLB). Len was a builder, so his role was obvious. Bernie's was somewhat evolutionary. He had done so much during those horrific days after the earthquake using the internet and social media to get and give information. He was always a computer kid, so he fell into the role of the technical person for BLB. Len and I had no experience whatsoever with that kind of thing and really had no idea what to do—but we knew it was important to spread the word that way.

When Len wanted something done on Facebook or when we started talking about a web page, he'd grab Bernie and have him do it. The ever-loyal son, Bernie was always eager to please Len and would do anything to help him and our foundation. Although he had no training in website development and design, he built BeLikeBrit.org.

As time passed, he further developed our virtual site while Len was involved in the early planning stages of the physical site location.

I checked in with Bernie regularly to see how he was doing, both on the virtual end of things and—more important— emotionally.

He told me that he missed Brit, of course, and that he knew his life wasn't ever going to be the same, but it was helpful that he had her friends to talk with. Even though not all of them had been in Haiti with her, some, like Lindsay and P.J., had. The one thing they'd all had in common was their experience of loss. Also, they could talk about real Britney and tell real

Brit stories and laugh. This gave them some kind of emotional intimacy and connection they'd not shared before. I was grateful that Bernie had other people he could go to, people closer to his own age, and not just me.

I also liked the idea that he was developing a life outside of the house and his family. While he had started doing this even before the earthquake, I wanted to make sure that Brit's tragic death did not stop him from experiencing life. Bernie was now eighteen, and by that age, Brit had really experienced the world, traveling to Italy and Greece. That girl lived every moment of her time on Earth, and I wanted that same thing for Bernie. That he chose to spend his time in Haiti and not on some beach looking out over the Aegean Sea was his decision, not because anyone made him go.

Richie didn't even have his driver's license when Brit died. Not that that's the only marker of a kid's maturity, but you get the idea. His relationship with his big sister, as I've pointed out, was different than his brother's was with Brit. He so looked up to her, and he's so much more like Len in one obvious way: Richie wears his heart on his sleeve, and he feels things deeply. I had to keep a close eye on him, and my check-ins with him were more frequent, more heartfelt, and more heartbreaking. There was a hole torn in his life that nothing could fill.

I especially hurt for him when Brit's funeral was over. His school was on a weeklong semester break, so he was around the house all the next week—alone with Len and me since Bernie had gone back to school already. When Richie got home after his first day back at Eagle Hill School, I asked him how it went. I was hoping that school, getting back into a routine, being out of the house with all the memories of Brit everywhere, would help him to begin healing. Instead, Richie broke down and cried.

"They forgot that my sister was dead," he said.

How do you comfort your child in that situation? I knew I wanted the boys to realize that life went on even after your sister died. I knew that those kids at school meant nothing malicious about not bringing up Brit to him; they were probably being careful not to hurt Richie and wound up doing it anyway. Even adults find it hard to know what to say, so they say the wrong thing, or avoid you so they don't have to say anything. That's how life is, I guess, and you don't want your kids to have to learn those hard lessons too soon. All I could do was hold Richie and let him know things would get better eventually—it would take a very long time—but no matter what, Brit wasn't going to be forgotten. Now we all had to go on with our lives for her as much as for us. He knew his sister well enough to comprehend that if the situation was different, Brit would have been telling him to just forget about it—don't let other people get to you. Go out and have some fun.

I wondered if Richie would ever be able to have fun again. I hoped so.

I had the same worries about Len. He was so sad so much of the time. I knew that the planning for the orphanage was his therapy; it was too painful for him to be at home.

In ways very real and surreal, our lives were being focused and relocated to a foreign country—from the wealthiest country in the world to the most impoverished in the Western hemisphere—and without the bright light of Brit's presence among us. Just how dark and difficult those days might be, I had no way of knowing. I was continuing the practice we had developed during those thirty-three days of hell: hope for the best and prepare for the worst.

* * *

Len is a big believer in signs and following your intuition. The way we found the site for BLB definitely would fall into the category of seemingly disconnected events falling strategically into place.

Through the Red Cross in Massachusetts, we had met a couple with land in Les Cayes, Haiti, who had been trying to build a medical clinic there for six years. Purchasing property there is tricky—you really need a Haitian national there, someone trustworthy, to represent you and your best interests. This couple used Lex Edme, the pastor Len talked about, so we scheduled a scouting trip with him to go down to Haiti and look for land. Les Cayes was on the ocean in southwestern Haiti and sounded like the perfect place for the orphanage. However, it was quite a distance from Port-au-Prince on roads that were very difficult to drive, and would take several hours. It was suggested we take a helicopter or a small plane, which was a rather scary thought.

We had our scouting group set and were going to leave in late June, but our trip was cancelled at the last minute because of an impending hurricane. One day turned into two or three, and then we finally had to wait another month.

Len was not able to go on the rescheduled trip, so I was going with Jodi, Bernie, Lex, Paul, and Andy. Because of the distance from Port-au-Prince to Les Cayes, we were going to stay one night at a hotel in Lex and Renee's town (their place had crumbled in the earthquake), which was about halfway there.

The evening before I was leaving for Haiti I was speaking with Gary Brozek, who helped us write this book, and he wanted me to fill him in on some details.

"Where were Brit and her group supposed to go the day after the earthquake?" he asked.

I told him I had no idea but that I still had her itinerary of the trip and would get right back to him. I sorted through all the papers and found the itinerary and where was she supposed to go: a fishing village in a town called Grand Goâve.

As fate would have it, Lex and Renee's home was in . . . Grand Goâve—the very place Brit was supposed to have gone. In Haiti, Bernie got to spend time with Lex and really took to him. He also got to meet some of the kids who worked as missionaries for his organization. They told Bernie about land owned by another orphanage high up on a hillside, somewhat near Lex's Mission of Hope church and school. They said it had spectacular views of the ocean and the mountains and went on about how peaceful it was up there.

The next day we visited Les Cayes. As beautiful as the land was, it was very far from the airport, and we knew we would be having a lot of people coming to our place. I realized it would take too long to get there.

When we got home I told Len that Les Cayes just wouldn't work for us. I was disappointed but ready to go back to the drawing board—knowing that it's better to be cautious and spend extra time now than to be hasty and regret a bad decision forever.

Bernie could not stop talking about Lex, how much he liked him, and how much he liked Grand Goâve. He told us about his conversation with Lex's missionaries and their description of this beautiful piece of property up the mountain. "This is where we should build," Bernie kept telling us. He was persistent, like a bulldog with a bone. The property he talked about, however, was owned by another established orphanage and was not for sale.

The more Bernie talked about it, though, the more we realized that Grand Goâve was the place we needed to be. It just seemed fitting, given that Brit was supposed to have gone there, and she loved the ocean. It's not like the whole hillside was developed and there was no buildable land. Surely there was something similar to what the kids had been so taken with that was for sale.

We had a good idea of what we wanted. The vista from the Hotel Montana, where Brit spent her final days on Earth, was spectacular and peaceful. Far above the mayhem of Port-au-Prince, there was none of the typical noise from the city—just the trees rustling and the birds singing with a breathtaking view of the ocean and the surrounding mountains. We envisioned that same thing for Be Like Brit, so that the children we would nurture there would know that same feeling of tranquility.

A few weeks later in August, Lex and Renee came to our

house, and Len asked him to find us land in Grand Goâve like the property of the Hotel Montana. Whether it be the hand of fate or Brit, I was grateful for the events that led us to find the perfect home of BLB.

LEN

I know it's a cliché to say that your heart is broken, but in my case that's literally true. In 2001, I had two stents put in my heart because of a congenital defect. I was forty-one years old, and Cherylann and I were really worried. My father had died of a heart attack in 1989 when he was sixty-five years old. Fortunately, I'd never had a heart attack, but the congenital artery disease that I'm prone to has been a bit of a butt-kicker, to put it mildly. In 2005, I underwent angioplasties, and except for having a recall notice on my stents—I had to go back in the operating room having them bored out like you would a cylinder head in a car's engine—and having an artery completely blow out while on the table, things had been pretty stable for a while. As a result of that little misadventure, I have five stents in my heart. I'm also on eight medications for various heart and circulatory issues, but I'm still up and kicking, holding up my end of the bargain I've made with Cherylann. She's known the score for a while, and she always thought she'd be burying me long before she passed. Neither of us figured we'd ever be putting one of our kids in the ground. So, whatever butt-kicking I'd been receiving because of my health issues was nothing compared to what Cherylann has gone through. It's easy being the unhealthy one. I've told Cherylann time and again, I wouldn't trade places with her. I've also promised her that I won't mess around with any of this, and at the first sign of trouble, I'd drop the big tough-guy thing and ask for help.

So, on the night of August 13, shortly after Cherylann had returned from Haiti, I'd had a really nice visit with P.J. and Lindsay (those Lynn U. kids have become like our own). Later I went to bed and woke up feeling like someone was stabbing me in the chest. I wasn't going to mess around. This wasn't just my usual anxiety and tension about Brit's death; this was clearly something else. I nudged Cherylann awake and said, "Get me an ambulance. It's like somebody's using a pick on my chest."

Even though the EMTs tried to tell me otherwise (and in defiance of my drop-the-tough-guy act promise) I insisted on walking down the stairs and into the ambulance that Cherylann had called. My blood pressure was through the roof at 202/104. Admittedly, under the best of circumstances, I carry a bit of stress with me, and the past seven months I had been acting like a backhoe operator digging at the same trench of my habit. I got some meds in the ambulance, and that immediately brought down my pressure. I was a little ticked off that only two months after having my heart monitor removed, here I was again, having more troubles.

After being admitted, I saw my backup cardiologist, and he agreed that a heart catherization was in order. By four o'clock on the 14th, I was under. My right ventricle was 100 percent blocked again! The good news is that the heart muscle itself is in great shape, and I'm now the proud owner of two new stents. Seven better be my lucky number. The next day, I woke up feeling good, and by the afternoon was feeling great. Who knew how good free-flowing oxygenated blood could be!

That night, Bernie and Richie were in the room while Cherylann went for a cup of coffee. I knew they had been through their share of the crap the past few months, and I told them how proud I was of how they'd been dealing with it all.

Richie tugged out his earpieces and offered me his iPod. "Some good stuff on there. It'll help you sleep if nothing else."

I thanked him and set the music player on the nightstand. Later that night, I woke up and couldn't fall back to sleep. I started to listen to Richie's music. Some, I fast-forwarded through, but one song was so beautiful that I had to keep listening. I flipped on the light so I could see who the group was and the title of the song. Mumford & Sons could have been the name of a butcher shop or a florist, but the refrain of their song "Timshel" really got to me.

The song was about someone on death's doorstep, and the refrain was, "You are not alone in this. As brothers we will stand, and we will hold your hand."

And it ended with, "I will move mountains for you."

As somber as the song could have seemed, I found it very moving, and even though I had no idea what the hell a Timshel could be, it seemed to put my mind at ease. The next day I was feeling even better and was eager to get back home.

I did feel bad about a couple of things. We had to postpone a trip to Philly and to California. On the other hand, all of this was actually good news for my heart. As I said to Cherylann when I came out of the anesthesia fog, "I just got another tune-up, that's all. I'm good to go for at least another five years. Did the doc give you any kind of warranty information?"

Cherylann rolled her eyes. "You'd think they could implant a better sense of humor in you."

Gotta' love that woman.

I also knew I was going to have to do some resting up. We were still on the hunt for property in Haiti. Though the idea was for me to slow down a bit and take it easier, that was nearly impossible—we had too much work to do.

Rebuilding Our Lives and Remembering Brit

"Oh, do you know who I am?"

—Brit

Len

In the two years since we began building Brit's orphanage, people have asked me over and over why take on such a huge undertaking? I just felt we had a responsibility as parents to honor and respect our children. Our lives have changed in ways I never could have imagined in the years since Brit passed, and I have to say I've undergone some changes personally. It wasn't like I was completely unprepared to make changes in how I operated, but Brit not being with us put them in a different light.

I came from humble beginnings and over time built C&S Builders into a company where constructing twenty houses a year was about par for the course. With that came a lot of hours of hard work and some real rewards and, I'm not ashamed to say, some of them financial. I was fortunate to have people who mentored me, Carla among them, who I'm sorry to say died in 2011. There were people in my life who helped give me a leg up, so I've tried to do the same thing for others. I've been asked to speak to various groups formally, and I've spoken informally to friends and others at various times. I've had the opportunity to really think about what it means to have a career, at least in my case, in the home-building industry.

As I see it, your career breaks down into three phases. In the first phase, you're learning. I can't catalog for you every mistake I made, but there were a lot of them, and I learned from each one. Growing pains and having your own business go hand in hand. In phase two, you enter into the earning portion. You take those lessons learned earlier and apply them, don't repeat the same mistakes, and reap the benefits of them. That's an exciting and rewarding time in anyone's life. I know that being able to provide for my immediate family, to get to the point where we had three homes in three states, really made me feel good. I'm not alone in thinking this way, and a lot of people I've talked to have said that as you enter the third phase of your life, what I call return, those rewards change. By return, I mean you begin to focus more of your efforts on giving back to your community, to the world at large in whatever ways you see fit. I don't mean to imply that those first two phases are completely selfish times. It's just that the balance or the proportion changes.

As we've mentioned, as a family we've stressed the importance of contributing to your community. We haven't just paid lip service to this but have walked the walk and talked the talk. Whether it was through our church and some of the charitable functions we've run or contributed to, or my serving as president of our local Habitat for Humanity board, we've done what we could to help out. Now, with our mission clear—to build and to run this orphanage—we've had to make some changes to adjust the balance, to put an even greater emphasis on the return portion of our lives. Believe me, that hasn't been easy, and we've had to make some sacrifices to see this job through to the end. I use the word job on purpose. At first, I approached the mission to complete Brit's journey in much the same way I would as I did when running C&S. Now that I'm in the process of slowly selling off, piece by piece, that machine I'd invested lots of blood, sweat, and tears in, I realize a few things.

First, I'm back in the learning phase of the cycle again. By leaving behind the world of residential construction in the U.S. for the most part, I'm kind of starting over. Even so, in some ways I'm just relocating—focusing my building efforts in a different country, one that I never would have expected to be concentrating my efforts, but one that I've grown to love.

One moment in particular strikes me as a lesson that Haiti and its people taught me.

As a builder, you're constantly facing challenges. Every day in my work life, I had to put out at least a fire or two—deal with an emergency of some kind or another. I thought that would prepare me well for what we faced in Haiti. It did, but not completely. One of the first challenges we faced in getting the site prepared for excavation was that there was no road that led to it. That meant that before we could even begin, we had to put one in. Now, when you develop a subdivision, you have to put in roads. We understood that. One of the problems that Haiti has had in rebuilding after the earthquake was that what little construction equipment existed had been lost or damaged. Building supplies, tools, and nearly everything else that goes into putting up a structure were also in short supply or couldn't be had at all.

For most Americans, a Home Depot or other building supply place is within easy driving distance of their residence. Not so in a third-world country. Haiti's efforts to rebuild itself are hampered by more than just the poverty that exists there. While that is the root cause of much of its struggles, that lack of funds means that the kinds of businesses that we take for granted don't really exist there. You also have to have a work around things to solve your problems. How do you work around an entire country?

Well, where there's a will, there's a way, right? For me, that way involved gathering supplies, tools, and machinery, loading them into a box truck, and sending them there in advance of our intended date to begin establishing a road to the site. We had planned on being there in mid December of 2010, but before we were scheduled to leave, the U.S. State Department issued this advisory bulletin:

December 9, 2010

The Department of State warns U.S. citizens of the risks of traveling to Haiti and recommends against non-essential travel. This notice replaces the Travel Warning dated June 24, 2010 to reflect continued high crime, the cholera outbreak, frequent disturbances in Port-au-Prince and in provincial cities, and limited police protection and access to medical care.

The Department of State strongly urges U.S. citizens to avoid non-essential travel to Haiti. The level of violent crime in Port-au-Prince, including murder and kidnapping, remains high, and Haitian authorities have limited capacity to deter or investigate such acts or prosecute perpetrators. While most kidnappings are financially motivated, some kidnapping victims have been physically abused, sexually assaulted, shot and even killed. No one is immune from kidnapping, regardless of one's occupation, nationality, race, gender, or age.

In a number of cases this year, travelers arriving in Port-au-Prince on flights from the United States were attacked and robbed a short while after departing the airport. At least two U.S. citizens were shot and killed in such incidents. Police believe criminals may be targeting travelers arriving on flights from the United States, following them, and attacking them once they are out of the area. Travelers are advised to use extra caution in arranging transportation from the airport.

We couldn't let that dire warning keep us from going, but we had to be wary and take as many precautions as possible. Bernie and I, and my nephew, Ross, who had just finished an internship with Senator Scott Brown, were the Americans scheduled to go—the Anglo Americans, I should say. What was going to help us was the fact that we had a number of Haitians on our team who we hoped would be able to protect us, assure our safe passage from the airport to the site, etc.

One of the Haitian-Americans who joined our team was a man by the name of Kervince (Gama) Parayson. Gama grew up in Léogâne, the next town over from Grand Goâve, and is well connected to the area. He has lived in Athol, Massachusetts, (he married a local girl, an LPN named Angela, who we just love) for the past five years and became an American citizen just before our re-scheduled departure date. Gama is the nephew of Lex and Renee Edme who serve as our representatives (NGO) in Haiti. Gama lived and worked at Mission of Hope for six years prior to going to the U.S.—that's where he met Angela! The BLB Board met with Gama and voted unanimously to hire him, and he accepted the offer made to him and will live/work in Haiti as our Clerk of the Works for the next two years. I never realized that Gama would become Mr. Incredible to our mission

One of the great joys of this construction experience was getting to know so many people in Haiti and also being able to hire them. At the height of the work, we were employing as many as one hundred twenty people to do all different tasks. Almost without exception, the people we hired and most of the others we came in direct contact with were delightful. Brit's assessment that the people in Haiti had so little but seemed so happy rang true; this has resonated with me on every trip into Haiti. What the State Department warned us about was also true. Port-au-Prince, in particular, was a danger zone, and traveling from the airport to Grand Goâve was its own version on some trips of our thirty-three days of hell. That it was actually thirty-four and a half miles didn't matter. Even with Lex as our guide and a Port-au-Prince Policeman as needed, I saw things and felt emotions I never thought I'd experience.

Prior to Christmas 2010, though, none of that mattered. Whether it was that I was so relieved to finally be doing something to make Brit's dream come true or the novelty of traveling to Haiti was still fresh, I'm not sure. But I do know that when we arrived in Haiti on December 24, I was certainly full of the Christmas spirit. The box truck had arrived and we came bearing gifts for thirty-two of the orphans from the Mission of Hope. The warm reception we received, the hospitality that Lex provided, our Christmas dinner the next day under the choukun—a type of tiki hut—with ham, Haitian turkey, mashed potatoes, and all the fixings was absolutely wonderful. The Edme's gave us a piece of home!

That didn't mean there weren't some dangers. The two-thousand-pound generator that we were unloading got away from the crew. Only a tree—and God—prevented it from rolling over on one of the men, named John. We were able to set up the site with latrines, a kind of warehouse, and a construction center in a trailer where Gama was to work. Soil testing and preliminary site work, clearing and leveling the land, were on the schedule. Though I was in a completely foreign environment, I was in a familiar place—feeling that buzz of joy and anticipation I felt whenever we began a project. At times I couldn't believe that I was there in Haiti, using the money that so many people so generously had donated. This thing was really happening!

The contrast between what we'd been warned about and our reality was hard to fathom in those first few days. I didn't speak their language, French or Creole, and Gama often served as my interpreter, but I felt an immediate bond with the new people I was meeting. We were coming up on the first anniversary of the earthquake and Brit's death. I'm generally not a very patient man, but even I was amazed that in less than a year we'd gotten to this point. There were times when I thought that we'd never get the project going. During that first construction trip, I was reminded immediately that I shouldn't and couldn't expect everything to go smoothly. Gama gave me great words of advice: "Leo, not to worry, the first week is the toughest, then you'll get use to the Haitian way of doing things!"

Not only had I been given a new name, "Leo," I'd been given a new perspective on things. Even though Brit's words had foreshadowed how wonderful the attitude of the Haitian people is, seeing it up close and personal on the more than thirty trips I've taken there through the fall of 2012, has given me enormous insight, great pleasure, and a real reason to hope that our efforts won't be in vain.

When Bernie and I were in Haiti in September 2010, that learning cycle took on a new meaning. Not only would I have to adjust my expectations about the how-to aspect of the construction, in a way I had to readjust my vision of the "who for" of this project. The last night that we were there, after seeing the location of the property, how beautiful it was, and how challenging it was going to be to build what eventually became Brit's driveway just to have access to the site, we were guests at a gathering that Lex was hosting to honor twenty-six of his students who had passed a national qualifying academic test.

One of the ways to reward them, Lex and I decided, was to present them with a Be Like Brit T-shirt. It doesn't sound like much, but given who these kids are and the kind of poverty that ravages that country, this was not an insignificant gift. As Brit had let us know, these people have so little, and this was a real reminder of that sad reality. The evening's activities were conducted in Creole. Like all languages of this type, it is a mix of a variety of languages but is mostly based on French. I don't speak French, so the language is even more impenetrable to me. So, Bernie and I had that odd experience of being in a foreign country and participating in an event during which we were mostly lost.

I stood on that stage and looked out at this assembled group of a hundred or so people. Bernie and I were up there so that we could shake each recipient's hand and present him or her with the T-shirt. At one point, I heard the word, Montana, and I looked at Lex and he was looking back at me. I figured out he was talking about me, and I also heard him use Brit's name a few times. He was telling the entire story and talking about how heartbroken we were. The funny thing is, the people in the audience just sat there in silence, looking completely unaffected by this.

At this early stage—and this hasn't changed all that much since—people who recognized us back home, especially in Florida and Massachusetts, would come up to us and offer their heartfelt condolences. I remember the first day that I went back to work, and I wanted it to be as normal as possible. A car seemed to be following me, and when I stopped in the development and got out of my truck at one of the building sites, a man got out of that car and followed me. He looked a little out of it, and my first reaction was to be worried, but then he stopped a few feet from me and said, "Mr. Gengel, you don't know me." At that point, he started to openly cry. He leaned over a bit and I was afraid he was going to fall, so I let him put his hand on my arm to steady himself. He went on to talk about how he'd followed our journey and how his heart was broken, knowing about our terrible loss. He saw me in the truck, and he just had to let me know how he felt.

In the days before that ceremony and certainly in the days and years after, Haitian people have expressed their sympathy in powerful ways. So what was it about that night that was so different? I have to admit that at first I was puzzled. I mean, Lex was telling these people some of the details of our gut-wrenching ordeal, and they essentially sat there stone-faced. I could have been angry, but I did something that I hadn't done for a while. I put myself in someone else's shoes. I'd been so focused for so long on what I'd lost, how I was hurting, what I had to do to complete Brit's mission, and how we had to find the right site for this orphanage, that I lost sight of something else. As I stood there, I could almost feel a physical change in me. Ironically, given what I realized, I felt a bit of the burden lifting.

The people had no expression of emotion not because they felt nothing, but because they all had experienced the same tragedy. All of those people in the audience had suffered a loss, many of them far greater than mine. Every one of them had lost at least one family member. Every one of them had been affected by the earthquake. Their home could very well have been destroyed, and they might be sleeping in a tent at a refugee camp. In that moment, I realized that building this orphanage was about more than just completing Brit's journey;

it was about returning something to these people who'd had their lives torn apart. We had something in common, and instead of feeling sympathy for them, I felt empathy. Our mission arrived at a pivotal point, and I knew then that this was about more than honoring Brit's last wish; it was something much, much larger than even that.

That lesson was reinforced that night when a man approached me afterward and offered his thanks for what we were planning to do. In halting English, he told me his story, how he'd lost his wife and three children, and now he was alone but not alone. He had many brothers and sisters in sorrow, and I realized after he said those words that this orphanage we planned to build would be a refuge for so many more people than just those sixty-six kids.

CHERYLANN

As I said, from the beginning Len and I agreed we would not judge each other on how we grieved and on how we would handle things. This included how we chose to deal with the holidays. Len had dreaded the end-of-the-year holidays from day one—Christmas, New Year's, Brit's birthday, and what wasn't a holiday at all but still a new marker in our lives—the anniversary of the earthquake. The closer we got to December, the more anxious Len became. He was restless and certainly more on edge. That was how Len felt, and I couldn't disagree with what he was feeling. I tried to talk with him about the rational approach to this, but I knew deep in my heart that I could help him understand things intellectually—that life goes on, that he should still find enjoyment in it, and all the rest—but I couldn't ever, and didn't want to, get him to feel differently than what he was experiencing.

Len made it clear to me and other family members that he couldn't deal with celebrations; for him they would be too much of a reminder of Brit's absence from our lives. That went for birthdays, weddings, and everything else. We could just count him out.

I also knew this wasn't just about what Len and I felt. I worried about what I was saying to my boys if we didn't at least give them the option of celebrating. "We only celebrated the holidays because Brit was alive . . . sorry you don't get any more holidays." I want grandchildren some day, and what would I say to them? "Sorry, no celebrating. Your aunt died years ago, and it was really all about her."

So, when Len made the decision to go to Haiti to work on the orphanage at the holidays in 2010 and early 2011, and Bernie followed him because he didn't want his dad to be alone, I fully supported their choice. I felt the same way about Richie's choice not to go. Of course, I missed them, but I also knew the pain that my husband was in, and I understood he wanted to be anywhere but home. Having something to focus on, some task to get done, was therapeutic for Len. The closer it got to Christmas, the more difficult it got for Len— memories of Brit and Christmas popped up around every corner. We had an old pick-up truck that Brit drove. She had bought a red fuzzy nose that you attach to the grill and antlers that you slide on the windows for it, so it looks like your car is Rudolph the Red-Nosed Reindeer. It was funny to see that Rudolph-mobile on the road. We still had the truck, and the memory of the way it was dressed up at the holidays the year before was funny but excruciatingly sad. We never used those attachments again.

I looked at the situation like this. If you have a kid who was so into the holidays that she'd even decorate a rust bucket like that so it would help spread Christmas cheer, then maybe I owed it to her memory to keep some of her spirit alive here while Len and Bernie did the same in Haiti.

We always had Christmas Eve at our house for the entire family. We would visit Carla, the woman who started Len in business, at 3:30 p.m. then go to the 4:15 Mass at St. John's then come back to have dinner and open presents. It was about being together. Brit had a large presence during the holidays. It was about family and, yes, presents but really about the memories—making cookies, buying gifts. Brit was in charge of wrapping all the presents. The scene is still so fresh in my mind. We'd have Mariah Carey singing, "All I want for Christmas is you . . ." in the background. We'd sing, dance and just laugh and laugh, grateful and giggling at the same time.

I let Richie make the call: If he wanted Christmas Eve at our house, I would have it again; if it was too much for him then I wouldn't. He said he definitely wanted it at our house. To explain why, he told me that Brit would have said B.S. if we didn't! He was right about that, but I also told him that we didn't have to do it because Brit would have wanted us to, but because he wanted it that way himself. He told me that he did. I'd been struggling all along with the idea of normal. I wanted things to feel the same as they had before, but I knew that they could never be that way again. I also didn't want Brit's passing to feel "normal" either, like it was something that we'd moved beyond already.

Strange as it may seem given both our families, having to deal with something feeling off and unfamiliar and odd was going to be our task. Nothing about this Christmas would be the same as before. Len and Bernie would be working in Haiti instead of celebrating at home; Richie and I would be home going through the motions of Christmas, surrounded by the familiar, but feeling like we were in a foreign land—with no Len, no Bernie, no Brit. There were memories in every ornament, in every Christmas carol, in every seemingly insignificant holiday tradition. In some ways they were comforting, but at the same time they underscored how much we had lost. Sometimes I would feel okay, like I had the strength to get through these few weeks on the calendar; then a wave of grief would wash over me and drag me under, making me wonder if I could ever enjoy the holidays again.

I would do what I needed to do, but my focus was on Richie. I had to make sure he was doing what he really wanted to do and not what he thought he had to do. I told him that even if he changed his mind at 4:00 p.m. Christmas Eve, we would understand; I wanted him to know he had options. We did not go see Carla that year, but we did go to the 4:15 Mass, and I have to tell you it was extremely emotional. I didn't know how I was going to get through it.

Len's told you this story, but it bears repeating. The Christmas before was when Father Madden had thanked Britney in the church bulletin for all that she did to help with the gifts for the less fortunate. She ran up to him in front of everyone after Mass started with that HUGE smile of hers and hugged him and said thanks!

He did it because he had thanked Bernie and Richie for helping and had forgotten Brit's name a few weeks before. She wasn't going to let him forget about his oversight. When he apologized, she said, "Oh, do you know who I am?"

Father Madden gave it right back to her, "So, who are you again?" It was hysterical. He said, "How can I make it up to you?"

With a straight face, Brit said, "Oh, just my picture next to Jesus on the altar and put a note in the bulletin."

So as I sat there I remembered all of that; I was frozen. I was a little out of sorts anyway. We always sit on the left center in the third row from the back. Don't ask me why, but like most people we're creatures of habit, and we had fallen into that pattern a long time ago. The comfort of that spot was something I'd come to count on in the times since Brit died and we'd attended Mass. I knew that for Christmas Eve we needed to get there extra early. Well, we were late (for us), and I still wanted to sit in the back in our usual spot. I also wanted an end seat in case things were too tough so I wouldn't have to crawl all over a bunch of people to get out. Our usual seats were taken, so Richie and I found an end seat on the far left. I never sat there before. So Mass started and I tried to concentrate the best I could on why we were really there.

Just after the "Lord Have Mercy" part and the "Glory to God," Richie nudged me and said, "Mom, look." He nodded toward the main altar at the front of the church. And there it was: a picture of Brit next to Jesus in the front of the church for all to see. Even though I know she is always with me, I really felt like she was there at Mass.

Father Madden has kept her picture there ever since, so now every Sunday I go to Mass with Brit! I later learned that Len had asked Father Madden to do that as a gift to all of us, and he made it possible. What a present! I also was pleased and embarrassed by how many other people reached out to us. Before Mass, during Mass (while exchanging greetings of peace), after Mass, so many people wished us a Merry Christmas with an extra-long look into my eyes. I knew they were saying, "I know it's your first Christmas without Brit." That was so kind of them, but I also knew that many of them had their own painful memories, ones less public than ours, but certainly no less meaningful in their lives.

I can't say that Brit's absence in our lives made the meaning of the season more clear, but without what Len and Father Madden had done, without our fellow parishioners going out of their way to let us know they hadn't forgotten, the void could have expanded but didn't.

We all came back to my house and had dinner. Everyone was hurting and unsure if they should be happy; should they enjoy the night? It was awkward at first, but we managed as best we could. I think everyone was looking at me to take the lead and to set the tone. I decided to tell a story about Christmas the year before—about how Brit tried so hard to win her own gift, a Snuggie, in our family Yankee Swap, and in true Brit fashion she got it!—and the ice was broken. We didn't laugh as much as we had in years past, but we did laugh and share stories. I could imagine Brit sitting there at the start, screwing up her face in frustration and saying, "C'mon people, lighten up! It's a party!"

The dinner and the conversation proceeded by fits and

starts. The laughs were sometimes followed by silent pauses, all of us aware of the fact that we wanted to say that we missed the hell out of that girl and wished she were there with us.

The night came and went, and we made it, thank God! Everyone left, and it was just Richie and me. I teased him that he had to go to bed so that Santa would come. It was something we said every year: "Santa can't come until you go to bed and don't get out of bed until 7 a.m.!" I still had the same rules this year, except with Richie I knew he wasn't getting up before 7 a.m. —he likes his sleep too much for that.

I was up early anyway, trying to avoid thinking about being at my house on Christmas without Brit. I did, and then re-did, a few of the dishes from the night before, the things left to soak overnight. I did everything I could to avoid thinking about Len and Bernie in Haiti and their pain in thinking about what this day meant, and the emptiness of Brit not being with us. But I also knew that Len was doing what he needed to do to get through the holidays, and I trusted he would take care of Bernie. My focus was on Richie. I tried not to worry about how he was going to be when he woke up. Would he be so sad that he couldn't open gifts? Would it be too much for him to do this alone? But, of course, in Richie fashion he loved being the center of attention and loved opening gifts—it was all about him. Which I guess he really needed since it hadn't been about him at all for almost a year. It was just the two of us, and we laughed as he opened some gifts, and of course, he loved opening his stocking stuffers.

Actually, all three kids had loved that the most. When they were little, it was cute stuff in there, but as they got older the gifts got smaller and soooo much more expensive—even I wanted to open the stocking gifts!

Finally, the pile of crumpled wrapping paper signaled that we'd made it through our first Christmas morning without Brit. We then went to Jodi's house to open gifts with her, her husband, my goddaughter, Kara, and my mom. We have done that for the past few years, and it was another little bit of normalcy—

but different. My sister-in-law, Joan, has Christmas Day dinner, so after we spent most of the day at Jodi's, we went to Joan's, experiencing more tradition, yet different.

LEN

I've never doubted that we were doing the right thing in choosing to construct and fund an orphanage in Haiti. Despite what Gama told me about getting used to how things are done there, it took a bit more time than I expected. Progress was slower than I'd like, mainly because supplies and equipment in country are limited. In the States, you phone a ready-mix company and ask them to send out X number of yards of concrete on a certain date, and then have that truck come rumbling up to the site with its enormous barrel spinning. This is not possible in Haiti, so we basically had to go back to the old-school ways of doing things. We'd mix the concrete on-site, then shuttle it around the foundation in wheelbarrows. I look back to this now with pride.

As I said, I had more than a few lessons to learn, and one of them was about how to properly lay out and tie up the reinforcing rods (rebar) that you put in place before the concrete is poured over it. Hundreds of pieces of rebar have to be in place in a foundation and floor, and we'd labored over that task for weeks. There's something magical in my mind about that first pour, and I was eager for it to happen. You can dig the foundation, but essentially what you've got is a hole in the ground. The pouring of the foundation signals that you mean business, that this thing is going forward, that what was once a hole in the ground is now the start of an honest-to-God building that will provide people with shelter. In our case, not just shelter, but a whole new life.

Given what happened in January 2010, we wanted to build a structure that was as earthquake-proof as possible, so that meant that rebar had to be done in a very specific way. I thought we had it right, so I called our friend, Susan Wornick.

213

We wanted to capture the images so that word could get out about the progress and thus generate some buzz back home to keep the donations flowing. I called Susan on May 9 and told her we were good to go the following day. I then sent some photos to our structural engineers, SG&H, and they delivered the bad news. The rebar wasn't quite correct.

I wasn't happy. I wanted to get that story out, and now it was going to be delayed. The people at SG&H were doing their jobs, and I appreciated that, but still the frustrations of it were wearing on me. I'm not built for Haiti. I'm a big guy, needed to lose a few pounds, and the conditions we were living under—the heat, the humidity, and all the rest—made for stressful times. I was also a little out of my comfort zone. I'm originally a carpenter by trade, so overseeing foundation work and doing foundation work is something that I turn over to the experts. Fortunately, in this case, we did have another of our angels on hand. Joe Chiaramonte owns a masonry outfit, L.A.L., in Saugus, Massachusetts. He's a father of three, and he graciously volunteered his time—after seeing a news story about us on television—to help teach us everything we needed to know about the work. It wasn't his fault that we didn't quite get the rebar right—something was lost in the translation between him and my Haitian rebar crew. He was such a valuable asset to us, and we were very fortunate to have him.

We got things straightened out, and on the morning of May 12, Pastor Lex and my nephew, Ross—who'd done yeoman work for us in the earliest days on-site but had had to go back to Florida—returned. Pastor Bouvier (the elder of the church at Mission of Hope, where Lex is a pastor), who found us the original land and the previous owner of the property, gathered us around for a brief prayer of thanks to commemorate the day. It was a beautiful moment, and much of my anxiety about the delays started to fade. As the two ministers spoke and offered their words of praise and thanks, in the background I could hear the concrete-batch machine running, and I added Perini Construction to the list of those angels on Earth to be thankful for because they donated that machine.

To me, the scraping sound of shovel going into newly

mixed concrete, what once had been separate bits of sand and stone now transformed by water into something that would harden and support the structure, is a joy to behold. It was music to my ears when that first bucket was passed along and then thudded to the ground with another deeply satisfying sound that plucked the tied rebar like a series of piano strings. We finally were getting there, and we were getting it all on tape. Watching those buckets get passed from hand to hand, seeing the workers feeding the raw materials into that batch machine, had me feeling pretty darn good. I had to restrain myself a bit from thinking too much about how much faster this would have gone if we had those trucks lined up.

With the footing pour under way, I decided that I'd be more helpful to everybody if I could improve our accommodations. I asked Matt, one of the college missionaries who was working nearby and assisting us, to help me build a bunk-bed frame. As I said, I'm a carpenter by trade, and the concrete work was better left to those who truly knew what they were doing. Matt and I worked inside the guesthouse (or was it the bunkhouse?) The sound of the circular saw, and then the drill securing the screws, added to the happy sound of a construction site in full throttle. Matt and I seemed lost in the rhythm and pleasure of the work, occasionally making some comment, but mostly just doing what we needed to do. We were just finishing up the frame, adding a couple of angle braces to firm up the legs, when I heard a truck roar past.

Matt heard it too, and we stopped and looked at each other.

"Why is that truck so close to the building?"

Matt shrugged and shook his head, his puzzled expression matching mine.

I looked out the window. I didn't see a truck, and then the building rumbled and shook. We went outside and stood there. Progress on the pour had stopped for a minute, and then resumed. I didn't think I was imagining things, but then again, my lack of sleep and the heat could have been playing tricks on me. The sun was angling lower in the sky, and I looked out at the sea down toward the fishing village, and everything seemed to be normal.

Ross came up to me with his cell phone in his hand. He held it out to me, telling me that it was Renee, Lex's wife.

"So, how did you like your first earthquake?" she asked.

I chatted with her briefly, but my mind was really someplace else. I stood there in the tropical afternoon, my hand in my pocket, my fingers working over those angel wings I'd found. This was May 12, 2011, sixteen months to the day from the events that so altered the course of my life. We finally were getting the concrete poured, I'd been agonizing over the many delays, and that temblor stopped me in my tracks. Call it divine intervention or what have you, but in that moment, I again felt Brit's hand at work. Okay, I told myself, I need to take a moment here. Stop and catch your breath. You've got a plan. Execute it. Do not hurry. Do not grow impatient. Do not be tempted to cut corners. Haiti will be here. You need to make sure this building can survive whatever Mother Nature throws at it—earthquake, tropical storm, hurricane. This thing will withstand it all, but only if you just let things take their course, pay attention to the details, but don't let your eagerness to be done end up being your undoing.

CHERYLANN

When we moved out of our house into the model home, I had to do a lot of packing and unpacking, including a lot of the stuff that was Brit's. That was more difficult than I'd imagined, but I'm very grateful that among the many things that Brit accumulated in her life was her enormous collection of friends. They helped to fill the void I was feeling. They still keep in touch but especially did so the first year. They would call just to check in; they would Facebook me and contact me on Skype; they would come by, or we would make plans to go to see them. I loved it! I loved (and still do) being with them. For me, it is like being with Brit. At first we really didn't share a lot of Brit stories but before you knew it, Brit was in every story! You just can't help it. She was a funny person who always had a story or was the story! It has given me such great comfort. I love listening to the stories.

I don't go to the cemetery a lot—in the very beginning I actually forgot about it! To me, Brit is just not there. Shortly after we buried her, the spring was coming and it was time to put flowers on the grave.

Really, I have to decorate my daughter's grave?

That's just not something I believe I have to do! Since I was a little girl, I always went to the cemetery and planted flowers—for my great aunts (my grandfather used to take us); for my dad; for my grandparents. That was something that I did. I was raised to show respect for those elders who have passed on. That was okay to me—that was the way it was supposed to happen. But I was not supposed to do this for my daughter. Brit and the boys were supposed to do this for us!

Even though I know she's not there, I hate going and then I hate leaving. It really hurts, like I am leaving her. It's such an awful feeling. A mother abandoning her child, how unnatural that feels.

Sometimes blessings find us when we do something we don't want to do.

One day when I was at the cemetery, a gentleman, Mr. Lynch, (whom I'd never met before) was driving by and stopped and asked me if I was related to Brit. I told him I was her mom. He got out of the car and came over to talk. He said how he had followed the story and so on. He told me that he was at the cemetery every day to visit his wife's grave (she had passed the previous year) and that he had been watering Brit's flowers. He wanted me to know that Brit always had a ton of visitors. How wonderful that he had been doing that! I was so thankful that he shared that people were there all the time. It made my leaving there a lot easier!

Also, a friend, Michelle, works at the cemetery and she went on her angel walks during her lunch. She included Brit on her walk—so incredibly kind!

* * *

Once Len started to go to Haiti he knew what his job was. I didn't know what mine was and I still struggle with that uncertainty. I pray that I am doing what I am supposed to being doing, but I just don't know. I'm like a work in progress—though as more of the building is being completed and is becoming a home I am slowly figuring out where I belong in the picture. My focus is Bernie, Richie, and BLB. I am doing what I can back here for BLB. I speak at schools (elementary, high school, and colleges), women groups, church groups, anyone that wants to hear about Brit and BLB. I LOVE when young kids raise money for BLB and then want to hand-deliver it to me—that's such an incredible feeling! Here are these kids (most who never met or knew Brit) raising money for her! That's when I know BLB is really so much bigger than the orphanage. It's people helping people. I don't know if anyone who donates can understand how much they are doing for the kids in Haiti, but also what they're doing for Len, the boys, and me.

Even today, as I write this in the summer of 2012, I still receive messages from people reminding me of just how much influence my daughter has had on people. Sometimes the details of building the orphanage remind me of what we had to do to furnish and decorate the various houses we've lived in. So many details, though this is for a big facility and not just a house.

I went on Facebook and posted a picture of Brit on the Be Like Brit page. It's one of my favorites of her time in Haiti. She is standing in shadows, but her smile is electric. A group of schoolgirls surround her and they all have ribbons in their hair, blue and white. I love the image of Brit. I'd like to think that one part of the reason why she's smiling so brightly is from the delight of being in the presence of those laughing and chattering girls; they are so genuine and filled with joy. That photo also reminds me of the girls who continue to surround me, Brit's friends, and how much they mean to me.

I lingered on the site for a while and then got back to work. Later that day, I got an email from one of Brit's Facebook friends: "WE ALL MISS YOU BRIT. You were and still are the best. I am trying to carry on your tradition of working with the special ed kids. Not only were you a friend, but you were a mentor. You inspired all of us to strive to look for the best in others. Your good heart and hard work will not be forgotten . . . EVER." That young man, who had been in special ed when he was in high school, now works as a janitor at that same school where he and Brit went. He later added to his note: "I came from the Special Ed group. Britney was more than a person. She was and is a great friend to all."

What I admired about Brit was that she was a popular girl, but she wasn't into cliques. She didn't care about what "category" others might have thought you belonged in; she just liked people for who they were. That email reminded me of that fact. She was very kind and respectful to the special-needs kids—certainly not typical for a high-school student. Here was a girl who, by her own admission, basically had everything she could need or want, but she empathized so much with those impoverished kids in Haiti.

I have to say, the hardest part of my travels to Haiti, even though they are far fewer than Len's, is still seeing the kind of grinding poverty and the awful conditions under which so many people there have to live. In a way, it's kind of like the have and have-nots at school—whether it's the smart kids versus special education kids, the jocks versus the klutzes in gym class, or whatever.

Photos and images on television can show you how people live, but you don't really comprehend it until you see it for yourself, face to face. There are so many families who live within a stone's throw of BLB in huts smaller than the typical American two-car garage, with tin roofs, tarp walls, and dirt floors. In the driving summer tropical rainstorms—of which there are many—those floors are turned to rivers of mud. There is no running water—no toilets, no showers, no drinking water. They have no electricity. It takes a lot of hard work, all day and every day, just to get the basics people need to live. They have to bathe in the open public bath at the ocean's edge. They have to get their water in buckets from a public well (we open ours to our neighbors every evening) and then carry it up the hill, usually on their heads. They grow their own vegetables and keep goats for milk.

There is no such thing as free public education. If you have any hope for a better life for your children, you have to pay for school—tuition, books, uniforms, and fees. The children who are able to go to school never complain and would certainly never ditch class—they are up in the pitch black at 5:00 a.m. walking or waiting for the bus, eager to learn. They sit in open-air classrooms. The lucky ones have desks: some sit side by side on wooden benches with no backs.

Students from the Lynn group who survived the earthquake told me that Brit was very troubled by what she saw. Just being born in the United States gives a child infinite possibilities that many Haitian children cannot even comprehend, let alone make happen. Orphans, especially, have no chance unless someone comes to their aid.

Having seen this for myself, I understand why Brit felt so strongly about these people and the children, in particular. The thought that we can make a difference for them keeps me going through long and difficult days.

* * *

It seemed as if our lives were taking on a new pattern as 2011 ended. Those times weren't any easier without Brit in them, but we took comfort in knowing that Len was in Haiti with another group of Britsionaries and that progress continued on the building site.

Back in the States, Lynn University had been at work for quite a while erecting a memorial to its victims of the quake. As parents of one of those lost, we were included in the planning stages. We were grateful for opportunity. We learned the dedication was to take place on March 16, 2012, at the campus. We made plans to fly in early. The closing on the sale of the vacation house on Ossipee Lake, New Hampshire, was complete, and we took the proceeds—nearly $500,000—and put the money into BLB. Len was spending so much time in Haiti—twenty trips in 2011 alone with many more to come—that we were considering the purchase of a place in Fort Lauderdale to make the commute easier. So we also would need to spend time in South Florida to go house hunting.

Being on campus again, so close to what would have been Brit's graduation, felt strange. It also brought back memories of the last time we'd been there, those joyful awful hours when we were told that Brit was rescued only to learn she wasn't.

I was very conscious that this trip was about Brit and the memorial, but I didn't want it to be completely about her. So much of our time and energy was devoted to BLB, but I was still very alert to the fact that we needed to do things that were about Bernie and Richie. As a result, looking at houses morphed into looking at schools that Richie might want to attend in 2013 as he began his college career. I had no trepidation about Richie being in Florida and that far away from the place we've called home. I wanted him to do what he wanted to do. So, we looked at Nova Southeastern University, and he loved it. It was good to see him excited about things, and that served as another reminder of just how far he'd come in the years since Brit's death. He had a rough go of it, but as more time passed, we could see him maturing from a boy into a young man.

That said, I still told the boys before the trip that they had to do what they had to do with regard to the ceremony. If that meant crying, then cry. If that meant retreating, then retreat. They should do what they felt like doing and not what they thought they were expected to do. They assured me they would, and that was that. The days leading up to the dedication of the memorial were a good distraction for us all. We got away from home, we got away as best we could from the day-to-day of BLB, but we certainly couldn't escape completely the reality about why we were going to Boca again.

My thoughts were as much about why we weren't there—for Brit's graduation—than they were about our reason for returning to Lynn University. I couldn't help but wonder what direction Brit's life would have taken if she hadn't gone to Haiti. We told her it would be life changing, and she was sincere in expressing her desire to do good in the world, but still I had to reflect on that. What form would that have taken? She was such a vivacious presence, and I had to wonder what the future would have held for her.

That Friday as we made our way across the campus, past the all-too familiar buildings that had been transformed from a campus structure into something more, those thoughts ran through my mind. We were all silent, lost in our thoughts, and as we made our way from the parking lot into the memorial space and were seated. It was almost as if I had blinders on. Just look straight ahead, try to stay in the moment, appreciate this for what it is going to be.

The funny thing is, that lasted about ten seconds. We'd been handed a program for the Remembrance Plaza dedication, and wanting to keep my mind focused, I opened it. There on the first page were words that in a lot of ways answered my questions about Brit and her future. They were from the American poet Ralph Waldo Emerson:

This is what I want for you.

· *To laugh often and much;*
· *To win the respect of intelligent people and the affection of children;*
· *To earn the appreciation of honest critics and endure the betrayal of false friends;*

· *To appreciate beauty; to find the best in others;*
· *To leave the world a bit better, whether by a healthy child, a garden patch or a redeemed social condition;*
· *To know even one life has breathed easier because you have lived.*

This is to have succeeded.

After reading those words I thought that Brit had done all those things. She'd only gotten nineteen years to do them, but she'd succeeded. I supposed that it wasn't the length of her life that mattered but what she did in those years. Selfishly, of course, I still wanted her to be around, to still be succeeding. I also knew that no dedication of any memorial—the one at Lynn or the one in Grand Goâve—could ever provide me with that false thing known as closure. Brit's loss would always be an open wound, but more importantly, it was proving to be a way to open my heart, my sons' hearts, my husband's heart, and the hearts and minds of so many people who we will never be able to thank.

LEN

The night before the dedication, before the Remembrance Plaza was open to the public, the families of the victims were granted a private viewing of the site. I'd seen the drawings that Louis Souza and his team had prepared, but nothing could really compare to seeing it in person. The sun had set and the rest of the campus was dark except for the security lights that reminded me of fireflies. The donated granite, a blue-green nearly translucent polished stone, nearly sixty thousand pounds of it, stood there shimmering in the distance. A reflecting pool captured that light and color and scattered it around the plaza, refracting and magnifying it. The effect was stunning.

The four of us stepped forward and walked up to the part

of the memorial where the six prisms stood. There was one for each victim, with those representing the professors on the outside, symbolizing their efforts to protect the others from harm. Each prism had colors representing the personalities of those named nearby. We weren't there for more than few seconds, my throat nearly clamped shut and Cherylann squeezing my forearm, when Richie said he wanted to take a photograph. He is very much a Gengel in that regard!

He used his iPhone and we stood there waiting for the flash. A moment later he brought the phone over to us so we could see it. We took a look at it and were stunned. I've never seen such a clear photo at nighttime. There were the four of us, looking fairly somber, of course, but behind us was this amazing display of light. It was as if there was a kaleidoscope on display in the background. We were sort of dull looking, but behind us was this dazzling, shimmering thing. Of course, we immediately thought of Brit and how she sparkled, and one of us, or maybe all of us—I was so caught up in the moment that I can't really recall—said, "Fabulous" without a hint of sarcasm.

I stepped away for a moment to gather myself, and I was struck by how far the reflections of light carried across the plaza and out into the dark of the night. It seemed as if they could have gone on into infinity. All those thoughts—maybe they were clichés, but who cares—came flooding in. The memorial was doing exactly what it was designed to do: to spread the light and the word about what these six people had been doing when they lost their lives.

I've always felt bad for the professors—Patrick Hartwick and Dr. Richard Bruno—because so much attention was paid to the girls' story and not as much to theirs. They'd been there leading the Journey of Hope group, setting an example for the students and the rest of the faculty about what it meant to not just teach, to mouth words, but also to show what it meant to give of yourself. I was glad they were going to be honored along with the students at the dedication ceremony, especially because this would happen in front of the entire Lynn community, their colleagues.

The ceremony was beautiful, from the opening invocation

by Reverend Martin Devereaux to the Boynton Beach Community High School choir singing "America the Beautiful." In some ways I didn't want that song to end, and I couldn't wait for it to be over. I knew that once their voices fell silent, the part of the ceremony I dreaded was going to arrive.

After they all spoke, we were called up in alphabetical order to get our daughters' diplomas. The Crispinellis were first. I was really sad to see the pain on Lenny's face and in the way he held the diploma. And there it was, supposed to be this beautiful graduation day for us. Here we were getting the diploma for our daughters, which they'd never see, but there was beauty in it. There was beauty in the fact that they honored them with a degree.

We were next. I just had so many raw emotions going through me—sadness, relief, some anger, frustration. I couldn't believe we were standing there doing this. Still, I was able to hold it together somehow—barely.

Since then I've see a picture of that moment, and my body reveals what I was thinking right then: I would have rather been back in Haiti humping a wheelbarrow or buckets full of concrete. My shoulders were slumped, and I looked like that was what I was doing. And that diploma, it felt heavy in my hand like a cinder block, I could barely hold it. Cherylann and I were just a mess because all of a sudden, reality had hit when we were handed that diploma. I was thinking about the first time I brought Brit to Lynn University. We were standing next to the sign outside so I could get a photo of her, which I loved having, but she was bitching and moaning, "I don't want the photo." I said, "Well I do. I'm paying whatever, $45,000 a year; I want the photo!"

Thinking of that, all these emotions came through. And so we got our daughter's diploma without tripping and falling, got off the stage, and then watched the Gianacacis and the Hayeses and the professors' families, and it was really, really sad. Heartbreaking. Hopeful. Horrific. Healing. Humbling.

We made our way back to our seats for the next portion of the program. Each of the mothers was going to say something about their daughters. I wasn't worried about Cherylann.

In the years since Brit passed, she'd become a very confident speaker. Like anybody, she had her nervous moments in front of a group, but she found an inner strength that really made me even more proud of her. I was glad, however, that she got to speak first so that she could gather herself and be there by me for what was to come next.

Then Lynn University did this beautiful thing when President Kevin Ross declared the memorial officially dedicated. They did a great job. We were very happy. We didn't know what was about to happen. We hadn't rehearsed any of this.

The professors—there had to have been about one hundred faculty members—lined up on each side of the pathway. Then the six families were the first of the thousand people to walk through. And as we did they handed us white roses.

Walking through that beautiful pathway they formed to the memorial and giving us roses to put at our daughter's prism just blew me away.

I made my way around the corner out of everyone's line of sight. And this one professor, who I did not know, grabbed me and said, "I would not let anyone sit in Brit's chair all semester. That was Britney's chair."

I lost it. I stood there holding this woman—I didn't even know her name—and we stood there sobbing and hugging. I don't think I've lost it like that since I first visited the Hotel Montana. I just couldn't keep it together. I just sat on the bench in front of Brit's prism and wailed out loud. Thankfully, as my family and others stopped to read each prism, the line stopped and allowed me some time to pull myself together.

Then a thousand people came through over the next half hour. I mean it was just beautiful to see them all. And some of Brit's friends, her roommates, of course, and even some of her friends from Massachusetts who were down there for spring break and had emailed me and asked permission to come over. It was just so moving to see them.

As beautiful as it all was, it sucked the life out of me emotionally. I think I probably lost a year off my life. Maybe it was the finality of it. Would I ever go back to Lynn? The beautiful memorial is there but we'd never have a real graduation.

And I didn't go back for the ceremony when her friends graduated in May. I couldn't because I know we would not have that joy. And I think that was going on in my head—just the raw reality of it.

12

ON ANGELS' WINGS

"We could have, individually or as a family, rolled into a protective ball, but instead we're out there experiencing new things and stretching our limits."

—CHERYLANN

LEN

Whenever you begin a project, you always look for signs of progress. I think that since Brit passed, I've been looking for all kinds of signs, and they've come to us in various forms. Sometimes, though, a sign is just a sign—a literal one—but even then it has immense meaning for me. In December 2011, reporters from the Associated Press came to Haiti to do a story on us. I gave them the grand tour of Grand Goâve since they had asked me why that particular location. I explained about Brit's trip and how she was supposed to go there and all the rest. I took them on a boat tour of the fishing village (thanks to Robin Mahood of Food for the Poor who made the arrangements), hoping these journalists could get a sense of the beauty of the place.

Food for the Poor has been wonderful in support of the orphanage, and they even donated their services to do the landscaping. That was incredibly generous of them, but I did have one request. I asked that they incorporate a memorial plaque into their design. I wanted them to tell the story of the students and faculty and the Journey of Hope they all began that January in 2010. I hadn't thought much about it since, but when I was on the tour with the reporters, talking to them about Father Gus and the establishment of the village known as Pierre Marie, I was stopped in my tracks. In front of me was a beautiful black polycarbonate plaque—something that could withstand the corrosive seaside air—about two and a half feet by four feet. Along with words of explanation about the events of January 12, 2010, and how Journey of Hope and this fishing village tied into it, the sign was also laser-etched with photos of the four students and two professors who lost their lives.

In my mind, I was visualizing a simple wooden sign with names, dates, and a brief explanation, but there in front of me was this gorgeous work of art. I nearly lost it in front of those reporters. I was so overcome with emotion, because of the generosity and incredible consideration that Food for the Poor put into creating that memorial, but also because my daughter's image was in front of me, right there in Grand Goâve. I imagined her standing there on January 13, part of me wishing that time could be reversed and the earthquake had never happened. Another part of me, the part that has come to accept this new reality, stood there and ran his fingers along the outline of his daughter's beautiful face, letting the tears come. So many people were contributing to making sure that Brit was here in spirit. That plaque's images of those students and faculty members were so lifelike that I once again felt like Brit was present there. In my mind, she was telling me that she was glad that we'd chosen this spot, that she absolutely loved it, and was glad this was where we were building that orphanage.

Brit loved the water, the beach, and we'd found a great spot where she could enjoy those things.

What Brit most loved in life was people. As a result of working on this project, this mission, I've come to meet so many people who've demonstrated the beauty of humanity. There are the folks from back home in the U.S. who came back and forth to Haiti, often on their own dime and on their free time. John Picard, electrician, and Greg Smith, vice president, of Granite City Electric, did an incredible job wiring the first-floor rough in a week, then back to do the second-floor rough before we poured the roof. John not only went in with me in September 2011 to assess the site and make sure this was doable, but he designed the electrical system for the entire orphanage and has overseen the installation on top of doing all the services and major components to the building. Greg, as I said, is the vice president of Granite City. He rough-wired the building in a week without John because John had a heart attack last February and had many stents put in. Still, he was back in June to rough-wire the second floor. Greg also worked his tail off getting suppliers to donate materials.

Alan Roseberry, the plumber, is another incredible person. He came back before we poured the roof to install his chases and then came twice in the fall of 2012 to install water piping and finish the apartment baths! He made a weeklong trip in late October 2012 to hook up the eastern-side water tank and then returned in December to install all the toilets and vanities—truly making Brit's Orphanage livable.

After this trip to Haiti, Bernie and I flew back to Ft. Lauderdale and were then to go back to Boston. While waiting for our connecting flight, I noticed a dignified gray-haired man looking at me. "I know you. Do you own a restaurant outside Boston?" he said.

I told him he must have me confused with someone else. Bernie was with me, of course, and we'd just spent an emotional weekend in Grand Goâve; I didn't want to make him hear me going over again for who knows how many times the story of who we are. Fifteen minutes later, still waiting at the gate, the man approached me again, this time certain of how he knew me. He thought that we had an argument at his Central Chrysler-Jeep dealership in Norwood. I laughed. I'm a tough negotiator and all, but no I didn't have a fight with him there. He walked away, and Bernie, bless him, told me that he was okay if I told the man who I was, let him off the hook, and identified myself. So, when the man returned five minutes later, I played the I'll-give-you-a-clue game with him. So I said, "Personal tragedy in Haiti."

Almost instantly the man's expression went from curiosity to anguish. Tears streamed down his face. "I knew it. I knew it. You're the man who lost his daughter in Haiti." He asked me to wait right there while he went to get his wife. She came back along with another friend of theirs. The man walked up to me and said, "I am Peter Catanese and this is my wife, MaryAnn. We lost our son in a car accident a month before he was supposed to graduate from Boston College. The accident was one block from our house."

I stood up and hugged him, and felt an instant connection with him. Only people who have lost a child can relate to this kind of pain.

Peter Catanese has turned out to be another of our angels that Brit brought into our lives. We shared our stories of loss, anguish, and our attempts to actively do something to make a difference and not let that loss defeat us. Peter and his wife established the Christopher Catanese Children's Foundation in their son's honor. At our first meeting in that airport, he told me that he wanted to do anything he could to help Be Like Brit. Later, I told him about our need to get a box truck so that we could drive our supplies from the Boston area down to Florida to have them shipped to Haiti. His dealership didn't carry commercial vehicles, but he'd see what he could find.

A week after Thanksgiving, Cherylann asked me what the name of that foundation was, the one the guy at the airport had told me about. I told her, and she said, "Well, he just sent us a $10,000 check." A year later, they were hosting a fund-raiser and wanted to present us with the money there, hoping to raise additional funds for us. What an amazing man. As it turns out, on the night of the event, things went as expected to a point.

Father John McLaughlin, who runs the Catholic Center at Boston University was there, one of Peter's good friends, and he introduced us and previewed our story.

Cherylann delivered a moving speech about Brit, then I spoke of meeting Peter and MaryAnn in front of an audience of four hundred people—even though we had no idea beforehand that we were going to have to speak. We learned it when Father McLaughlin was at the podium while we were having dinner—talk about a surprise! While there was no time to prepare, there was no time to get nervous either. After a standing ovation, people came up to us with more donations. As the saying goes, there wasn't a dry eye in the house, and I had an awakening moment: I realized I could speak publicly about Brit without breaking down. This was a big deal. I'm pretty much an open book—what you see and hear is what I am feeling—but being able to talk about Brit and coherently tell the story of what happened to her, and how we had chosen to honor her last wish, was vital to our fund-raising efforts, as well as my ability to move beyond the tragedy.

Father John got up after the dinner portion of the evening was over and announced that the Catanese family had decided to double their initial donation and were committed to contributing $100,000 over the next three years. I was stunned—that chance meeting at the airport had led to this. It also affirmed my belief that we were on the right path, and that I could get up in front of people without breaking down in tears, raise money, and become an advocate for kids in Haiti. I'd been focused on the fund-raising and the building, but I don't think until that moment I truly realized that our lives were never going to be the same. We were going to have to spend the rest of our lives promoting Be Like Brit, Haiti, and its many orphans, and that we now had a new calling in our lives. Cherylann and I drove home that night, and we talked about our sense of purpose and how our life path had been altered. These things really began to sink in. Sometimes change is frightening; sometimes it is horrific when it is forced on you as it was when we lost Brit, but this was different. I accepted this change and this challenge. This was the return portion of the cycle, and I realized those three elements—learn, earn, and return—didn't have to be separate parts of our lives, that they didn't have to necessarily follow one another in that exact sequence.

You know, the raw reality is that life is messy. I don't normally like messes. I like order, precision, sequences, and control. The truth is there is a lot to be said for learning to recognize what you can control and allowing some things into your life to take control over you. The Catanese family's generosity is extraordinary, but it isn't the amount that matters. Every dollar helps; every dollar counts. And we account for every one of those dollars because we want to make sure they go toward the purpose for which people gave them to us: to get that orphanage built and to house, feed, and help educate those kids. One thing I won't relinquish control of is those purse strings.

I say this because, like a lot of people, one of the things I had heard about Haiti was that it was a place where corruption was rampant and honesty was rare. I haven't found that to be the case, at least with the people I've directly dealt with in Haiti. I've already mentioned Gama and my regard for him. Well, it's time that I sing his praises even more clearly. Gama is the quiet leader who keeps the ship afloat at our site in Grand Goâve. For the past two years, he has done a phenomenal job of making this orphanage happen.

I'd only met Gama—a man who I call Mr. Incredible and introduce him to other people as such—three times before he made the commitment to come to Haiti, leaving behind a good job in the States to do so. He's a tireless worker, taking on everything from mundane but necessary tasks, like being sure the generator at the guesthouse has diesel fuel in it to ensuring the electricity stays up and running to keeping our books. Gama is not an accountant, but my CPA and comptroller, Deb, at C&S spent a week with him in the States establishing systems and training him so that he could do that work for us in Haiti. Brit's text to us spoke about how the people in Haiti are so poor, yet are so appreciative for everything they do have. That's the spirit that is embodied on the site and has been translated into the kind of can-do attitude that permeates the place. Gama is the main reason why. He cares passionately and goes to extraordinary lengths to make sure there's no waste, no oversights in how those precious dollars that come in get used.

Sometimes that means gathering all the workers in the middle of the night to rescue $30,000 of rebar that lay in the middle of the road when the delivery truck tipped over. There is a fair distance from the main road to the orphanage. Our unpaved road is a series of steep inclines. The steepest grade is the final approach to our gate at the BLB entryway. The truck got to the top, but halfway up that very last steep hill, the driver downshifted and couldn't get into gear. The truck, with that extremely heavy load, rolled backward into the hill on the side of the road and tipped over! Gratefully, the driver wasn't injured, but when you've got that much valuable steel lying there, anyone could have come along and helped themselves. This was another one of the moments where I shrugged my shoulders and said, "It's Haiti!" Luckily, Gama oversaw that operation to make sure that every single piece was accounted for and carried up the long, steep hill.

I've been in business most of my adult life, and I've hired dozens and dozens of people, and no one has ever done what Gama did recently. We have a bank account in the U.S., and we do regular wire transfers each week to take care of payroll for the workers in Grand Goâve. We have people who volunteer their time, but we also have full-time employees. I'm thrilled that we can offer Haitians an opportunity to earn good wages. It isn't a question of lack of trust but simply best practices that each month when I'm down there, I conduct an audit of the books. Two months ago, I noticed there was a credit of $5,000 whose source I couldn't identify. I asked Gama where that money came from.

"Leo, the wire transfer was late. It was a Friday, and the workers needed their money on Saturday. I put the money in there. You can repay me whenever you get the chance."

My jaw dropped. Out of his own pocket, well, his own account, Gama had made sure that the people he supervised would get their regular salary. He wouldn't have said a word about his actions except for the fact that I asked him during this review of the books. It is easy to believe the worst about people and a country, but when you work with individuals and not broad-stroke assumptions and perceptions, it is amazing what you will witness. I'm so grateful that Brit has introduced me to such wonderful people.

CHERYLANN

I have to say that the big holidays aren't the things that I get upset by or that make me miss Brit the most. It's actually the everyday things. I miss her coming into the house smiling and singing with some dramatic story of something that happened that day. I miss making Duncan Hines cakes with her—no frosting. I miss her making dinner and leaving all the pans in the sink. I miss tuning the radio to Kiss 108 and blaring the music, and her and I and the boys and their friends breaking into dance and singing along. I laugh every time a Chris Brown song comes on. Brit was trying to convince me to take hip-hop classes with her and her girlfriend. The first hip-hop dance they learned was to Chris Brown. I always loved to dance but hip-hop, at my age? Brit would beg me, "Pleeeaaase, Mom?"

She never was ashamed of me and really wanted me to do it with her. However, when Brit went off to college, the local dance studio offered a hip-hop class and I went with my girlfriend. When we were younger, we could dance like Janet Jackson and in my mind I thought I still could; however, the reality of watching my body in the mirror confirms I am no Janet Jackson! I would call Brit and laugh about what I was doing.

I even missed yelling at her to clean her room.

The first time I walked into a Forever 21 store during the bathing-suit season I thought I was going to have a breakdown. Brit had about twenty bathing suits and had to have new ones because the old ones didn't fit (yeah, right). To see all the bathing suits hanging there, knowing that I would never buy her another one again was just too much!

As much as I miss everything there is to miss about Brit, the saddest thing for me is that she will always only be nineteen. She will never get to grow up.

In 2012, I really was aware of that. I've watched her friends from elementary school, junior high, high school, and college all grow into wonderful young adults. I remember when they were all so little and listening to their dreams of growing up. They'd share what they wanted to be doing, and many of them are living those dreams. I've watched a lot of her friends do the drinking, not making the greatest decisions, etc., but they grew up. They learned from it and moved on. I am thrilled for them—honestly—but I'm just sad for Brit that she doesn't get that opportunity. She will always be Brit, nineteen.

I have to say one of the hardest moments so far was college graduation season. It caught me by surprise. One day I was working in my office on BLB stuff—actually stuffing envelopes with T-shirts. Over one hundred twenty students had ordered shirts and needed them for a concert. I was sitting there thinking how wonderful it was that these kids who don't even know Brit were willing to help us. Their school was putting on a concert and the proceeds were going to BLB—terrific, right?

I was on the computer getting one of the student's addresses and hit the wrong button, and my Facebook page came up. And there was a picture of all Brit's friends with their caps and gowns on. They had just been confirmed that they were graduating. They were thrilled, as they should be, but out of nowhere I lost it.

I could not control myself. It was the first time since Brit died that I couldn't stop crying. I was sitting there stuffing envelopes for my dead daughter's foundation. The tears and overwhelming grief instantly came pouring out of me. Len heard me from the other room and asked if I was okay, and I just couldn't answer him. I literally couldn't answer him; I couldn't make my mouth form words. He came into the office, and I think he was in shock that I had lost it! He is not used to me being so emotional and not used to me needing him to hold me, but I needed him! I needed that pain to go away. But it couldn't; it didn't. I had to get up and walk away. I went into the shower because I didn't know where else to go. My fists hit the tile walls.

I screamed.

I swore.

The reality was this: Britney wasn't here! She wasn't coming back! She wasn't in Florida.

She was dead!

I allowed myself that time to just collapse and not care if anyone knew what I was really thinking and feeling. After a while, I pulled myself back together, and I kept in perspective what I'd been thinking and feeling wasn't anything abnormal or wrong. I also wasn't somehow being resentful or angry about what all those other girls were getting to experience.

Brit's friends had been through so much themselves, and I was thrilled for all of them! I love them all so much—talking with them; communicating with them is like having my daughter around. They had earned their degrees, their ongoing lives. My outburst was never about "my daughter not graduating;" it was about me missing my daughter so profoundly.

I suppose that Len and I could have read this in a book and learned it, but I'm not sure I would have fully understood what it meant until it happened to us. When you lose a child, so many of the things that once gave you great joy are now tinged with sadness and longing. That was particularly true for Len when it came to people reaching out to our family and to Be Like Brit as a way to honor her memory. Throwing out the first pitch at a Boston Red Sox game—I should say, our beloved Sox—would have been an unimaginable thrill under other circumstances. Brit and the rest of the family and I had spent a lot of time at Fenway over the years, experienced the jubilation of their long-overdue World Series championships. After Brit passed, the Red Sox organization was so kind to us, and Len's friend at Granite City Electric, Steve Helle, held a fund-raiser at Fenway and invited Len to throw out the first pitch. Len said he couldn't help but think of Brit when he stepped out on that diamond. Steve knew Brit as a young girl, and like so many people, he wanted to help out. As I said, under normal circumstances Len would have been jumping for joy, but knowing the reason why we were there took most of that pleasure away for him. I don't mean to diminish what was done for us—and something similar occurred at a Boston Celtics game, and the outpouring of support was amazing—but it was as if a filter was placed over a camera lens recording these events.

Only Len, Bernie, Richie, and I probably saw that veneer of regret on our faces, and maybe only those people who'd lost someone close to them, a child or an adult, could fully appreciate how off it felt that day. His nerves, not wanting to bounce one in there or throw one over the catcher's head, were pure, as was our gratitude for the organizers of the various events that made the orphanage possible.

The best way that I can think of this is that you've made a dish for a lot of years, kept the recipe the same, and then one day the meal doesn't taste quite the same. Most everyone else eating it wouldn't know, wouldn't be able to tell that this wasn't the same, but we could. In time, though, as Len has gotten involved more in the fund-raising and spends more time in Haiti, he's healing. The heartache is still there, and it will always be there, but the hope is lifting him and all of us up.

* * *

In keeping with that idea to Be Like Brit and to do the right thing, we instituted a program called Be a Britsionary, like missionaries but with our own twist. This first group of volunteers made the trip to Haiti in June 2011. Many people had helped out with funding, construction equipment, and their expertise, and so many others asked us what they could do to help. As a result, we came up with a plan that answered that question and also achieved something we'd hoped would happen as a result of Be Like Brit. The idea behind the Britsionary program was to bring people to Haiti and the orphanage site to help with the construction, but also to educate them about and expose them to the reality of Haiti.

This was not going to be a trip to Disney World, obviously, but we did everything we could to make sure the volunteers were safe and had fun. I joked with Len that this wasn't about how much work we could get out them, it was about how much we could expose them to the idea of doing good works. We had no idea if anyone would volunteer for the program, and we knew the cost could be a problem. For that reason, once we received applications and a person was accepted into the program, we provided help in organizing fund-raisers to offset the cost of the seven-night stay in Grand Goâve.

We had to be as realistic as possible to make sure everyone understood that life in Haiti was not like it was at home. Even though they were going to be staying in the guesthouse at the Mission of Hope, we made it clear that even the basics—clean drinking water, electricity, etc.—could at times be a problem. Mostly, though, with the help of Lex and Renee and others who were veterans of the project, we put together a list of cultural differences that covered everything from the fact that they were likely to see Haitians bathing in just about any water source, to children being naked, to men holding hands, to not rewarding begging, to not giving gifts to anyone without a BLB representative's approval beforehand. We had to make sure they and we did nothing to harm the delicate relationship we had with the people of Haiti.

To our delight, we did receive applications and did send our first group of Britsionary volunteers to Grand Goâve. A group of thirteen individuals from Becker College, led by our own Kristin Hervey Musser, worked there for a week, assisting in the pouring of floors in ten rooms as they manned the bucket brigade and shovels. Seeing these young people being like Brit, hearing and reading their enthusiastic reports, was deeply gratifying. How much I wish that Brit could be among them, but knowing this work was being done to honor her memory and to make a difference in a part of the world that needs an outpouring of hope, made that less painful.

In December 2011, another group, this time eleven volunteers, spent part of their holiday break at Grand Goâve and were led by our nephew, Ross Pentland. The construction had proceeded to the point they were helping to pour the cement for the columns that would support the second floor. We were expanding skyward, and these angels were making it all possible. Universally, the response the volunteers had was that the experience was life-changing for them, words that echoed what we had told Brit prior to her leaving for Haiti. Knowing that we were helping to make a difference in the lives of people here and in Haiti, keeping to the theme of Be Like Brit, enriched my life in ways that I don't know if I yet fully understand.

In 2012, we've had even more Britsionaries at work, and this is one program that, even when the building is complete and the orphanage is operational, we expect to continue. Not only do we have to honor Brit's dream, but we also have to make certain that the work so many other people have done along the way is honored as well.

LEN

Ask any builder and they'll likely agree with this statement: Once the roof goes on a building, you begin to feel like you're in the home stretch. When those four walls are up and you've got a ceiling over your head, you have a place to go to get out of the bad weather. There's a sense of security and satisfaction that, pun intended, can't be topped.

On July 3, 2012, we spent the entire day and night prepping for what I humbly consider to be one of the finest achievements in this building project. As I've told you, much, much of the work that was done on the building was done by hand, employing some of the most labor-intensive methods to mix concrete, mortar, and to make the cinder blocks that comprise the walls. To make the building stand the test of time and the worst of Mother Nature, it also was designed to have a cement roof.

I know that numbers may not mean a lot to people who don't have experience in construction, but we knew going into this pour that we'd need somewhere between four hundred and four hundred fifty yards of concrete. A yard of concrete is a measure of volume. A square foot is a measure of area. A cubic yard is twenty-seven cubic feet of stuff. (3x3x3) To relate volume to area, you must extend the area over a third dimension. One square foot that is one foot deep will equal one cubic foot. (1x1x1) So, a yard of concrete is twenty-seven cubic feet or three feet tall, three feet wide, three feet deep. Concrete weighs one hundred fifty pounds per cubic foot; twenty-seven cubic feet times one hundred fifty pounds is four thousand fifty pounds. This is one cubic yard of concrete.

So, now forget all that math and those numbers and remember this: four-hundred-plus yards of concrete is a BIG amount. We couldn't possibly do all that work by hand, and in something as close to a miracle as I can imagine, we managed to secure the use of a ready-mix company and their pumper trucks that would transfer the concrete to the roof where it would be spread and finished by hand. This was to be a monumental undertaking that eventually would take thirty-nine straight hours of labor and see us use four hundred forty-one yards of concrete to put a roof on the place.

This was an all-hands-on-deck operation, and Paul Fallon was there to help oversee the work. We were working nonstop, so we needed portable lights so that the concrete finishers could see. I was thrilled that everything was proceeding like clockwork. A truck would pull up, discharge its contents as the chute and pumper tube were moved around, and nearly as soon as it was empty, we'd get started on another truck. Eventually, you fall into a rhythm, whether you're someone who is raking the concrete, leveling it with a float, or doing what I was do-ing—testing each batch of concrete to make sure it was the proper consistency and collecting the slips documenting the amount of material coming with each delivery.

We began in the early morning hours and worked steadily until nightfall without incident. Over time you grow accus-tomed to all the sounds of the trucks, the directions being shouted, the men working, and later, the generators. I stood there wondering what anyone flying over the site would see. I smiled at the thought of the darkness being penetrated by this circle of light and emerging form of the letter B. I didn't want to, but I knew I had to get some rest, and I grabbed a quick two hours of sleep before returning. Later, Paul needed some shut-eye, too. As we traded places, I shook his hand as well as my head, marveling that in a country where we'd struggled to find any kind of building supplies or tools, we were doing something that would be considered a tough act in the States, and it was all coming off without a hitch.

I looked over and saw that all that work and lack of sleep had gotten the best of Gama. He'd been there throughout but was now dozing in the cab of the truck. I told Paul that I could manage from there. I went back to collecting slips, stuffing the ever-growing number of them in my left front pants pocket. We were about two-thirds of the way through the pour, and I told myself that I needed to be careful. Every time I got a new slip, I'd pull the others out and add it to the wad, and then stuff the pile plus one back into that pocket. I had my angel's wings with me in that pocket, and I didn't want to lose what was left of them.

I've said so many times, probably too many, that what I was witnessing was surreal. Somehow, though, as I stood on the roof of the building charting our progress so that just a few sections remained to be filled, I could see the sun coming up, the horizon going from light blue to orange and red, the light looking like a hand reaching out to either present something or to take it away. In that moment, bleary-eyed but happy, I decided that was how life worked in many ways. Something taken. Something given. I felt a tear welling in my eye, but I wasn't fully sad, just a bit. I knew Brit could see what was taking place and that she was happy for us all, proud of us for the effort we'd put out there.

Paul came up to me, and I handed him the slips, grateful he was there to relieve me. I didn't go to the guesthouse immediately. I wanted to stay on the site, be there when the last truck roared out of there and the men came down the scaffolding with the job done. I wanted to shake everyone's hand, thank them personally for the awesome effort. Seeing their smiles of pleasure, feeling their sense of accomplishment, was a thrill.

I took Bernie aside, wrapped my arm around his shoulders, and said, "Come here, son," as I led him up the hill that overlooks the building. "Almost two years ago we walked up this hill together, looking down on this place, dreaming of what it could be. Now we have all this . . . this dream of Brit's and ours coming true!" Bernie and I had spent a total of nine weeks together on different trips in and out of Haiti, twice through the Christmas holiday. "It's been a trying time for all of us," I said, then I reminded him of what legendary Green Bay Packers coach Vince Lombardi said: "'Everyone in life gets knocked down; it's how you pick yourself up that defines you as a human being.' I'm blessed to have had your love and support through all of this. I'm so proud you are my son!" and I hugged him and held on tight.

Bernie didn't need say anything—he didn't need to—I knew what he was feeling. He was happy for all that we had accomplished. You could see it in his face and sense it in his demeanor. This was a momentous occasion.

Having run on sheer adrenaline for the past few days, I was nearly delirious. I decided to go back to the guesthouse to take a trickle shower to clean up and revive myself. There was still more work to be done, even while the concrete set.

As I was taking off my pants, I remembered the wings. Paul had all of the slips, so my pants pockets were no longer bulging. I reached inside that left front pocket, and my heart skipped a beat or two. The wings weren't there. Thinking that maybe in my sleep-deprived state I might have transferred them to another pocket, I began a frantic search while fighting a rising tide of panic. That didn't last long. I remembered I had been on the roof with Paul and handed the slips over to him. I figured the wings must have slipped out then. I was okay with that. I knew that we were standing on the two-by-six boards that served as a walkway spanning the joists that helped frame the roof and support the freshly poured concrete. I was certain the wings had fallen out of my pocket there and were imbedded in the roof. What better place for them to end up. They were now a permanent part of the building, a structure that we'd made sure would weather any storm or upset that could occur. I stood feeling Brit's presence again, as I had before, and as I knew I would until my life ended.

I was at peace with the loss of those wings. They'd gotten me to this new place in my life, somewhere that I wasn't prepared to go initially but someplace where I'd learned a lot, a place that I had earned, a place where I knew I would return. Even though the roof was poured, work remained to be done. I was eager to get at it. Somehow, that trickle shower felt more refreshing than ever, and when I drove back up to the orphanage, I saw what we had all done, and I smiled and thanked God for all his many blessings.

CHERYLANN

It's never been easy for me to ask for help. The same is true of Len, though when it came to the work on the orphanage, he was willing to work as hard as ever to get other people to help him work harder. I think you know what I mean by that. Amazing people kept coming into our lives. In addition to the formal Britsionary program, family members, friends, and people who found out about Brit and what we were doing wanted to help out here and in Haiti. One of those people who became an integral member of the Be Like Brit team is Kristin Hervey Musser. I already mentioned her in connection with one of the Britsionary trips. We knew Kristin as a little girl, but we hadn't seen her in years. In August 2011, she reached out to us. She was in graduate school and wanted to do an internship with BLB.

Anytime someone offers to help, we're thrilled. Kristin was (and is) terrific. By the time her internship was done, we decided we couldn't afford NOT to have her working for BLB. Len and I didn't realize how much help we really did need until we started to receive it. Our days working at BLB were getting longer, and we just couldn't fit everything in. BLB is a foundation started from grief and heartache. We never wanted it to become a business—we wanted Brit's spirit to guide us and that always has to be in the forefront! However, as we moved forward, we came to the realization that BLB is not a mom-and-pop shop. We want to make sure that every dollar that people raise for us is used the most effective way. We truly feel blessed that people chose to donate to us when they could have chosen another organization. We were pushing back on doing some things and saying no to things, but Kristin has allowed us to open the doors and is helping us to move the foundation into what we want it to be.

With her help, we've developed innovative programs for reaching out to the community, whether that's soliciting donations for mattresses, building blocks, or helping as a liaison with all the other groups that are hosting events on our behalf. Kristin has been invaluable. Inevitably, as time has passed and the construction has continued, we've realized something else: Once the building is complete, the work for us doesn't stop. Staffing and funding the organization and the orphanage, making sure the kids have what they need, is going to become a full-time job for us. To that end, Len and I decided it was time to end his work as a builder in the U.S. That was a difficult choice made easy by the fact that giving up something you've spent most of your adult life building into a success wasn't an end. It was just a start. Throughout 2011 and 2012, Len had been transitioning away from his daily workload here in Massachusetts to splitting his time in Haiti and here. For him the choice was between doing what he loved and doing what he loved more. That's never a bad place to be.

Len has put so much of himself into BLB and the orphanage, that I'm glad that in some ways his workload will be different—not necessarily lighter, but certainly not driven by the same needs as before. Our lives are always in process, and with Richie on the verge of starting college and Bernie already away from home at school, we've had to keep pace with that ourselves. Be Like Brit is the next phase of our lives. To complete the construction, we've had to make some sacrifices ourselves. One of Len's true labors of love was the lakefront log home he and Bernie, along with Gary and Jeb, built for us in New Hampshire. It was a great vacation getaway spot for us all. We decided to sell it to help fund the last phases of the exterior construction. I can't say it wasn't a sacrifice, but in our time in Haiti we've come to realize that happiness isn't always found in things. That's such a commonplace idea that I hesitate to even make that statement, but one of the benefits of our work on BLB is that many of those ideas that we all know but seldom act on, have served as catalysts as we continue on our journey with faith, hope, and love!

I've said before how sad it makes me that Brit died at nineteen and didn't get to grow and evolve into a young woman we'd loved to have seen. Yet, by her passing, she's enabled Len and I to grow together and for our lives to take a direction I don't think either of us would have predicted. If Len says so very often, "It's Haiti." Well, from my perspective, "It's life." Things change, and opportunities present themselves. We could have, individually or as a family, rolled into a protective ball, but instead we're out there experiencing new things and stretching our limits. We are doing our best to Be Like Brit.

13

You Just Can't Make This Stuff Up

"There are so many amazing stories of Haitian children we have met in the past three years, that I could easily fill up another book."
—LEN

CHERYLANN

The expression goes, "Time flies when you're having fun." I can't say that all the time Len was in Haiti in 2011—twenty trips there—was fun, but we made good progress on the building during that first year. It had its frustrations, to be sure. The number of "It's Haiti" moments was far greater than he would have liked, but they were always offset in some way by, "You just can't make this stuff up," or "We are truly blessed" moments. An example of the first of those was this: There are approximately four thousand five hundred colleges and universities in the U.S. and every year two and a half million freshmen go off to college. With that many choices and those millions of students, what are the odds that Michel Martelly Jr. (Sandro), the son of the Haiti's President Michel Martelly, would choose Suffolk University for his freshman year of college. Pretty large odds, I would guess?

The story goes like this and involved a string of coincidences. Bernie was going back so Suffolk for his sophomore year. A friend, who was supposed to be his roommate, decided not to go back to Suffolk at the last minute. It was too late for Bernie to find someone because everybody he knew already had chosen their roommates. He had to go with the luck of the draw, having the school choose, almost like freshman year.

A few days before move-in day, Bernie came down the stairs with his computer and announced, "I found out who my roommate is, and I think he's Haitian."

I laughed and said, "Oh, sure Bern . . . what are the chances of that happening?" Bernie wanted to get in contact with him to figure out who would bring the dorm-room essentials: the TV, the fridge, etc. He also wanted to find out what time he was moving in and so on. Bernie finally got in contact with the roommate, and he was an international student, so he had already moved in (international students move in the week before). Bernie talked to him for a while. When he got off the phone he came over and said, "Yup, my roommate is Haitian. His name is Sandro and I think he's the president of Haiti's son." Bernie had friended him on Facebook and, sure enough, Sandro, Michel Martelly Jr., was indeed the son of the Haitian president Michel Martelly.

We didn't meet Sandro that weekend—he was out with the other international students when Bernie moved in to his room on the nineteenth floor, by the way—but we did eventually. We had lunch with Bernie, Sandro and his best friend from Haiti. We were so impressed. He was such a nice kid, a real gentleman, and we were thrilled. He and Bernie started a nice friendship, giving each other a hard time in a joking, funny way; it was nice to see.

As Len said, "I can't make this stuff up." Bernie and Sandro are doing well together; they have a few things in common! Bernie recently texted me to tell me he Skyped with the first lady of Haiti last night, and she was pretty cool.

The second category is far too broad to include everyone and everything that happened to make us realize that though we lost so much in Brit's dying, we have gained so much as well. The number of people who volunteered their time and effort is so staggering that it qualifies as an "I can't make this stuff up!" as well.

Personally, I felt blessed to speak in front of many groups, schools, and organizations throughout the year. Two that really stand out were in Worcester. One school I went to did a Blocks for Brit campaign. We had started a campaign for ten-dollar donations—the cost of a cement block with which we were constructing the building's exterior walls. This was a fairly modest amount and a tangible reward for people who donated. We liked the idea that they would know exactly what their donation was going toward.

I had gone to the school, which was a K-4, and told them about BLB and Brit. The principal was a phenomenal leader, and this school raised over $4,400 for us, $10 at a time. The children were able to color a paper block representing a real one, bring it in, and hang it on the wall. They had me back to present the check to me. The principal had told me how excited the kids were (ahead of time) and that they raised a lot of money, so I had asked Len to spray-paint the name of the school on one of our walls in Haiti, take a picture, and send it to me. He did, and I had the picture blown up and brought it with me—a little surprise for the school. After they presented me with the check, I showed them their wall. They were ecstatic! The principal brought the picture around to the children—about six hundred students were at the assembly.

The principal told me that one of the girls who presented me the check wasn't able to give $10 for a block but wanted to be part of it. She had reached into the bottom of her backpack and dug out 29 cents, and that's what she gave. How awesome is that? She stood there so proud and I was beside myself. I wasn't able to keep the tears in. After the assembly was over I went up to the young girl and thanked her for helping BLB and told her she was going to help a lot of children in Haiti. She smiled at me with her huge gorgeous smile and looked up at me and said, "I want to go to Haiti with you."

I told her when she got older I would take her and she said, "Because I want to help the children."

She gave me a hug and I didn't want to let go. This little girl doesn't have a lot and she still wanted to help. This is what I love about BLB! People wanting to help people.

From the very beginning, Susan Wornick was so instrumental in getting us media exposure, and Bernie's Facebook page for BLB has also gotten us a lot of attention. Without those outlets, who knows how much money we would have been able to raise? It breaks my heart sometimes to tell people who want to donate clothes and toys that it's too early in the process for that. At some point we will be able to accept those things, and I know those donations will come pouring in. We know the news business is just that—a business. Stories come and go, but thanks to Susan and many other people, BLB continues to receive coverage. That means so much to us, and as our thoughts turn to not just opening the orphanage, but operating it, we know how important it will be to stay in front of the ever-changing news cycle.

Just today as I write this, I learned that a ten-year-old girl had a birthday party and told her mom she didn't need presents this year, so they decided to buy gifts for BLB. They thought maybe books or backpacks, but being the non-student that I am, I thought of games for the kids—things that they could use and learn from, and just plain have fun. They invited me to the party to pick up the gifts, and I gladly went. Five beautiful girls greeted me at the door, so excited to give me the gifts when usually it is the other way around. It was a strange feeling to go to the party empty-handed and walk away with my arms full of presents. But I have to tell you, being with those girls made me so happy! It's just such a time of innocence. I thought so much of Brit and her friends at that age—when they just loved being together, giggling about nothing, singing songs, not afraid to dance in public. Beautiful!

LEN

One of the highlights for me in our first year working in Haiti was having my sons there with me in June 2011. Bernie and Richie had been there before, but this solid stretch of summertime was special. Shortly after we arrived, I had one of those aha! moments where I saw the future of BLB. We went to Mission of Hope International (MOHI), Lex's school and church, and I saw two boys who had become my favorites there: Makinlove and Chrislove, or as we call them the Love Brothers. They were so happy to see us. I was talking with someone, and I turned around and Bernie had Makinlove in his arms and Richie was just picking up Chrislove.

I took a photo of the four of them, and it occurred to me that these two Haitian brothers and my two sons would be at Brit's orphanage for decades to come. The Love Brothers are not orphans, but Chrislove is HIV positive, as is his mother, Clara, so we are planning on making them all part of our family, and also giving Clara a job. They live just down the road from BLB, where we built them a small but comfortable house. I consider these kids my Haitian boys. I was so happy at that moment, experiencing that awakening realization that this was the reason why we were here in Haiti, to help the children, as Brit had wanted to do. Seeing Bernie working with Renee to update the website and Richie helping with the construction made me so proud.

There are so many amazing stories of Haitian children we have met in the past three years that I could easily fill up another book. One is a nine-year-old boy named Anji, whom my nephew, Ross, befriended on his three trips in and out of Haiti. Anji has several siblings, but only he and his brother, K.B.—who are inseparable and go everywhere together—share the same mother and father, not uncommon in Haiti. Their father passed away years ago after he fell out of a mango tree. Their mother, who has at least six children, is deaf and mute. She and Anji created their own sign language to communicate with one another. Anji and K.B. recently started to attend school but previously had no education. As Ross said, "Even with all these troubles, a kid who basically raised himself and has had no form of schooling, Anji is one of the happiest kids I have ever met with the biggest smile! The fact that he wants nothing more than to have a friend is beyond incredible to me and shows how big the Haitian heart can be."

Speaking of my nephew Ross, he was just amazing and came to Haiti on three different trips. Incredibly, and through the help of his friend, Anji, and the other kids, he learned how to speak Creole. The first time, Ross came with Bernie, Gama, and I in December 2011 for three weeks. We had just purchased the land and were just beginning to clear and flatten it. Bernie and Ross were very eager to contribute and argued with me about using the chainsaw to cut down trees; even Ross later admitted that neither of them had any business using a chainsaw. I handed that job over to people who knew what they were doing and wouldn't lose a limb in the process!

Ross and Bernie helped out where they could and borrowed the workers' machetes to cut some down small bushes. It took them at least ten hacks to chop this one puny bush. The Haitian workers saw this and could hardly stand up laughing so hard. They came over and cut down a much bigger one in only three swings. Everyone had a great laugh, and even though all these guys could not yet communicate with each other, this was no different than the guys busting each other's chops back on the construction site with C&S back in the States. They're regular guys, no matter how poor they are or difficult their lives are, and they enjoy a laugh and hanging with their friends like everyone else, everywhere else in the world.

* * *

Ross, along with my other nephew, Pat Kalagher, and P.J. Tyska—one of the Lynn University students who had gone to Haiti with Brit—were our first Britsionaries. They organized and mapped out the early Britsionary programs, and helped recruit people to come down and help. Pat made two trips to Haiti, the first for almost two months, but then he contracted malaria ,and we insisted he go home and recover in the States. Undaunted, he went back to Haiti again to continue construction at BLB.

Ross and P.J. spent nine weeks in Haiti in the summer of 2011. Words can't explain the amount of courage it took for P.J. to fly back to Haiti, after all he had been through in the earthquake, to help us out. To dig that deep into one's soul, to find the strength to bring yourself to overcome that fear, amazed me.

A difficult but necessary part of our trip was a visit to the Hotel Montana, sacred ground to all who lost loved ones there. P.J. came with us and I gave him many avenues out, but he felt he was ready. I knew it would be an emotional day for Richie also; he had never been to the Montana. Bernie had been there with Cherylann and Jodi the previous summer. This was also Ross's first trip there.

I talked to everyone about the day ahead and made sure to keep an eye on P.J., asking him occasionally how he felt. We talked, but the conversation was forced. Ross was quiet, and the anxiety level in the SUV rose as we approached the Montana. I asked P.J. if he recognized the name Huguette. I said, "She worked for Food for the Poor, and she is going to meet us at the Montana." P.J. said he didn't recognize the name, but then a few minutes later said, "Len, she might have been the tour guide for our group!"

The last time I was here days after the earthquake, it had been hell on Earth. We had to park at the gate and walk up the rubble-strewn hill past the morgue. My heart was in my throat as I remembered this—something I could never forget. I swallowed hard as I stared out the window. Today, Lex was able to drive in and up to the top of the hill, so it was a different feel. The morgue was gone and with it the unmistakable smell of death that I also could never forget. We made the turn off the main road, and there was the wall and gate I remembered so vividly. It was open with a shotgun-wielding guard standing by. We checked in and off we went up the hill.

P.J. told me later that he had flashbacks seeing all this, "But the weird thing is they were all happy ones. I remembered all fourteen of us driving up the first time looking out the window smiling at how beautiful it was."

Waiting for us was Huguette from Food for the Poor, along with a niece of the owners of the Hotel Montana. They were very nice ladies. We all introduced ourselves and when it came to P.J., Huguette answered, "P.J.? Like P.J. P.J. P.J.?!" Then she hugged him. She was the tour guide for their group that day, and all the girls in the famous picture at the orphanage had chanted his name when they first met him. It was good to see him smile, and I hoped that put him at ease; I knew this was going to be as difficult for him as it was for me.

I went right to the railing I had stood at ten days after the earthquake. A modest peace garden now stood there. I can't tell you the disappointment I felt when I saw the way the owners of the Hotel Montana had chosen to honor those people who passed away on this sacred ground! I had hoped to find something significant: a wall or something permanent listing the names of all who had perished here and where they were from. The niece was very nice, and she told me of her family's losses and how the insurance company wouldn't pay anything to help rebuild! Everything on the Montana site was under construction except for two areas that had already been rebuilt.

It was very surreal being there again! I checked on Richie who had had enough. He wanted out of there: it was just too painful. I asked him to take a couple of photos, like where Brit's room was and in the peace garden.

Bernie said he loved how the property was so beautiful,

above the poverty line, looking over the ocean, so much like the site of the BLB orphanage. P.J. called his girlfriend Lindsay Doran, another survivor of the earthquake who was Brit's roommate and best friend, and I called John Gianacaci, Christine's father. He has been there for me, and I prayed for all four of our daughters on that site. I prayed for the two professors and I prayed for the other souls and all their families. I prayed that someday they find the peace and serenity that this sacred ground brings to us, knowing this was the last place that our loved ones took their last breath and left this Earth.

As we drove back down the mountain into downtown Port-au-Prince, P.J. started recognizing various places. He said, "The last time I was on this road I was running down it, literally tripping over dead bodies." I couldn't imagine what those kids had gone through.

We drove toward the all-girls orphanage that the Journey of Hope had traveled to the day before the earthquake. P.J. was filling in the blanks for us as to what time they were there and what place they went to first. He said these girls were a lot of fun to be with that day, so we all looked forward to it! I was hoping to see one girl in particular. She was one of the children in the photo of Brit with the orphans that I've looked at a thousand times; it's the wallpaper on my laptop computer.

When we arrived at the orphanage, all the girls, over a hundred, all under the age of fourteen, were waiting for us at the gate. We followed Hugette, and when we got out of the car, all the girls started chanting in unison, "P.J., P.J., P.J.!" as he exited the SUV. It was amazing; they immediately remembered him, seventeen months later. You could tell he loved it because his face lit up like a Christmas tree. There is something special about the pure, unvarnished joy of children that I wish I could bottle up and drink in when I am feeling down. We felt like visiting celebrities. The girls sang for us, we got a tour of the orphanage, and then we went to the backyard where they play and where Brit sat in the photo with all the orphans. This too was just surreal. Were the boys and I really standing there in the courtyard where the photo was taken? I saw the cement pavers, and I knew we were there in that same spot. I have the photo on the back of the BLB business card, and I saw some of the girls today that I had seen all these months.

There was one girl in particular who always grabbed my attention; she was sitting to Brit's right in the photo and had this smirk that I will never forget. In that photo with Brit there are twenty-seven girls, if you count them all, as I did on many occasions. I just wanted one of them to be there and never expected what would happen next! Lex was taking photos with my camera when a little girl was brought toward me by older girls that I showed the photo to! She was very timid. I showed her the photo, and when she looked up smiling, I couldn't believe my eyes: There she was, the little girl who was right next to Brit in the photo. She was standing right in front of me with her photo with Brit in her hand.

I scooped her up in my arms, and I yelled to the others, "It's the little girl in the photo!"

Bernie captured that moment in a photo. I just didn't want to let go of her; I can't even explain the connection. I put her down, and some girls tried grabbing my card out of her hand, I said, "No, no, no!" and I closed her hand over the photo, and she put it in her pocket. I was beyond words!!!

I looked over and Richie was smiling with a group of young girls all around him, chanting "Richie! Richie!" or as they say in Haiti, "Witchie, Witchie!" They were also fascinated by the hair on his legs and were pulling on it. I don't think he cared for that so much, but I was so happy for him at that moment. Whatever sorrow he was feeling at being at the Hotel Montana was now washed away by the attention these girls lavished on him. I wanted to freeze-frame that moment, hoping those feelings would stay with him for a long while. We all left feeling pretty high on life. The mood had changed from everyone thinking of Brit and being sad, to seeing the happiness of the kids. You could feel her calling to us that this was why were all back in Haiti.

In my mind, a moment of divine intervention took place in that courtyard on June 12, 2011. The date was exactly seventeen months after the earthquake. We'd wondered if the little girl in the picture with Brit had survived; not only did she survive but we also got to meet her. In fact, not one of the one hundred twenty girls at the orphanage had been injured in the earthquake. In all the excitement, as I was driving away from the orphanage and on the way to the airport, I realized I never got the little girl's name! I thought to myself, no problem, I will email Huguette!

A few days later I heard from her that the child's name was SaBernie. Brit's grandfather, my father, and Brit's brother and my son are named Bernie! SaBernie is the feminine for Bernie, and on that Father's Day, I took this as another sign to believe that Britney is safe in heaven with her grandfather, Bernie. I just can't make this stuff up. I continue to keep the faith.

14

FAITH, HOPE, AND LOVE

*"We did not realize it at the time but Britney, herself, helped light
the way through the darkness for us when she sent us that
fateful text message on January 12, 2010."*

—LEN & CHERYLANN

LEN &
CHERYLANN

In early October 2012, we made a trip to Haiti, this time together, and as we end this book we speak with one voice, unified as we take on the new challenges that await us.

* * *

By now, the orphanage was nearly complete with most of the stucco work on the exterior walls completed and painted.

261

An entire section of staff rooms was complete—painted, tiled, and wired. Bathrooms in this area were also finished, as was the small kitchen.

We were excited to see the progress, and were filled with anticipation as our plane touched down at the Toussaint Louverture International Airport in Port-au-Prince. Traveling with us was the man we had chosen as program director for Brit's orphanage, Jonathan LaMare; a news crew from South Florida television station WPTV, reporter Marissa Bagg and her cameraman Tom Anderson; and our book editor, Christine Belleris. We initiated them into the Haitian way of travel, giving everyone an assignment as we all helped corral the luggage as it came off the baggage carousel. It included twelve huge hockey bags loaded down with kitchen supplies, food, and donated linens. We receive donated items almost daily, and the sheets were no exception. One day we put a notice on the Facebook page and less than a week later the UPS man had cartons of bed linens at our doorstep.

Running the gauntlet of airport skycaps—many of whom aren't helpful airport employees, but just men who want to help themselves to your luggage—we squeezed ourselves and our bags into a big rented van, packed in like sardines. It was a Sunday and the traffic was surprisingly light, though it might not have seemed that way for our first-time American visitors. We weaved our way through the cars, motorcycles, trucks, and tap-taps—the brightly painted Haitian mass-transit vehicles. Lanes are non-existent; it is every driver for himself. The tent camps that lined every empty square inch of open space in Port-au-Prince—from the sides of the highway to the medians, to the soccer fields and parks—were finally starting to clear out. Over a million people were left homeless after the quake, and it was sad to think that anyone should still have to live this way, nearly three years later.

Our first stop was the Hotel Montana, and though we had made many trips to Haiti, we had never been to the place together, where Britney took her last breath. It will always be unsettling to be there. We drove through the lush, tree-lined streets of Pétionville—the Haitian equivalent of Beverly Hills—winding our way past artists selling beautifully crafted metalwork, then up the big hill. It was warm but not too hot yet, and the sky was a brilliant blue. After checking in with the armed guard, we drove in and up the steep driveway.

The hotel is operating again, though only a fraction of its former size. Piles of gravel and cement blocks seem to indicate that more reconstruction is being done. We stopped in the small, gated memorial garden, filled with lush tropical plants and a bench for contemplation. Hand in hand, we walked to the spot where Brit's room, #300, once stood. It is gone now, of course, the twisted wreckage of the building, but it is still hard to think about what was once here, what she had to endure, and all the souls who lost their lives that day.

Also difficult to see were the people enjoying themselves—splashing in the pool, drinking and eating at the bar under the canopy of white gauzy fabric. Looking back at us, they probably thought we were just other tourists, or NGO officials, or media people covering a story. They couldn't really know our pain and that we consider this sacred ground, where we lost our Britney. But life goes on, and so we took one last look at the scenic vistas across the mountains and out toward the sea, and remembered that we must keep moving too.

As we stopped at the gate on the way out so Tom could shoot some video, we thought of Len's promise to Brit when he came to this sacred ground ten days after the earthquake. We promised you, Brit, that you would not die in vain, that your beautiful spirit would live on by honoring your last wish, to help the children that you fell in love with in Haiti for whom you wanted to start your own orphanage. You gave the world a precious gift when you sent that text heard around the world.

Port-au-Prince can still be dangerous, and it is a place you want to get through as fast as you can without stopping. We hit the road and traversed the streets where people sold everything imaginable on the side of the road: mangoes and bananas, chickens both dead or alive, beans and rice, caskets, dining-room sets, blister packets of unmarked pills, clothing hanging on stone walls. We drove past pigs and goats and horses and cows and stray dogs. It was Sunday, so people were just leaving church wearing their finest dress clothes. Men and little boys in long-sleeved shirts and ties, women in tailored suits and high heels, little girls in beautiful lace dresses and crisp layered skirts wearing bright anklets and patent-leather shoes—walking through the endless piles of broken glass, rusty cans, and rotting garbage that is absolutely everywhere. This is a far cry from the serenity of the Hotel Montana, and is the paradox that is Haiti: great natural beauty, stunning poverty, and endless suffering.

An hour and a half later, we were finally in Grand Goâve. Up high on the hill, Be Like Brit shone like a beacon of hope, its bright yellow walls setting it apart from the surrounding trees. We had to unload everybody and reload all of us and our stuff into the BLB pick-up truck for the long drive up the hill. The Love Brothers, Chrislove and Makinlove, saw us and squealed with joy, so we gave them a ride up with us.

Our architect, Paul Fallon, was there to greet us. Together we gave our guests the grand tour, and he updated us on the progress he and our workers had made over the past two weeks. Seeing the tiled floors, the bunk beds, the installed fixtures, made this all that much more real. We put sheets on the beds. Then we loaded up the kitchen with food and utensils. The kitchen is the heart of the home, the gathering place that brings people together and sustains them. This was not just a building anymore; this was turning into a home for us and for so many children who had lost theirs and their families.

And in every nook and cranny, you could feel the soul of Britney: from the stars on the railings and decorative ironwork that represent our three children; to the radiant yellow exterior as bright as her spirit, that welcomes you in; to the pops of blue in the furniture, like the color of Brit's sparkling eyes. Buildings are not alive, but this place just has a certain feeling—happy and hopeful.

Our first evening there together was great. In the open veranda on the second floor, we ate a traditional Haitian dinner of paté—chicken and onions wrapped in dough and deep fried—and drank fresh-squeezed citrus juice. The blazing sun gradually sank in the sky toward the horizon, painting the sky and sea a breathtaking orange. As evening turned to night, we called it a day, thrilled to be the first people spending the night in our new home.

* * *

Over the next few days, we'd have a few other "firsts" together. We woke up together in our new home, high-fived, and began the new day. We'd never been to the fishing village, together where Brit and the Journey of Hope group were to have gone the day after the earthquake. Gama had taken the BLB truck to buy tile, so we had to take his SUV, which had major transmission problems and had to be push-started. We rocked the vehicle up and down, then pushed as the engine finally sputtered and started. Somebody said it felt like a ride at Disneyworld. We answered back, "It's Haiti!"

We drove through town, down the main commercial street in Grand Goâve, and then down to the Pierre Marie fishing village. Many people do not have running water and must use the public baths at the end of the street by the beach. We let them finish, then walked to the shelter, next to a pile of simple canoes made from hollowed-out tree trunks. Together we looked at the beautiful memorial sign made by Food for the Poor. We were so glad that the organization had done this. Now, people forever would see the faces of our four daughters and the two Lynn University professors who gave of themselves to come here and ended up giving up their lives. Brit loved the beach and would have liked this spot right at the water's edge with the ocean lapping at the shoreline. We looked at the brightly painted stucco houses that Food for the Poor had built here, something that Brit would have helped build as well. Taking in the view, we felt her presence all around us.

We had made the building, as you know, into the shape of a capital B and we wanted to take an aerial picture—our Christmas card for 2012 and for the back cover of this book—of us waving from the rooftop together. A neighbor back in Massachusetts had a remote-control toy plane called Blue Sky that had the capability to take video and still images that you could download into your computer. It sounded pretty sophisticated for a toy and might be the answer. If Plan A did not work, we would have to go to Plan B, renting a helicopter—luckily one we had found through President Martelly's son who, as we said earlier, was Bernie's college roommate.

Our editor, Christine, said her son had this toy, so she volunteered to work the controls while we posed on the roof. "We take this out into a wide, open field with no trees because when the wind gets it, you usually lose control," she warned. The terrain around BLB was hardly wide and open—it was mountainous, there was the big security wall, and trees! Nothing ventured, nothing gained.

We stood on the roof with the plane while Christine and Jonathan were on the ground. "Okay, throw it," yelled Christine and she pressed the throttle on the controller. The plane did a nosedive off the building and hit the dirt. On the next try, the plane got some lift, but scraped the ground again, going into the six-inch crawl space underneath the BLB construction office. We crossed our fingers for the next attempt. The plane went in the right direction his time, up in the air instead of on the ground, but then did a loop into the enormous mango tree. The tree seemed to get even bigger and denser when Jonathan and Christine ventured into the mud beneath it. "I can hear it!" Jonathan said. Eventually, some of our workers were able to locate it after climbing into its thick canopy.

Christine turned the controls over to Jonathan, saying, "Here, maybe you will have better luck!" As he gave it the gas, it soared high into the sky! He attempted to turn it so it would fly over the building, but then a gust of wind caught it, and it went soaring at least three football fields away out of range of the controller and out of sight into a field or God knows where. Obviously, Brit did not want the picture of her B taken by a toy; she wanted Plan B! Seconds later we were on the phone with the helicopter company. And as for the plane—believe it or not, we found it, but long after the helicopter was under contract!

The next day the workers scurried to clean up the front of the building and all the stuff that had been piled under the mango tree. The temporary construction office—a wooden building painted bright blue—would find a permanent use as the BLB guardhouse. First, it needed to be moved from its spot adjacent to the building down the hill and next to the wall by the front gate. This was a fairly large and heavy building, and relocating it would take some doing.

With no forklift available, we again had to go back to the fundamentals. Remember, it's Haiti! The Coliseum in Rome, the Pyramids in Egypt, and the Acropolis in Athens were built without forklifts—gigantic columns and stone blocks were moved the old-school way: using logs as a kind of conveyor belt. While our Haitian workers had thought they could actually lift this thing during an earlier and shorter move of the building, they were convinced otherwise after showing them this method. If it worked for the Roman Empire, it could work for BLB.

Today, however, we were on a tight twenty-first century schedule. The copter was scheduled to come at 9:00 a.m. and was charging by the hour. It was now 8:00. All the workers surrounded the building.Gama shouted instructions in Creole. The workers shouted instructions back and forth to each other. Some used boards to raise the structure while others moved the logs from the back to the front. It was working! Even though it was morning, the sun was getting higher in the sky and it was getting hotter. This was not easy work and everyone was drenched with sweat. Slowly, steadily, the building rolled along. Then came the moment of truth—the steepest part of the hill right next to the perimeter wall. A couple of wrong moves and the building would go crashing right through it. The blue wooden building rolled and lurched, and everyone screamed. Then, whew, it stopped just in the perfect spot and with twenty minutes to spare until the helicopter came. And another piece of the plan fell right into place.

Soon we heard it, the rapid chop, chop, chop of the helicopter's rotary blades. We actually see many helicopters flying over the building. They are either the powder blue of the United Nations, or the red and black of some NGO or commercial outfit. This one was definitely ours—we can't make this stuff up—it was painted the colors of BLB: bright cobalt Britney blue with cornflower yellow numbers! Once again, we knew Brit's hand had to have been in this. What an entry; as Britney would say, "Fabulous!" The copter landed on the flat top of the hill behind us, sending all the children who lived there squealing and running to see what was happening. Surely they had never been this close to a helicopter before. Gama loaded up onto it with his camera and then it took flight, circling overhead. We smiled and waved for the camera. Then we had an even better idea.

We did not build BLB alone. Along with the many people in the States who helped, there were hundreds of Haitians who made this possible, working from dawn until dusk in the scorching heat and stifling humidity, in the rain and wind, happy to help and never complaining. We gave them good jobs and took care of them, but they have given so much to us as well: hard work, appreciation, respect, and love. They were every bit a part of this as we were. We would not be standing on the rooftop were it not for them, so we called them up from the corridors of the building where they had been hiding out of sight, up the two flights of stairs to the top of the B.

The evening that we heard about the earthquake in January

2010, the sun was setting, it was winter, getting darker and colder. Now we were all standing together in the bright sunlight of a new day. The feeling in the air was electric up on the capital B that shouts "Britney" for all the planes and birds that pass overhead. We all raised our arms and shouted—in English and in Creole—waving at the helicopter, skyward, to heaven and to Britney.

* * *

Life never takes you where you expect. You can plan and prepare and make sound choices and still, it is the things over which you have no control that change the trajectory of your life and send you on a completely different course.

We never could have anticipated that an earthquake in the Caribbean would have such an impact on our lives. In an instant, we lost our daughter, Britney, and with her the life we had known and built together as a family. There have been many dark nights, many tears shed, but what gave us sustenance through those trying times—and even now—were three things: faith in God, hope for the future, and the one thing that no person or natural disaster could ever take from us: the love that we shared—and still do—with our daughter and sons.

We did not realize it at the time, but Britney, herself, helped light the way through the darkness for us when she sent us that fateful text message on January 12, 2010:

They love us so much and everyone is so happy. They love what they have and they work so hard to get nowhere, yet they are all so appreciative. I want to move here and start an orphanage myself.

Somehow, she knew that to help us heal from the pain of losing a child, we would need children. Our family suffered a horrific loss, and the people of Haiti have suffered a great loss as well—beyond anything that most of us could imagine. Over the past two and a half years of building Be Like Brit, they have taught us how blessed our life really is—we have had good fortune and the love and support of our family and friends. We lost our child, and the children who will fill Brit's orphanage have lost their parents, their families. Together we will enlarge the circle of our family, hold hands, and fill their hearts and ours with love. Where we once looked into the beautiful blue eyes of Britney, we will now see her reflection, her kind and loving spirit, in the hopeful brown eyes of the many children she led us on this journey to help. With the completion of the building, we are starting to build many new lives.

One of the stars in our family constellation is gone, and we will never be able to replace her, but when we look up from the roof of Be Like Brit into the clear night sky, we see millions of twinkling stars. We are at peace, knowing that Britney is one of them, safe and watching over us until we join her again for eternity, keeping the faith!

About the Authors

Len and Cherylann Gengel have been married for more than twenty-four years and for most of those years worked together to raise their beautiful family, daughter, Britney, and sons, Bernie and Richie. Len, who started C&S Builders when he was in college and then received the Massachusetts Home Builder of the Year Award in 1995, and Cherylann, a stay-at-home mom, had no idea their lives would be forever changed on January 12, 2010, when the Haiti earthquake devastated Haiti, burying their daughter Britney in the rubble of the Hotel Montana.

Len and Cherylann have redirected their lives to making their daughter's last wish of building an orphanage in Haiti a reality, and are building an orphanage in Grand Goâve, Haiti. The Be Like Brit Orphanage is designed in the shape of the letter B and can be viewed at www.BeLikeBrit.org. Len, Cherylann, and their family are committed to dedicating the rest of their lives to helping the children of Haiti.

Len and Cherylann reside in Massachusetts and are avid Boston Red Sox fans. They have hosted many events for Red Sox players at their restaurant, The Grand Slam Cafe, which Brit named. One of Len's most cherished memories is watching the Red Sox win their first World Series in eighty-six years in St. Louis on his birthday in 2004. He also saw the Red Sox clinch the 2007 World Series in Denver alongside Brit, Bernie, and his sister, Chris. Sadly, Cherylann and Richie were home in Massachusetts due to a state-mandated test, but will be there next time.

Help Us Keep Brit's Dream Alive:
Bring Joy, Opportunity, and a Voice to Children in Need

Britney Gengel was a typical teenage girl in many ways—but her humor, passion, and deep sense of caring for those less fortunate made her special to all who met her. It was her compassion for others that took Brit to Haiti, just a day before the catastrophic earthquake that claimed an estimated 230,000 lives, including her own, and devastated the small, poverty-stricken country.

As you have read in this book, Britney dreamed of returning to Haiti and opening an orphanage to help the children who so touched her heart. In Brit's memory, her family has established a nonprofit organization called Be Like Brit, whose mission is to serve the children of Haiti by establishing a safe, nurturing, and sustainable orphanage in an environment where they can grow, learn, and thrive. The 19,000-square-foot facility is built to the same seismic standards as San Francisco and houses 33 girls and 33 boys—symbolic of the 33 days Brit was missing—as well as six rooms for "Britsionary" groups. Be Like Brit also provides tuition for the orphans—there is no free, public education in Haiti—paving the way for a brighter future.

Your tax-deductible donation can help continue Brit's compassion by offering hope and a future to generations of children. If you would like to donate, or if you are interested in taking a trip to Haiti as a Britsionary, please contact us at:

www.BeLikeBrit.org
www.Facebook.com/BeLikeBrit
Britney Gengel's Poorest of the Poor Fund, Inc.
P.O. Box 355
Rutland, MA 01543
(508) 886-4500

Be Like Brit is an official U.S. Non-Profit Organization
501(c)(3). Tax ID #27-1857525